Sound Concepts

An Integrated Pronunciation Course

Marnie REED

Christina MICHAUD

Sound Concepts: An Integrated Pronunciation Course Student Book

Thank you to our friend and colleague Steven J. Molinsky,
who provided ongoing inspiration, encouragement, and feedback.

ACKNOWLEDGMENTS
The Authors and Publisher would like to thank the following individuals
who reviewed the Sound Concepts program at various stages of development
and whose questions, comments, and reviews were instrumental in helping
us shape the program.

- Judith Garcia, Miami-Dade Community College
- Patricia Heiser, University of Washington
- Giang Hoang, Evans Community Adult School, Los Angeles Unified School District
- Brant Kresovich, English Language Institute, University of Buffalo
- Dorothy Lynde, Center for English Language and Orientation Programs, Boston University
- Suzanne Overstreet, West Valley College
- Alison Rice, Hunter College, City University of New York
- Anastassia Tzoytzoyrakos, University of Southern California
- Colleen Weldele, Palomar College

ISBN: 0-07-293428-X
2 3 4 5 6 7 8 9 DOW/PCR 11 10 09 08

Editorial director: Tina B. Carver
Executive editor: Erik Gundersen
Developmental editor: Sheila Parsonson
Production manager: Mary Rose Malley
Cover design: BookLinks Publishing Services
Interior design: BookLinks Publishing Services
Art: Sean Riley, Gerard Damiano

Permission to use text has been generously granted by the publishers of the following copyrighted works: *The Blank Slate: The Modern Denial of Human Nature* by Steven Pinker. Viking/Penguin 2002; *Fatal Words: Communication Clashes and Aircraft Crashes* by Steven Cushing. University of Chicago Press, 1997; "Ben and Jerry's: About Us" from *www.benjerry.com/our_company*. Ben & Jerry's Homemade Holdings, Inc; "A Conversation with Paul Ekman: The 43 Facial Muscles That Reveal" by Judy Foreman. Copyright © 2003 by *The New York Times*. Reprinted with permission; "Before Kisses and Snickers, It Was the Treat of Royalty" by Kenneth Chang. Copyright © 2003 by *The New York Times*. Reprinted with permission. We apologize for any apparent infringement of copyright and, if notified, the publisher will be pleased to rectify any errors or omissions at the earliest possible opportunity.
Photo credits: pp. 13, 52, 60, 94, 126 (photo on left), 138, 152 (photo on right): courtesy of Getty Images Royalty-Free Collection; pp. 126 (photo on right) courtesy of Royalty-Free/Corbis; all other photos courtesy of Cory Mason

Contents

An Introduction to the Teacher

Like you, the authors of this book are ESL teachers. We know how busy ESL teachers are, so we've tried to keep this introduction short. This introduction covers four main topics:

1. The Case for Teaching Pronunciation
2. The Scope of the Task
3. A Short Course in Teaching Pronunciation
4. How to Use this Book Effectively
5. Words of Wisdom

Each section addresses specific concerns teachers have voiced about pronunciation.

The Case for Teaching Pronunciation

How can I teach pronunciation without harming students' sense of identity or making them feel bad about their accents?

We know that accent and identity are inextricably linked, and that it's not politically correct to imply that there's something wrong with a student's accent. Therefore, some teachers and teacher-training programs shy away from addressing pronunciation errors. However, accents and mispronunciations can interfere with communication: students whose job security or academic advancement is at stake because of poor pronunciation are not well served by teachers who neglect to address it.

How can I translate research and theory about pronunciation into pedagogy?

Terrell (1989) writes that teachers using "communicative approaches have not known what to do with pronunciation" in the classroom, and many ESL and ELT teachers may share this view. However, teaching pronunciation *can* successfully be combined with a communicative approach. This book will help you put the theories of pronunciation into practice in a wide variety of classrooms.

How can I find time to teach pronunciation as well as vocabulary, grammar, writing, etc.?

Pronunciation is an integral component of language instruction, and work on pronunciation complements core instruction instead of taking time away from it. Many errors students make—such as not using past tense endings—may appear to be grammatical, but may, at root, be pronunciation problems. Addressing the underlying pronunciation cause of these problems leads to tighter grammatical control in speech and in writing.

How can I teach pronunciation effectively? I've tried it before, and it just doesn't work.

Most teachers spot correct, ignore, or recast student errors, but often find these methods ineffective. We believe that teaching pronunciation *can* be effective, however, when done in a systematic way, and when teachers and students share responsibility for identifying and correcting errors.

The Scope of the Task

Think of pronunciation as an umbrella term. In order to teach or learn it, teachers and students need to understand its sub-skills. Unit 1 contains much of the following information, in simpler language, for students.

Pronunciation: An Integrated System

Pronunciation is an integrated system that consists of speaking and listening (or production and perception). Speaking and listening inform each other and must be discussed together.

A Challenge to Conventional Wisdom

Traditionally, pronunciation teaching moves from listening (aural) to speaking (oral). We believe that this is backwards, and that teachers should instead focus first on speaking (production) in order to improve students' speaking *and* listening.

Conventional wisdom holds that language learners comprehend more than they can produce. However, ESL/ELT learners often begin speaking English before they have time to internalize its sound system; as a result, they are soon able to produce more than they can comprehend. Because language learners use their speaking (their own output) as input, in a closed-circuit process, it's only when their pronunciation converges with the target sound that learners will finally be able to notice and understand that sound. We call this idea **convergent production.** Speech production precedes and facilitates speech perception—or, as we tell students in chapter 1, *speaking helps listening.*

The Two Components of Listening

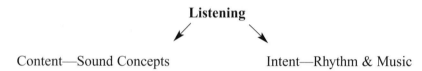

Good communication involves listening and understanding on two levels. The first level is listening for what the speaker said (the communicated content, or in linguistic terms, the locution—the actual utterance). When students can reconstruct the speech signal despite distortion caused by linked, deleted, reduced, altered, or contracted sounds (the "Sound Concepts" of our title), they can understand the content of a message—the words the speaker said. However, while comprehending the content is progress, it is not sufficient for complete understanding.

The second level is listening for what the speaker meant (the communicative intent, or in linguistic terms, the illocution). Students often don't realize that it's possible to understand every word someone said and still miss the point; they believe that if they understand all of the individual words, then they have understood the entire message. However, communicative intent includes stress, intonation, and timing (the prosodic or suprasegmental features of language), as well as body language and facial expressions (paralinguistics).

The Two Components of Speaking

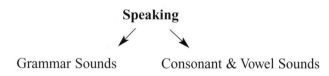

Good communication also involves making yourself understood in two different areas: Grammar Sounds (verb and noun endings) and consonant and vowel sounds. Students may be more familiar with a focus on consonant and vowel sounds (segmentals), but more serious speaking errors occur when students omit or mispronounce verb or noun endings. Our title for this part of pronunciation, "Grammar Sounds," draws on the popular misconception that errors with verb or noun endings are grammatical in nature.

However, since students very often *know* the rule for applying these endings in writing, yet often fail to *produce* these endings when speaking (or even reading aloud), we believe that these errors are actually pronunciation errors.

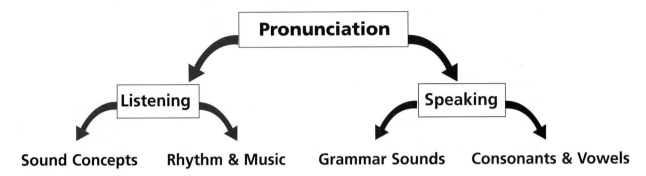

Why do we divide pronunciation into these four parts?

We have schematized the divisions between the different sub-skills of listening and speaking in order to enable students to conceptualize the scope of the task, to prioritize their pronunciation goals, and to make their work in this course manageable. Each chapter contains explanations and exercises for topics in each of the four components of pronunciation. However, because pronunciation is integrated, our chapters interweave the four components of pronunciation, moving from one component to another and building on one another within a chapter.

Do I have to focus equally on every part of pronunciation? Are all equally important for both listening and speaking?

No. Some components are more important than others, and some are important for both listening and speaking.

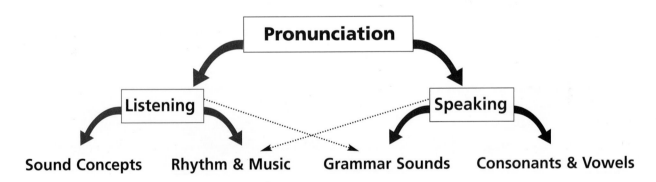

A Short Course in Teaching Pronunciation

What does a student's progress in this course look like?

Our goal is to get students to take responsibility for their errors—to identify them and to learn to self-correct. To get to this point, students must first become conscious of their errors, and then learn to correct them.

We schematize the learning process this way:

Level 1: Students make errors but don't realize they're making them.

Level 2: Students begin to understand the errors they are making.

Level 3: Through conscious effort, students sometimes manage to avoid making errors.

Level 4: Students use the correct forms without having to consciously monitor their speech.

	Consciousness	Competence
Level 4	–	+
Level 3	+	+
Level 2	+	–
Level 1	–	–

Level 4
Unconscious competence

Level 3
Conscious competence

Level 2
Conscious incompetence

Level 1
Unconscious incompetence

How do students reach Level 4?

Students reach Level 4 through a combination of explicit instruction in a sound or concept; practice, which forms mental and physical habits; teacher intervention, which lets students know when they have made an error and when they have said something correctly; and metacognition, which allows them to monitor their own pronunciation and self-correct.

Students make so many errors—how do I know which errors to correct?

Do not correct any errors until you have introduced the concept or sound. Students must be able to refer back to something in order to process your correction, or else your correction will go in one ear and out the other. Only when students understand their specific mistake and are able to supply the correct form when prompted will they be able to correct their mistake in the future. Therefore, bringing students' attention to problems that they cannot yet name doesn't result in lasting changes to their pronunciation.

Remember that some mistakes are more serious than others: look at the following chart for an explanation of which mistakes to correct.

Pronunciation component	Other ways to think about it	More about this component	Important for	Should I correct students' errors with this component?
Component 1: Sound Concepts	Message Content; Locution; Utterance	In connected speech, sounds are linked, reduced, deleted, altered, and contracted. Students need to understand these Sound Concepts, but they do not need to use them in every-day speech.	Listening	Probably not, outside of the specific exercises that teach students to produce these Sound Concepts for the purposes of improving their listening.

Pronunciation component	Other ways to think about it	More about this component	Important for	Should I correct students' errors with this component?
Component 2: Rhythm & Music	Message Intent; Illocution; Force of the Utterance; Suprasegmentals	The message is in the music: syllables, stress, intonation, and timing all carry meaning. Students need to be able to notice, understand, and produce these suprasegmental aspects of the language in everyday speech.	Listening and Speaking	Yes: their errors in this area, especially errors with syllable structure and standard word- and sentence-level stress, can seriously impair students' communication.
Component 3: Grammar Sounds	Noun and Verb Endings; Inflectional Morphology	English speakers listen for verb and noun endings for grammatical information and rhythm. These endings are essential, and students need to be able to notice them and produce them correctly.	Listening and Speaking	Yes, always: even when an exercise, discussion, or activity does not target these endings.
Component 4: Consonant & Vowel Sounds	Individual Sounds; Segmentals	Though most students believe that this area is where their most important pronunciation problems lie, these errors usually do not interfere with students' communication.	Speaking	Sometimes: It depends on the severity of the error and the focus of the class.

A Principled Approach to Error Correction: A Teacher-Student Partnership

Error correction is most effective when students themselves correct their error, rather than when teachers merely recast it for them. The following steps help students correct their own errors:

1. **Stop**—Stop students when they make errors that have already been addressed.

2. **Find**—When students are new to this process, identify their errors explicitly: "You said 'use-ed,' with two syllables. Look at your log or the checklist—how do you say that ending?" When students get used to this process, use a shorter prompt to help them find their mistake: "Something's not right there. Go back over what you just said—where's the mistake?"

3. **Correct**—Require that students always correct their own errors, even if this only means repeating the correct form after you or a classmate have provided it.

4. **Freeze-frame**—Tell students immediately when they have said the correct form. This "freeze-frame" lets students create a motor-memory of their pronunciation and leads to a change in their understanding (acoustic image) of the sound.

The flow chart below shows this process of error correction in more detail.

When a learner's acoustic image of a sound, concept, or ending doesn't match the target, **the learner makes an error.**

If the sound or Sound Concept has not yet been introduced …	If the sound or Sound Concept has been introduced …
Do nothing: ignore the error.	Alert the learner and ask the learner to correct his or her error: 1. Immediately stop the learner. 2. Identify the error (if necessary). 3. Ask the learner to say the word or sentence again correctly.

Prompt the learner to freeze-frame the correct pronunciation.

How else do students take responsibility for their own progress?

We give students three primary tools to help them participate actively in their learning. You may need to encourage individual students to refer to one or more of these tools at different times.

1. Journal activities (for reflection and observation)

2. Checklists and strategies (for self-monitoring and self-correction)

3. Logbook pages (for individualized error tracking)

How to Use This Book Effectively

How does this book differ from other pronunciation texts?

This book takes into account many aspects of the latest theories of pronunciation, including:

- the importance of paralinguistics to pronunciation
- the use of a student logbook to improve error correction and promote student responsibility
- the use of journals, checklists, and strategies for better metacognition
- the integration of all components of pronunciation within each chapter
- the use of listening exercises *after* speaking exercises, in order to allow learners' production of a sound or concept to facilitate their perception

What level students will benefit from this approach?

This book is helpful to three levels of students: false beginners, who have multiple years of study, low productive ability, and higher knowledge about the language; intermediate students, who can produce more than they can comprehend; and advanced students, who may never have had a systematic approach to pronunciation.

Why do some of the exercises and activities seem so basic? My students are beyond this!

Your students may well have a conceptual grasp of many of the targeted structures. However, most ESL/ELT students (even high-intermediate and advanced) do not consistently produce these structures correctly. Though many language teachers no longer notice these errors, many advanced students continue to say things like "He drive to school everyday" and "Teacher, how to say this word?"

My students already studied verb and noun endings, so why should I cover them again?

If students are still making errors with verb and noun endings—as many intermediate and advanced students are—they may need a more systematic and cognitive approach that will change and correct their existing pronunciation patterns.

Can I use this book with both small and large classes?

Yes. Most of the exercises and activities can be done in pairs or small groups, which will work even in large classrooms. When an activity is more complicated, we provide specific instructions on using it successfully in both small and large classes.

What choices do I have about how to use this book? Can I skip around?

This book can be used as the main text in a pronunciation or listening/speaking class, or as a supplemental text in a general skills class. Chapters 1 and 2 provide a general introduction to the book, complete with preview mini-lessons and diagnostics. After this, teachers may skip around in the text, picking and choosing individual sections or exercises to meet their students' needs. Our Grammar Cross-Reference (appendix 3) provides additional help in coordinating this text with a standard grammar-based syllabus. The **focus** icon next to exercises lets you see at a glance what students will be working on in a given section. The **recycle** icon lets you see what students need to already know in order to have success with the new material. Together, these icons let you skip through the book, using exercises and sections in any order you wish.

How should I use the student logbook?

Chapter 1 introduces students to the idea and format of their logbook. Several other places in the text prompt students to add entries to their logbook if they are still having problems with specific concepts or sounds. Students' logs will vary, since different students will need to work on different areas. However, no student's log should recapitulate the entire book. If errors persist for one or more students after you have introduced a concept in class, you should prompt those students to add an entry to their log if they have not yet done so. *The log is not meant to be a time-intensive "journal" or homework activity.* Adding an entry to a log should be quick once students are familiar with the task. Students can then refer to their logs when they make errors in spontaneous speech.

What's the purpose of the Preview of Pronunciation chapter?

The purpose of this section is to give students a sense of the scope of the course and a feeling of success after the first one or two class sessions. It is not intended to provide specific controlled exercises to practice every topic introduced: it is a preview of various concepts. Later chapters explain these concepts more fully and offer additional exercises.

Words of Wisdom: Theoretical and Research-Based Foundations

Why does the Principled Approach to Error Correction (p. xi) work?

Research with a theoretical base in both language learning and psychology suggests that learners retain something better when they produce it than when they merely hear it. Swain's second language acquisition output hypothesis and related studies suggest that students must self-repair in order to make progress.[1]

What evidence supports the closed-circuit theory (p. viii)?

Traditionally, pronunciation was taught in a listening-first, "repeat-after-me" method (aural before oral). However, studies on segmentals in second language acquisition suggest that production can indeed precede and facilitate perception.[2] Additional studies from neurolinguistics suggest that mere exposure (listening) is not enough for successful acquisition: interaction is essential.[3,4]

Why are suprasegmental errors (syllables, stress, intonation, and timing) considered more serious than segmental errors (individual consonant and vowel sounds) (p. xi)?

Recent pronunciation theory argues that segmental errors simply have a less serious effect on intelligibility;[5] therefore, students' problems with stress, etc., are more likely to cause communication breakdowns than a mispronunciation of the consonant /r/, for instance.

Do students really not know what their mistakes are (p. x)?

One recent study found that 39% of ESL/ELT students surveyed could not name a single pronunciation problem.[6] When students can identify a particular pronunciation mistake, it's most likely a less serious problem with individual consonant or vowel sounds.

How can I help students use all their resources to listen and comprehend effectively?

Research suggests that ESL/ELT learners "have a tendency to process language with minimal reference to contextual cues and instead to focus primarily on the acoustic signal" (Jenkins 171). Since the acoustic signal is distorted (sounds are linked, reduced, deleted, altered, and contracted), students need to be more active, learning to draw on background information, language information, and paralinguistics: "In fact, even when the context is manifestly clear, [ESL/EFL learners] still seem more likely to place their trust in an acoustic signal (in other words, the exact speech sounds which are transmitted)" (Jenkins 35).[7] We tell students about the Three Kinds of Information on p. 7, and we remind them of it at multiple points in the book.

What research supports teaching stress patterns as on pp. 76-81?

Sources for the relative frequency of stress patterns and the x-y notation for signalling word syllables and stress come from the work of John Murphy.[8]

[1] Swain, M. (1985). Communicative competence: Some roles of comprehensible input and comprehensible output in its development. In S. Gass and C. Madden (Eds.), *Input in Second Language Acquisition,* (pp. 235-253). Rowley, MA: Newbury House.

[2] de Bot, K. (1996). The psycholinguistics of the output hypothesis. *Language Learning 46,* pp. 529-555.

[3] Gass, S. (1984). A review of interlanguage syntax: Language transfer and language universals. *Language Learning 34,* pp. 115-132; Sheldon, A., & Strange, W. (1982). The acquisition of /r/ and /l/ by Japanese learners of English: Evidence that speech production can precede speech perception. *Applied Psycholinguistics 3*, pp. 243-261.

[4] Sachs, J., & Johnson, M. (1976). Language development in a hearing child of deaf parents. *Neurolinguistics 5*, pp. 246-252.

[5] Dalton, C. & Seidhofer, B. (1994). *Pronunciation.* Oxford: Oxford University Press; Brown, A. (1991). *Pronunciation Models.* Singapore: Singapore University Press.; Hahn, L. (2004). Primary stress and intelligibility: Research to motivate the teaching of suprasegmentals. *TESOL Quarterly 38 (2),* pp. 201-223.

[6] Derwing, T.M., & Rossiter, M.J. (2002). ESL learners' perceptions of their pronunciation needs and strategies. *System 30 (2),* pp. 155-166.

[7] Jenkins, J. (2000). *The Phonology of English as an International Language: New Models, New Norms, New Goals.* Oxford: Oxford University Press.

[8] Murphy, J.M. (2004). Attending to word-stress while learning new vocabulary. *English for Specific Purposes Journal 23* (1), pp. 67-83. See also Murphy, J. & Kandil, M. Word Stress Patterns in the Acedemic List. *System 32* (1), pp. 61-74.

A Preview of Pronunciation

The English Alphabet	The International Phonetic Alphabet (IPA)	Mini-Lessons 1 and 2 *Sound Concepts Rhythm & Music*	Mini-Lessons 3 and 4 *Grammar Sounds Consonant & Vowel Sounds*

A Preview of Pronunciation

An Introduction to Language, Sounds, and the Alphabet

What do you think?

How many languages are there in the world?

60   600   6000

How many sounds are there in the world's languages?

100   600   1100

How many sounds are there in English?

26   44   62

(Answers on p. 13)

Talk with a partner

What languages do you know? _____

How many sounds are there in your native language? _____

How do you write your language? Does it have an alphabet? _____

How many letters are there in your alphabet? _____

How many letters are there in the English alphabet? _____

How many vowels are there in your language? _____

How many vowels are there in English? What are they? _____

 Eye-Opener: English is written with symbols that stand for letters, but some other languages are written with symbols that stand for syllables or words. How is your language written?

D

ム

福

Language: English
This symbol is a letter. It can be part of many syllables and words.
Say it: "dee."

Language: Japanese
This symbol is a syllable. It can be part of many words.
Say it: "mu."

Language: Chinese
This symbol is a word. It means, "good luck."
Say it: "fu."

LANGUAGE STRATEGY
Using the International Phonetic Alphabet (IPA) to Talk About English Sounds

The English language has 44 speech sounds, but the English alphabet only has 26 letters.

The same letters sometimes represent different sounds.

Example: The letter c can stand for different sounds: **c**ake; o**c**ean; i**c**e.

The same sounds can also be written in many combinations of letters.

Example: The sound /f/ can be spelled differently: i**f**; o**ff**; **ph**one; lau**gh**.

We need a tool to help us talk about sounds, not letters. This tool is the International Phonetic Alphabet (IPA) (appendix 1). Use IPA symbols to understand the way this textbook and your dictionary mark pronunciations.

One symbol stands for only one sound.

The sound of the letter **c** in **c**ake is /k/.

The sound of the letter **c** in o**c**ean is /sh/.

The sound of the letter **c** in i**c**e is /s/.

Write sounds between slashes: the letter is k, but the sound is /k/.

LANGUAGE STRATEGY: Saying the Names of the Letters of the Alphabet

Before continuing, you need to know the English alphabet and how to say the names of the letters. There are 26 letters in the English alphabet: 21 consonants and 5 vowels. The vowels in English are a, e, i, o, and u. Be careful! If your language has an alphabet, you may say the names of these letters differently.

Eye-Opener: The names of some letters are also English words: bee, see, gee, eye, jay, oh, are, you, and why.

Letter	Say it	Letter	Say it
1. A a	ay, as in "say" or "day"	14. N n	en
2. B b	bee	15. O o	oh, as in "go" or "slow"
3. C c	see	16. P p	pee
4. D d	dee	17. Q q	kyoo
5. E e	ee, as in "eat" or "meet"	18. R r	are
6. F f	ef	19. S s	ess
7. G g	gee, as in "jeans"	20. T t	tee
8. H h	aytch	21. U u	yoo, as in "to," "do," and "you"
9. I I	eye	22. V v	vee
10. J j	jay, as in "James"	23. W w	duh-bul-yoo, like "double-you"
11. K k	kay	24. X x	ex
12. L l	el	25. Y y	why
13. M m	em	26. Z z	zee

PRONUNCIATION GOAL:

Try to say the names of the letters of the English alphabet correctly.

Exercise 1: Word Ladders

 Focus on the letters of the alphabet

Change the word at the top of the ladder into the word at the bottom by changing only one letter at a time. Use the definitions to get started. Remember to say the letters aloud for practice.

Change COLD to WARM:

1.	C	O	L	D	opposite of hot
2.	C	O	R	D	a piece of rope
3.	__	__	__	__	smallest part of language
4.	__	__	__	__	area in a hospital
5.	W	A	R	M	not very hot

Change HERD to SEAT:

1.	H	E	R	D	a group of animals
2.	H	e	a	d	top part of the body
3.	D	E	A	D	not alive
4.	__	__	__	__	how to start a letter
5.	__	__	__	__	be afraid
6.	__	__	__	__	listen to
7.	W	A	R	m	make something hot
8.	S	E	A	T	a chair or bench

Exercise 2: More Word Ladders

 Focus on the letters of the alphabet

Change the word at the top of the ladder into the word at the bottom by changing only one letter at a time. Write definitions for each word. Remember to say the letters aloud for practice

Change MORE to LESS:

1. M   O   R   E   in addition, extra

2. __ __ __ __   _____

3. __ __ __ __   _____

4. __ __ __ __   _____

5. L   E   S   S   _____

Change FLOW to CRAM:

1. F   L   O   W   move like water

2. __ __ __ __   _____

3. __ __ __ __   _____

4. __ __ __ __   _____

5. C   R   A   M   _____

USAGE NOTE: ACRONYMS

Acronyms are groups of letters that stand for words. English has many acronyms, and we often pronounce them by saying the names of the letters.

     Example: **CD – compact disc**   Say it: "see-dee."

At work or at school, you may hear acronyms you don't know. Use one of the questions below to ask for their meaning:

     Example: **I got an invitation that says to RSVP.**

Q: What does that mean?   A: It means you have to tell them if you're coming.

Q: What does that stand for?   A: It stands for four French words: it means you have to tell them if you're coming.

Exercise 3: Using Acronyms

 Focus on the letters of the alphabet

1. Match the columns below.

   1. The sign says my bank is closed but I can use the ATM. What's an ATM?   A. It means "for your information."

   2. I got an invitation that says RSVP. What does RSVP mean?   B. It means your date of birth.

3. I got a memo that says FYI. What does FYI mean?

4. I'm filling out a form that asks for my DOB. What does DOB mean?

5. I hear there's a meeting of the WTO next month. What's the WTO?

6. There's an article about world politics that talks about the UN. What's the UN?

C. It's an automatic teller machine that you can use anytime.

D. It's the United Nations.

E. It's French. It means you have to tell them if you're coming.

F. It's the World Trade Organization.

2. Look at the following lists. Which of these organizations are you familiar with? With a partner, list more acronyms in each category.

Colleges and Universities	Political Organizations	Government Offices/Services
UCLA (University of California at Los Angeles)	UN (United Nations)	MTA (Metropolitan Transit Authority)
LSE (London School of Economics)	WTO (World Trade Organization)	NYPD (New York Police Department)

Exercise 4: More Alphabet Games

 Focus on the letters of the alphabet

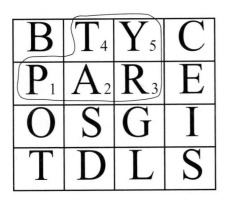

1. **The Game of Boggle:** Make as many words as you can by connecting letters. All letters in a word must connect. Do not skip over any letters. For example, you can make these words from the board at left: POT, POTS, PARTY and BAG. You can't make the word RICE because the "I" does not connect directly to the "C." Use the board on the right to make as many words as you can. Make up your own boards or play a version of this game on the Internet for more practice.

2. **Wheel of Fortune:** The first player thinks of a word and draws a line for each letter in the word on the board or a piece of paper. Other players take turns trying to guess the word by guessing letters. If someone guesses a letter correctly, the first player writes it on the appropriate line and lets the player make another guess. The first player to guess the word wins. Use the question "Is there a _____?" or "Is there an _____?" to ask for letters.

> ### Journal
> You need to say the names of the letters of the alphabet in many real-world situations. Here are just a few. Talk with a partner and think of more.
> - In a chemistry class: elements on the Periodic Table
> - In a newspaper article: Congress is debating the acceptable level of CO_2 emissions.
>   (CO_2 = carbon dioxide. Say it: "see-oh-two.")
> - In a math class: algebra (x, y, z)
> - When meeting new people: Many popular names have two or more different spellings: "Is that Catherine with a C or a K"?
> During the week, find at least one situation to practice the alphabet. Take notes about your experience and be ready to report to the class.

Four Mini-Lessons in Pronunciation

This book deals with four parts of pronunciation: Sound Concepts, Rhythm & Music, Grammar Sounds, and Consonant & Vowel Sounds. You will practice each part in every chapter of this book. The four mini-lessons that follow give you a preview of the four parts of pronunciation.

Sound Concepts

Mini-Lesson 1

English doesn't sound the way it looks. Native English speakers change the sounds of the language when they speak it. These changes may explain why you have difficulty understanding spoken English. You need to know how to make sense of the sounds that you hear in order to understand the content of spoken English.

 Diagnostic

Listen to the business meeting. On a separate piece of paper, write down each statement or question you hear.

After Listening

Did you find listening to this conversation difficult? What do you think caused the problems?

 Eye-Opener: English doesn't sound the way it looks.
The sounds you hear—and the sounds a speaker says—may not match the dictionary pronunciation. This book will help you learn the five patterns that English speakers use to change and omit sounds. We call these patterns Sound Concepts.

Introduction to the Sound Concepts

Sounds are linked.

Some sounds in the conversation you heard were linked. Sounds are linked when sounds in one word connect to sounds in the next word. Everyday speech is linked speech: it has many linked sounds.

Example: Is everybody here? Where's Albert?

Sounds are deleted.

This conversation included words with sounds that were never pronounced, such as the sound of the letter "h" in words like "he" or "his." You didn't hear these sounds because the speaker didn't say them! These sounds are deleted.

Example: Is ̶He in ̶His office? Try ̶Him on ̶His cell phone.

Sounds are reduced.

This conversation included words that were shortened, or reduced, such as some sounds in the word "and." These words are reduced.

Example: Susan ̶and Catherine are here.

Sounds are altered.

Some sounds in this conversation were altered or changed, such as the sound of the "t" in the middle of the word "meeting." This sound is changed so that it sounds more like the sound of the letter "d." This sound is altered.

Example: Meanwhile, can we start the mee͟t͟ing without him?

Sounds are contracted.

Some sounds in this conversation were contracted, or combined across words and written with an apostrophe. These sounds are contracted.

Example: Albert's missing.
            No, he's not.

 Eye-Opener: Linking is the most important Sound Concept. You must link sounds in order to be able to reduce, delete, alter, or contract sounds across words.

LANGUAGE STRATEGY
Using the Three Kinds of Information to Increase Understanding

Sometimes understanding English is like breaking a code. Use three kinds of information to decode a message:

1. Background information—what you already know about the topic of conversation

2. Language information—what you know about how the English language works
   (the grammar, the vocabulary, and the sound system)

3. Sound information—the sounds that you actually hear someone saying

You don't have to depend on just the sounds of the sentences—the other kinds of information can help you too!

✓ CHECKLIST

Use these three steps to decode the dictation sentences here and throughout the book.

1. What did you hear? Write it down.

2. Reread what you wrote. Does it make sense?

3. What was really said? Use the three kinds of information above to make sense of what you heard.

Exercise 5: What did they say?

 Focus on Sound Concepts, using the Three Kinds of Information to decode what you hear

Go back to the diagnostic. Your teacher may ask you to listen to it again. Write what you heard on a piece of paper or the board. Use the checklist above to decode these sentences with a partner or the whole class.

Do your best to use the list of Sound Concepts on the previous page to help understand the sentences. For each sentence, try to list at least one Sound Concept and circle the part of the sentence where sounds are linked, reduced, deleted, altered, or contracted. Talk about your choices. You will learn more about these Sound Concepts in the rest of this book.

Consonant & Vowel Sounds

Mini-Lesson 2

Talk with a partner: Where do speech sounds come from? What parts of your body do you use to form them? What terms do we use to describe individual sounds?

Eye Opener: You use over a hundred different parts of your body to make speech sounds. The following section discusses the main parts:

1. your lungs
2. your vellum (the back of your throat)
3. your vocal cords (or your voicebox)
4. your glottis (the space between your vocal cords)

5. your teeth
6. your tongue
7. your lips

Three important things help us to describe consonant sounds:

1. Place of articulation—where in your mouth (teeth, tongue, lips) you block the air to form a sound

2. Manner of articulation—how much air you block when you say a sound

3. Voicing—whether you turn your voicebox on or off for a particular sound

1. **Place of Articulation**

Speech happens while you're breathing out. For individual consonant and vowel sounds, air comes up from your lungs and passes through your mouth. When we talk about the place of a specific consonant sound, we mean the place where the air is blocked when you say that sound.

2. Manner of Articulation

Some consonant sounds are called stops, like the sounds /t/. Think of these sounds as a red light: you *stop* the air completely when you say them, just as you stop at a red light while driving.

Example: the sounds /t/, /p/, and /k/

Other consonant sounds are called continuants (or fricatives, like the sound /sh/). When you say them, you let most of the air *continue* out of your mouth, but your mouth blocks part of it, creating friction. Think of these sounds as a yellow light—you slow down the air and make friction when you say them, just as you slow down and start to brake (use friction) at a yellow light.

Vowel sounds are unblocked sounds. Think of these sounds as a green light—the air is not blocked at all. You don't make friction when you say them, just as you don't brake or stop at a green light.

- All vowel sounds: air completely unblocked

- Consonant sounds that are continuants: air partially blocked, with friction

- Consonants sounds that are stops: air completely blocked (stopped)

3. Voicing

When you're speaking, the air passes through the voicebox in your throat before it reaches your mouth. The voicebox has vocal cords that can move back and forth or stay still, so your voicebox is either on (moving) or off (not moving). If your voicebox is on, you can hold your hand to the front of your throat and feel it move, or vibrate. If your voicebox is off, you won't feel it vibrate.

Your voicebox is like a switch. When it's on, sounds are voiced.
When it's off, sounds are unvoiced.

All vowel sounds are voiced. Some consonants, like /d/, are voiced and some, like /t/, are unvoiced. Sometimes using your voicebox is the only difference between two different words with different meanings.

English has the following eight unvoiced consonant sounds. Your voicebox is off when you say them.

/k/–the sound at the end of "look"	/p/–the sound at the end of "stop"
/f/–the sound at the end of "laugh"	/s/–the sound at the end of "box"
/sh/–the sound at the end of "wash"	/θ/–(say this symbol "theta") at the end of "with"
/tch/–the sound at the end of "watch"	/t/–the sound at the end of "sat"

Eye-Opener: Minimal Pairs

When there's only one difference between the pronunciations of two different words, the words are minimal pairs. The difference between them is minimal, or very small: it only depends on one individual segment, or sound. Otherwise the words are the same.

Example: "to" begins with an unvoiced sound

"do" begins with a voiced sound

Introduction to the "th" Sounds: /θ/ and /ð/

In English, one spelling—"th"—can make two different sounds. Now that you know about place, manner, and voicing, you can understand the difference between these two sounds.

What are the sounds?

/θ/ —————————→ Say this symbol: "theta."   /ð/ —————————→ Say this symbol: "eth."

These sounds are minimal pairs: the only difference between them is voicing.

How do you spell them?

/θ/:   **th**ink   /ð/:   **th**em

How do you form them?

	/θ/, "th" as in "thanks"	/ð/, "th" as in "that"
1. Place	Touch the tip of your tongue to the bottom of your top teeth. If you look in a mirror, you should be able to see the tip of your tongue.	same as /θ/
2. Manner	This sound is a friction sound—a continuant. Make sure to let the sound continue; don't stop all the air.	same as /θ/
3. Voicing	This sound is unvoiced (your voicebox doesn't vibrate).	This sound is voiced (your voicebox vibrates).
Examples:	think, Thursday, both, with	those, these, the, mother, then

Trouble Spots

1. Don't say /t/ or /d/ for these sounds. Use friction when you form these sounds and make sure your tongue is between your teeth.

2. Use your voicebox for the sound /ð/, but do not use it for the sound /θ/.

 Eye-Opener: Many languages don't use "th" sounds, which are difficult to form. Even children who grow up speaking English usually learn to say these sounds last, after every other English sound.

Exercise 6: Practice with /ð/

 Focus on /ð/

Work with a partner. Use the frame below to practice the sound /ð/ in these words: this, these, those, the. Remember to form the sound by touching the tip of your tongue to the bottom of your top teeth. This is a voiced sound. Continue the sound, don't stop it: don't say the sound /d/ or /z/.

Example: books to do my research
  A: I need those books to do my research.
  B: *These* books?
  A: No, *those* books.

No, *those* books.

1. ingredients to make this dish

2. handouts to study for the test

3. papers to fill out this form

4. CDs to take on the trip.

Exercise 7: Practice with /θ/

 Focus on /θ/

Work with a partner. Use the frame below to practice the sound /θ/ in words and numbers. Remember to form the sound by touching the tip of your tongue to the bottom of your top teeth. This is an unvoiced sound. Continue the sound, don't stop it: don't say the sound /t/ or /s/.

> Example: clinic / south on 5th Avenue
> **A:** Excuse me, am I going in the right direction for the clinic?
> **B:** Yes, just continue south on 5th Avenue.
> **A:** Thanks!

1. **Th**ree Pines Inn / sou**th** on 20**th** Avenue
2. supermarket / sou**th** on 4**th** Street

3. drugstore / nor**th** on 140**th** Street
4. library / nor**th** on 15**th** Avenue

 Rhythm & Music

Mini-Lesson 3

There's more to understanding English, or any language, than just the sounds of the language. Try to use the rhythm and music of the language to understand the speaker's intent, or meaning. With different intonation or stress, the same words can mean different things. In these sentences, intonation (the changing music or melody) and stress carry meaning.

Exercise 8: How do they feel?

 Focus on intonation and stress

 A. You will hear three sentences. How does the speaker feel? Choose the best word from the box. Discuss your answers with a partner.

1. What do you know about that? The speaker is _____

2. What do you know about that? The speaker is _____

3. What do you know about that? The speaker is _____

sarcastic	sad
annoyed	pleased
happy	afraid
upset	thrilled
curious	surprised

B. If you had difficulty with this exercise, what do you think caused it? Would this exercise have been easier if you could see the speaker? Why or why not?

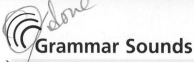

Grammar Sounds

www . npr . org

Mini-Lesson 4

Talk with a partner

1. How do you talk about the past in your language? Do you use words like "yesterday" or a part of a word, such as a verb ending?

2. Is the word or the ending required (you must use it) when talking about the past, or is it optional (you can use it if you want to, but you don't have to)?

3. How do you write the past tense ending of regular verbs in English?

In English, the regular past tense verb ending is a required piece of information. You must add this ending when talking in the past tense.

You may also use words such as "yesterday," "last week," or "ten years ago." These words are optional. You may use them if you want to, but you still need to write (and pronounce) the "-ed" ending.

> **Eye-Opener:** A famous linguist once said that a verb is like a king who rules the sentence completely. The past tense ending is part of the verb, and you must say it.

Introduction to the Pronunciations of the Past Tense Ending "-ed"

Some students have problems with the past tense ending "-ed" because they don't know the logic behind the different pronunciations. There are three ways to pronounce the "-ed" ending. One pronunciation adds an extra syllable—an extra beat—to the verb. We will focus on this pronunciation here.

How do I know if I need to say "-ed" as an extra syllable?

If the final sound (not letter) of the verb is /t/ or /d/, say "-ed" as an extra syllable.

want (1 syllable) + ed (add an extra syllable) = wanted (2 syllables)

need (1 syllable) + ed (add an extra syllable) = needed (2 syllables)

decide (2 syllables) + ed (add an extra syllable) = decided (3 syllables)

In all other cases, don't say "-ed" as an extra syllable:

fix (1 syllable) + ed (no extra syllable) = fixed (1 syllable)

use (1 syllable) + ed (no extra syllable) = used (1 syllable)

borrow (2 syllables) + ed (no extra syllable) = borrowed (2 syllables)

PRONUNCIATION GOAL

Remember that Grammar Sounds are very important in spoken English. Say the past tense ending "-ed" as an extra syllable only when the final sound of the simple form of the verb is /t/ or /d/.

Final Chapter Activity

(HW)

 Focus on past tense endings   ♻ **Recycle θ and ð**

1. Underline all the "-ed" words in the short paragraph below. Make a chart like the one below to decide how to pronounce each "-ed" ending.

SEPTEMBER						
	1	2	3	4	5	6
7	8	9	10	11	12	13
14	15	16	17	18	19	20
21	22	23	24	25	26	27
28	29	30				

Last month I registered for a new school. Classes started on the 8th. On the 9th, I purchased all my books. I was worried about the cost, but I managed to find some used books. . .

/d/ */t/* */d/* */d/* */d/* */d/*

read and record.

Simple form of verb	Number of syllables	Final sound (check one)	Add an extra syllable?	Total number of syllables in "-ed" form
register	3	❑/t/ ❑/d/	❑Yes ❑No	
start	1	❑/t/ ❑/d/	❑Yes ❑No	

2. Repeat the excercise above with your own past-tense paragraph.

Journal

A. Look back at exercise 8, "How do they feel?" Imagine and describe the speaker's facial expressions for each different sentence. What does your culture think about expressing emotions through facial expressions and body language?

Observe some English speakers having a conversation on TV or in a public place. Don't worry about understanding everything they say. Just watch their facial expressions, their hand motions, and any other body language. What do you see? How do you think the people feel, and why?

B. Look at the section on consonant sounds /ð/ and /θ/ again. Remember that when you say these sounds correctly, you can see the tip of your tongue between your teeth. Some students think that this feels strange. You may wonder if all English speakers really stick out their tongues when they say these sounds. Watch some! What do they do? Try to notice specific words with these sounds and carefully watch a speaker's mouth when he or she says them.

C. Imagine that you're talking to a friend who isn't taking this course. Your friend is very interested in English listening and speaking. Your friend asks you what you learned today and how this course will help your English. What do you tell your friend?

Answers p. 1: 1. There are about 6000 languages in the world; 2. There are about 1100 sounds in the world's languages; 3. There are 44 sounds in English.

Getting Ready for Chapter 2

What You Need to Know About Pronunciation (An Integrated Approach)

Pronunciation works two ways:

You can understand others.  Others can understand you.

In order to understand others, you need listening skills. In order for others to understand you, you need speaking skills.

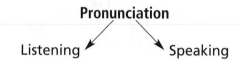

Pronunciation

Listening ← → Speaking

Listening: Three Kinds of Listening Skills

1. Listening for **message content:** you need to understand what the speaker said.

2. Listening for **message intent:** you need to understand what the speaker meant.

3. Listening for **Grammar Sounds** (noun and verb endings): you need to understand the information given by these endings.

Listening for Message Content: Sound Concepts

Content is what a speaker says. In written English, there is white space between the words on the page, and each word is clear and distinct. In spoken English,

    1. Some words are linked or run together

    2. Some words are reduced or shortened

    3. Some sounds are deleted or not pronounced

    4. Some sounds are altered or pronounced differently

    5. Some words are contracted or combined

In other words, speakers *distort* the sounds. Even if you hear all the sounds, you still may not understand every word a speaker says.

 Eye-Opener: The distortion of normal spoken English is like the effect of a lot of static on a telephone call. In both cases, it can be difficult to distinguish the words someone says.

Listening for Message Intent: Rhythm & Music

 *Intent* is what a speaker means. Imagine that your friend looks at your homework and says, "Nice job!" Until you understand the intonation, or the music, in your friend's voice, you don't know if your friend is complimenting your homework or insulting it. Speakers use the rhythm and music of English—stress, timing, and intonation—to help signal their meaning. The message is in the music. Even if you know all the words, you still may not understand what a speaker means.

 Eye-Opener: Stress, timing, and intonation carry meaning: the meaning is more than the sum or total of the words.

Listening for Noun and Verb Endings (Grammar Sounds)

The grammatical endings on regular nouns and verbs are important for listening. Listeners use these endings for valuable information about tense, person, and number. Grammar Sounds also help complete the rhythm of spoken English.

 Eye-Opener: Speaking helps listening.

Remind yourself of the Three Kinds of Information (p. 7).

What are the Three Kinds of Information?	Why is it hard to use this information to make sense of what you hear?	Can you improve your listening in this area?
1.	Conversation topics may change: You may not have any context.	No. You can't control the topic.
2.	You're still learning English: You don't fully understand how it works yet.	Yes, eventually, as your English improves.
3.	English doesn't sound the way it looks: Sounds are linked, reduced, deleted, altered, and contracted.	Yes, by learning about and practicing the Sound Concepts in this book. If you *say* something, you'll be better at hearing it.

 PRONUNCIATION GOAL

Since pronunciation is an integrated system, let your speaking help your listening. Practice saying linked, reduced, deleted, altered, and contracted sounds in order to make sense of what you hear.

Review: The Three Kinds of Listening Skills

LISTENING

Sound Concepts	Rhythm & Music	Grammar Sounds
Sounds are linked.		**Noun and verb endings**
Sounds are reduced.	Syllables	3rd person singular present tense verbs
Sounds are deleted.	Stress	regular past tense verbs
Sounds are altered.	Intonation	regular plural count nouns
Sounds are contracted.	Timing	possessive nouns

Case Study 1: The EMT

An English-language learner was an emergency medical technician (EMT) in his home country. When he came to the United States, he enrolled in an EMT training course to become certified to work in his field. He already knew a lot of the information taught in the course, but he had trouble understanding the teacher. He finally had to drop the course and enroll in an advanced ESL listening and speaking course in order to succeed.

Discuss the following questions with a partner:

1. What was the EMT's problem? Why couldn't he understand the class lectures?

2. Which of the three kinds of information did the student have? Which was missing?

3. Have you or someone you know ever been in a similar situation? What solved the problem?

Speaking: Three Kinds of Speaking Skills

1. Speak with correct syllables, stress, intonation, and timing (Rhythm & Music).

2. Speak with correct noun and verb endings (Grammar Sounds).

3. Speak with correct consonant and vowel sounds.

SPEAKING

Rhythm & Music	Grammar Sounds	Consonant & Vowel Sounds
Syllables		
Stress	**Noun and verb endings**	
Timing	3rd person singular present tense verbs	
Intonation	regular past tense verbs	
	regular plural count nouns	
	possessive nouns	

Think About It

What are your individual pronunciation problems? List them on a separate piece of paper.

 Eye-Opener: If you are like most language learners, you only wrote one or two items. In fact, most English language learners can't say what their specific pronunciation problems are at all!

Knowing *what* your problems are—what you need to improve—is the first step to improving.

Things you may have written	**Things you probably didn't write**
• problems with l and r	• syllable structure
• vowels	• verb and noun endings
	• altered sounds

In general, students make three kinds of speaking errors:

1. **Rhythm & Music:** Students use the wrong syllable structure (adding or subtracting sounds or syllables), the wrong stress, or inappropriate intonation or timing (pauses).

2. **Grammar Sounds:** Students also have trouble with the sounds of common grammatical endings, such as the sounds of the "ed" at the end of "moved" and "looked."

3. **Consonant & Vowel Sounds:** Some students mispronounce specific consonant or vowel sounds, such as the sound of the letters "th" in "something" (the sound /θ/).

Case Study 2: The Presentation

At an international conference, a well-known linguist (a nonnative English speaker) was giving a presentation to mostly native speakers of English. One important point the speaker made was about what he called "wa-ka-BYUL-er-ies." No one in the audience understood what he was talking about. In fact, the audience members were so confused and distracted that they missed much of the rest of his talk. After the talk, some of the audience talked together and eventually realized that the speaker must have meant "vocabulary." At the same conference the next year, many people who had heard the talk still remembered the mispronunciation of the word "vocabulary," but no one remembered what the speaker's point had been.

Discuss the following questions with a partner:

1. There is more than one mistake in the speaker's pronunciation. How many mistakes can you find? Which mistake caused the biggest difficulty for the listeners? Why?

2. Why was the audience unable to pay attention to the rest of the speaker's talk?

3. How did the listeners eventually figure out the speaker's mistake? What kind of information were they using?

4. Can you think of a time when you or someone else made multiple pronunciation mistakes in the same word? What happened?

Case Study 3: Alfredo and Junko

Two friends, Junko and Alfredo, are talking about Pam's new car. Junko says, "Gee, I really rike Pam's car." When Pam arrives, Alfredo says, "Oh, Pam, Junko like your car."

Discuss the following questions with a partner:

1. What kind of mistake did Junko make? What kind of mistake did Alfredo make?

2. In which case would listeners think the speaker needs English lessons? Why?

3. Which mistake is more noticeable? Why?

Summary

Pronunciation is an integrated system. Practice listening and speaking together.

1. **Sound Concepts:** Sounds are distorted, and the content can be lost. Practice Sound Concepts to improve your listening.

2. **Rhythm & Music:** Stress, intonation, and timing carry meaning. Practice Rhythm & Music to improve your listening and speaking.

3. **Grammar Sounds:** Noun and verb endings change the meaning (and sometimes the music) of a sentence. Practice Grammar Sounds to improve your listening and speaking.

4. **Consonant & Vowel Sounds:** Different sounds are difficult for different students. Practice Consonant & Vowel sounds to improve your speaking.

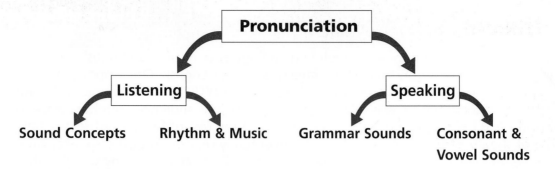

Think about the following questions and discuss them with a partner:

1. Which of these four parts of pronunciation do you think are more important? Which do you think are less important? Why?

2. Which areas have you focused most on in other English courses? Which areas have you focused least on?

 What's our focus? Many pronunciation courses focus on consonant and vowel sounds. But these sounds are just one part of pronunciation. Mistakes in the other three areas—Sound Concepts, Rhythm & Music, and Grammar Sounds—can cause much more confusion. This book focuses on Sound Concepts, Rhythm & Music, and Grammar Sounds.

 In this book, the camera symbol tells you the focus of an exercise or section.

 The recycling symbol tells you what's being reviewed or recycled.

DISCUSSION OF CASE STUDIES

1. **The EMT:** This student already had background information on the subject. He even had some language information because he had studied English before. But he wasn't able to understand the sound information—the linked, reduced, deleted, altered, and contracted sounds (Sound Concepts)—of connected speech in the lectures.

2. **The Presentation:** The speaker made four mistakes. The combination of mistakes and the serious mistake with stress caused problems for the audience.

   A. Rhythm & Music: The speaker stressed the wrong syllable of the word (third instead of second). This was his biggest and most serious mistake: stressing the wrong syllable often makes a word impossible to understand. Even if the speaker only made this mistake, his listeners still would have had great trouble understanding him.

   B. Grammar Sounds: The speaker added the regular plural noun ending to "vocabulary" even though "vocabulary" is usually used as a noncount noun, which shouldn't have a plural ending.

   C. Consonant & Vowel Sounds: The speaker made two mistakes: he used a /w/ sound instead of a /v/ at the beginning of the word, and he used the wrong vowel sound in the second syllable of the word. If these were the only mistakes the speaker made, his listeners probably would have understood him anyway.

3. **Junko and Alfredo:** Junko's mistake is with individual consonant sounds /r/ and /l/. Alfredo's mistake is with the third-person singular present tense verb ending "-s" (Grammar Sounds). In both cases, their listeners would probably understand them. Many English students think the bigger mistake is Junko's. Junko's listeners might notice she has a foreign accent, but most native English speakers think the bigger mistake is Alfredo's. Alfredo's listeners might think he's not very educated because he didn't pronounce the /s/ in the verb ending.

Diagnostics and Logbook

Beginning Diagnostics	The Teacher-Student Partnership	Learning to Use Your Logbook	The Key to Success in Pronunciation
Part 1 Listening Part 2 Speaking Part 3 Thinking about listening and speaking			

> ♻ **Remember: Pronunciation includes both listening and speaking.**
>
> The four parts of pronunciation are **Sound Concepts**, **Rhythm & Music**, **Grammar Sounds**, and **Consonant & Vowel Sounds**.

Diagnostics

Use the following three diagnostics (Listening, Speaking, and Thinking About Listening and Speaking) to make a record of your pronunciation at the beginning of this course.

Part 1: Listening

SECTION A: Sound Concepts

🎧 You will hear 13 sentences. Write the sentences you hear.

1. _____
2. _____
3. _____
4. _____
5. _____
6. _____
7. _____
8. _____
9. _____
10. _____
11. _____
12. _____
13. _____

SECTION B: Rhythm & Music

1. You will hear six words or phrases. Write the word or phrase you hear.

1. _____   4. _____

2. _____   5. _____

3. _____   6. _____

2. You will hear a sentence. What does it mean? Listen and choose the best paraphrase.

Example: **A.** Look! There's a very warm dog.

B. I'm hungry. I think I'll have one.

1. **A.** The doctor is late.   **B.** The patient is late.

2. **A.** The speaker is asking Bill for the phone.   **B.** The speaker is asking for the phone bill.

3. Choose the phrase that best matches the meaning of the sentence you hear.

1. **A.** CDs, not DVDs   **B.** Three, not four

2. **A.** Those tools, not these   **B.** Those four, not those six

4. Decide whether the person speaking has just heard good or bad news.

1. **A.** good news   **B.** bad news

2. **A.** good news   **B.** bad news

5. Decide whether the person speaking is uncertain (asking for information) or certain (asking for confirmation).

1. **A.** uncertain   **B.** certain

2. **A.** uncertain   **B.** certain

3. **A.** uncertain   **B.** certain

4. **A.** uncertain   **B.** certain

6. Listen to a brief dialogue that ends with a question. How do you think the speaker will answer it? Choose the best answer below.

1. **A.** Italian food   **B.** to cook

2. **A.** Los Angeles   **B.** California

3. **A.** On the 10th   **B.** Next month

Part 2: Speaking

Record yourself reading the following paragraph.

Last June, Veronica and Greg moved to Ithaca (a city in upstate New York). She was interested in studying Spanish at a four-year college, and he wanted to get a job. Veronica had already applied to some colleges and universities, so she started school right away and really liked her classes. But Greg had trouble with his job search.

"I've looked at job listings in newspapers and even used Internet job lists for months," he complained. "None of it's done any good."

Some people at Veronica's school said that local libraries could be good sources of information, but nothing helped Greg. They started to think he would never find something. Finally, after a year, he found a job in one of the offices at Veronica's college.

"It's really great—now, he works right on campus," Veronica said, "and in between my classes I can even meet him for lunch."

The speaking diagnostic records your pronunciation at the beginning of this course. In the periodic assessment sections, you will return to this diagnostic and work with some of your specific errors. Don't worry about trying to fix all your errors at once.
(See appendix 2 for reproducible speaking diagnostic)

Part 3: Thinking About Listening and Speaking

SECTION A: Sound Concepts

1. Native speakers use dictionary ("correct") pronunciations in conversation.

   Agree   **Disagree**

2. How acceptable are contractions (such as "can't") in everyday speech?

   Completely acceptable   **Somewhat acceptable**   **Not acceptable**

3. How acceptable are shortened forms (such as "gonna") in everyday speech?

   Completely acceptable   **Somewhat acceptable**   **Not acceptable (careless speech)**

4. When I listen to English speakers, I can understand the individual words even if a speaker doesn't exaggerate the space between words.

   Always   **Sometimes**   **Never**

5. When speaking, I link or connect one word to another.

   Always   **Sometimes**   **Never**

SECTION B: Rhythm & Music

1. How well can I explain the differences between English and my language in syllable structure?

   Very well   **Not so well**   **I never thought about it.**

2. How important is it to say the correct number of syllables in a word?

   Very important   **Somewhat important**   **Not important**

3. How important is it to use correct stress in words?

   Very important   **Somewhat important**   **Not important**

4. If I can understand every word in a sentence, then I've understood the meaning of the sentence.

   Agree   **Disagree**

5. In general, intonation doesn't change the meaning of individual English words. Therefore, intonation isn't essential to clear communication.

   Agree   **Disagree**

6. Intonation and stress change the meaning of sentences.

   Agree   **Disagree**

7. English questions use rising intonation.

   Always   **Sometimes**   **Never**

8. When I read aloud, I know which words to stress and why.

   Agree   **Disagree**

9. English has a standard pattern of stress, intonation, and timing.

   Agree   **Disagree**

10. I can tell when a speaker uses non-standard stress or intonation.

    Agree   **Disagree**

11. I understand the meaning of non-standard stress and intonation.

    Agree   **Disagree**

12. Most English speakers will pause in the same places when reading aloud the same sentence or passage.

    Agree   **Disagree**

13. When I read aloud, as in the speaking diagnostic, I think about (Check all that apply)

    _____ vowel sounds   _____ consonant sounds

    _____ stress   _____ intonation

    _____ pauses   _____ thought groups

    _____ pronunciation of new words or proper nouns   _____ number of syllables in words

14. True or false? Put T or F in front of each sentence.

Intonation, stress, and timing can…

_____ turn a statement into a question
_____ change the meaning of a sentence
_____ reduce the number of words needed to convey your meaning
_____ act as oral punctuation, quotation marks, and paragraph breaks
_____ signal an implied contrast

15. I use clues from a speaker's intonation and stress to help understand a speaker's meaning.

    Always   **Sometimes**   **Never**

16. I use clues from facial expressions and body language to help understand a speaker's meaning.

    Always   **Sometimes**   **Never**

17. One of the main reasons I have trouble understanding English speakers is that they speak too quickly. If they slowed down, I think I could understand them.

    Agree   **Disagree**

SECTION C: Grammar Sounds

1. Verb and noun endings are unnecessary because of words like "yesterday" or "many."

    Agree   **Disagree**

2. The "-s" or "-es" ending on regular third-person singular present tense verbs has different pronunciations.

    Agree   **Disagree**

3. The regular past tense ending ("-ed") always adds an extra syllable onto the verb.

    Agree   **Disagree**

4. I use correct verb and noun endings when I speak to teachers.

    Always   **Sometimes**   **Never**

5. I use correct verb and noun endings when I speak to my peers.

    Always   **Sometimes**   **Never**

6. How important is it to use correct verb and noun endings in everyday speech?

    Very important   **Somewhat important**   **Not important**

7. My teacher will correct my pronunciation every time I make a mistake.

    Agree   **Disagree**

8. Whose responsibility is it to keep track of my pronunciation errors?

    My teacher's   **Mine**

9. I keep a list or a logbook of my pronunciation errors.

    Agree   **Disagree**

SECTION D: Consonant & Vowel Sounds

1. How important is the correct pronunciation of consonant and vowel sounds?

   Very important   **Somewhat important**   **Not important**

2. How well can I explain the differences between English and my language in vowel sounds?

   Very well   **Not so well**   **I never thought about it.**

3. Compared to the number of English vowel *letters*, there are _____ English vowel *sounds*.

   many more   **about the same number of**   **fewer**

4. If I can correctly pronounce all the consonant and vowel sounds, my listeners will understand me.

   Agree   **Disagree**

5. My biggest pronunciation problems are consonant or vowel sounds.

   Agree   **Disagree**

6. Sometimes, correct pronunciations feel so strange to me that I prefer my own pronunciations.

   Agree   **Disagree**

SECTION E: Errors and Change

1. List your biggest pronunciation problems here:

   _____

   _____

2. What's one strategy you're using to improve your specific pronunciation problems?

3. I know I make pronunciation errors, but I want to improve my speech, not change it.

   Agree   **Disagree**

4. Complete the sentence by choosing the item that best fits the way you feel. There are some things I always get wrong,

   A. and I know this because my teachers correct me again and again on the same mistakes.

   B. but when my teachers say I get the pronunciation "right," it feels so strange and wrong that I think they can't be right.

   C. but I think I'm saying things the same way my teachers do, so I don't understand where my mistakes are.

   D. and I'm working on them: I know where my specific mistakes are, and I know how to fix them.

5. If people understand me when I speak, I don't need to make changes to my pronunciation.

   Agree   **Disagree**

6. I want to improve my pronunciation.

      Agree strongly   **Agree somewhat**   **Disagree**

7. I know what changes I need to make to my speech in order to improve.

      Agree strongly   **Agree somewhat**   **Disagree**

8. I monitor my speech to make these changes and corrections.

      Agree strongly   **Agree somewhat**   **Disagree**

9. I know when I've been able to successfully change part of my pronunciation.

      Agree strongly   **Agree somewhat**   **Disagree**

How to Use This Book: The Teacher-Student Partnership

This course will help you figure out what your errors are, learn how to correct them, and work systematically through your problems. Use the diagram below to think about your progress in this course.

> **Eye-Opener:** "Consciousness" means being aware of errors and thinking about how to correct them. "Competence" means not making errors.

THE FOUR LEVELS OF COMPETENCE

GOAL!

LEVEL 1

Unconscious incompetence

Before this course, you were probably here. You made mistakes and you didn't know what your specific problems were.

LEVEL 2

Conscious incompetence

At this point in the course, you are probably here: You still make mistakes, but you are starting to understand what kinds of mistakes they are.

LEVEL 3

Conscious competence

As you work on your English, you have a lot to do. You need to think about your errors and try to correct them. Your teacher and this book will help you.

LEVEL 4

Unconscious competence

This is your goal: At this level, you will listen and speak accurately, without thinking about it all the time.

Eye-Opener: Pay attention to your own speech. You need to be conscious of your mistakes, so that you can correct them. But you also need to be conscious of the correction, so that you can remember how and where to form the sound. When you form a correct sound, stop— "freeze" the feel of the correction in your mouth and in your mind (freeze-frame) so you can say it more easily in the future.

How You Can Learn to Correct Your Mistakes
The Teacher-Student Partnership in Action

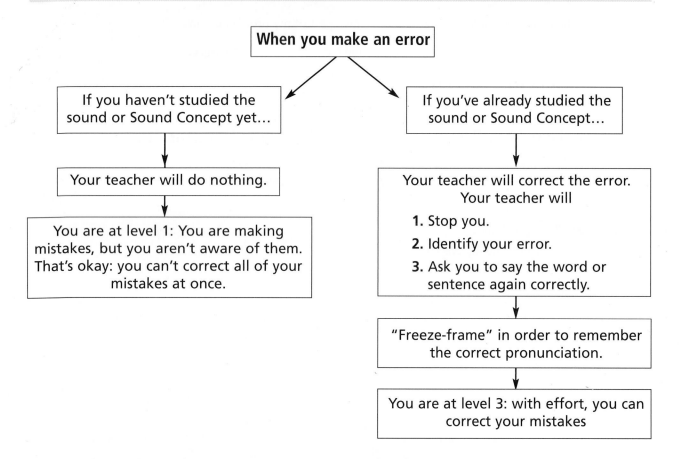

When you make an error

If you haven't studied the sound or Sound Concept yet...

Your teacher will do nothing.

You are at level 1: You are making mistakes, but you aren't aware of them. That's okay: you can't correct all of your mistakes at once.

If you've already studied the sound or Sound Concept...

Your teacher will correct the error. Your teacher will
1. Stop you.
2. Identify your error.
3. Ask you to say the word or sentence again correctly.

"Freeze-frame" in order to remember the correct pronunciation.

You are at level 3: with effort, you can correct your mistakes

How will your teacher and this book help you succeed?

1. **Freeze-Frame**

    In this course, you will do more than just imitate models of correct pronunciation. Diagrams show you how to place your lips, tongue, and teeth to pronounce a word. When your teacher describes what you are doing wrong and what you need to do to fix it, pay attention so that you don't keep making the same mistakes. When your teacher says you're doing something correctly, "freeze-frame" the moment so you can remember the right way to do it.

2. **Error Correction**

    Your teacher will not correct every mistake you make in the beginning. Your teacher will only correct mistakes *after* a topic is introduced in class.

How can you help yourself succeed?

1. **Try to produce the sounds and speech patterns correctly.**

   After a sound, pattern, or concept is introduced, you are responsible for making these changes to your speech. You should use the new speech patterns not just in a specific exercise, but also in all future classroom speech, and in your speech outside class. Your teacher will correct you if you make these mistakes in class.

2. **Keep track of your specific pronunciation trouble spots.**

   Use the log at the back of this book to help keep track of your errors and to think about why you make them. Enter any word, phrase, or idea you need to work more on. Only enter something in your log *after* you talked about it in class.

LANGUAGE STRATEGY: Using Your Pronunciation Log to Track Your Progress

Your pronunciation log is an important tool to help track your progress and improve your pronunciation. Read the steps below to learn how to record and study your mistakes.

1. Write down your mistake or problem and describe it.

2. Label your mistake so you can look it up in the table of contents and index.

3. If you make the same mistake later, look back at your log to remember how to correct it.

4. Remember, *your* logbook won't look exactly like any other student's logbook!

How a Pronunciation Log Works

Everyone has different pronunciation problems. Look at the sample log entries below to see the different problems three students had with the same word. Listen to the students say the word and follow along below. Don't worry about the individual mistakes. Instead, focus on learning how to use the log. You will learn more about syllables in "Getting Ready for Chapter 3."

Student 1:

Word or phrase	How to say it	How did I say it?	What was my mistake?	Other examples
speech	speech	su-peech	separating the first	su-trong/strong
	(1 syllable)	(2 syllables)	two consonants	

Student 2:

Word or phrase	How to say it	How did I say it?	What was my mistake?	Other examples
speech	speech	es-peech	adding a vowel	es-sport/sport
	(1 syllable)	(2 syllables)	sound at the front	

Student 3:

Word or phrase	How to say it	How did I say it?	What was my mistake?	Other examples
speech	speech	speech-ee	adding a vowel	each-ee/each
	(1 syllable)	(2 syllables)	sound at the end	

Practice Using a Logbook

 You will hear a student read a word, then a sentence with that word, then the word again. Work with a partner to fill out one row of the chart for each student's mistake in that word, using the sample entries above as a guide. Do your best to label each mistake. You will learn more about these mistakes in chapter 3.

	Word or phrase	How to say it	How did I say it?	What was my mistake?	Other examples
Student 4:	EYES				
Student 5:	LOOKED				
Student 6:	USED				

 Eye-Opener: When you have trouble with a sound or concept after practicing it in several exercises, enter the specific problem into your log.

Understanding the Key to Success: Speaking

PRONUNCIATION GOAL

Improve your speaking *and* listening by practicing speaking.

Remember, pronunciation works two ways: Your goal is to understand others and to be understood.

Imagine that this is your pronunciation:

but the sound of other English speakers is this:

There is a mismatch. This mismatch is why it is difficult to understand speakers of English and to be understood.

You can hear English speakers, but you don't sound like them, and you can't understand them. Hearing other English speakers isn't helping improve your pronunciation. If hearing others does not help, what will help? Hearing yourself will help, once your pronunciation begins to match the sound of English.

Your speaking and listening are like a closed circuit.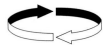

What you hear:

What you say:

If you say it right, you will start to hear it: Speaking helps listening. As your pronunciation improves, your listening comprehension will improve.

Speaking is the key to understanding others and being understood.

Final Chapter Activity

Context for Practice: Language Learning Case Studies

Case Study 1: Departures

A pilot and an air traffic controller were taking an English course to improve their on-the-job pronunciation and communication. When practicing talking about arrivals and departures, the two mispronounced the word "departure" in different ways.

Pilot: "I'm seeking clearance for a *de-BARCH-er* on runway 2E."

Air traffic controller: "Okay, you have clearance for your *de-PARCH.*"

Their teacher stopped them and told them that the word was de-PARCH-er. Each of them kept mispronouncing the word in their own way. The teacher kept repeating the word, and the students kept saying it wrong. Finally, the students asked the teacher to explain what they were doing wrong.

Discuss the following questions with a partner:

1. What was the pilot's mistake? What part of pronunciation is important to understand this mistake?

2. What was the air traffic controller's mistake? What part of pronunciation is important to understand this mistake?

3. Why was the teacher's repetition of the word not helpful? Why did the speakers keep mispronouncing the word?

4. What do you think the teacher could have done to help the students understand their mistakes and correct their pronunciations?

5. Have you ever been corrected by a teacher, but not understood the point of the correction? What did you do?

Case Study 2: Train Station

An American was living in Japan teaching English. One of the first Japanese words she learned was the name of her train station, but she couldn't pronounce it correctly. When taking the train, she counted the stops to get off at the right stop. There were announcements on the train in Japanese, but she couldn't understand them.

Whenever the teacher told her students where she lived, they didn't understand her. Finally, they would realize what she meant: "Oh, you mean _____ station," they would say, naming the station correctly. One day, the teacher's students decided to teach her to say the station name correctly. The students helped the teacher until her pronunciation of the train station matched theirs. That night, on the way home, she heard the announcements on the train as usual. But this time she understood one word: the name of her train station. She got off at the right station without needing to count stops.

Discuss the following questions with a partner:

1. Why did learning to pronounce the name of the station correctly help the teacher to hear it?

2. Have you ever been in a situation where you heard something many times, but never understood it until you learned to say it yourself?

What did we do in this chapter?

Diagnostics: Listening; Speaking; Thinking About Listening and Speaking

Understanding the Teacher-Student Partnership

Learning to Use Your Logbook

Understanding the Key to Success: Practice speaking to improve your speaking and listening

DISCUSSION OF CASE STUDIES

Case Study 1: Departures The pilot's mistake was using the sound /b/, a voiced sound, instead of the sound /p/, an unvoiced sound. He needed to turn his voicebox off for that sound in order to say it correctly. The air traffic controller's mistake was making the word a two-syllable word instead of a three-syllable word. He needed to say the final syllable in order to say the word correctly.

The teacher's model wasn't helpful to the students because it was blocked by the students' mental images of the word. The students were pronouncing the word according to their mental image of it. The students needed to be told specifically how to say the word correctly in order to change their pronunciation of it. Then their mental image of the word would change.

Case Study 2: Train Station The American pronounced the station name incorrectly because she was using English sounds and rules to pronounce a Japanese word. Her mental image of the name of the train station didn't match the Japanese pronunciation. Remember, speaking helps listening, but *hearing* isn't the same as listening. She *heard* the correct pronunciation of the word many times (from her students and every day on the train), but she never recognized that single word until she learned to say it correctly herself. When her pronunciation of the word matched the actual pronunciation, then she was able to recognize the word in the middle of a stream of Japanese.

Getting Ready for Chapter 3
What You Need to Know About Syllables

Introduction to Syllables and Counting Syllables

 Eye-Opener: A syllable is a beat. Just as music has a rhythm, spoken language has a rhythm. The smallest unit, or beat, of English rhythm is a syllable. Think of syllables in terms of sounds. A syllable in English usually has a vowel sound.

Exercise 1: Syllables Around the Room

 Focus on counting syllables

1. Work with a partner. Practice clapping or tapping the number of syllables in each of the three words below.

clock	clock	one syllable, one clap or tap
window	win-dow	two syllables, two claps or taps
thermostat	ther-mo-stat	three syllables, three claps or taps

2. Make a chart with three columns like the one below. Make a list of things you see around you and write your words in the correct column in the chart.

Words with 1 syllable	Words with 2 syllables	Words with 3 syllables
desk	pencil	computer

3. Work in groups of four or more students. Take turns reading a word aloud from your chart. Say the number of syllables the word has and count them.

   Example: pencil   2 syllables   pen-cil

The other students should listen, clap or tap the syllables, and decide if you are correct. When your group agrees on the number of syllables, move on to another word.

Exercise 2: Meet Your Classmates

 Focus on counting syllables

1. Work in small groups. Make a chart with your classmates' names, countries, and nationalities. Write the number of syllables in each word or name. Ask these questions:

   • What's your name? How do you spell it?

   • Where are you from? What's your nationality?

   Example:

Name	Country	Nationality
Ana	Spain (1)	Spanish (2)

2. Work with a partner. Use your chart to answer these questions.

   Who has a one-syllable name? _____

   Who has a two-syllable name? _____

   Who has a three-syllable name? _____

   Who has a name with four or more syllables? _____

   What countries have the most syllables? _____

   What countries have the fewest syllables? _____

3. Work with a partner. Read the usage note below. Write an introduction for your partner, and read it to the class or a small group. Make sure to say the right number of syllables in each word. Don't add or delete syllables!

   Example: This is Ana. She's a lawyer. She's Spanish.

USAGE NOTE: INTRODUCTIONS

Introduce people in different ways in different situations.

	In person	On the phone
Yourself	I'm Carlos.	This is Carlos.
Someone else	This is Ana.	– – – –

⚠ **BE CAREFUL!** Don't say "I'm Carlos" when introducing yourself on the phone.

Journal

Thinking about syllables is difficult for many students. Write answers to the following questions in your journal. Don't worry if you don't know the "right" answer—just write what you think.

What is the rhythm of your language? How does listening to your language differ from listening to English? What kinds of breaks, pauses, or beats do you hear?

Introduction to Syllable Structure

 Eye-Opener: The way we write a language—the letters or symbols—affects the way we think about syllables.

A language can be written using symbols that are alphabetic (one symbol = one letter), syllabic (one symbol = one syllable), or logographic (one symbol = one word). Some languages combine these systems. Which system(s) does your language use?

Alphabetic _____　　　　Syllabic _____　　　　Logographic _____

If your language uses a syllabic writing system, thinking about English syllable structure may be difficult for you. You need to try to think about English syllables without using your language's writing system.

Remember that a syllable is a rhythmic beat. You can think of all spoken languages in terms of syllables. Sometimes a syllable is a single word. Sometimes it's a part of a word.

A syllable has a combination of consonant and vowel *sounds*, not letters. Different languages allow different combinations of consonant and vowel sounds in a syllable.

V = a single vowel sound　　　　C = a single consonant sound

Word	Word in IPA*	Number of Syllables	Syllable Structure	Explanation
man	/mæn/	one	CVC	Each letter represents a single sound.
good	/gʊd/	one	CVC	The two letters "oo" together represent only one vowel sound.
box	/baks/	one	CVCC	The single letter "x" represents two different consonant sounds: /k/ and /s/.
this	/ðɪs/	one	CVC	The two letters "t" and "h" together represent one consonant sound, /ð/.
comb	/kom/	one	CVC	The letter "b" doesn't represent any sounds. We say the "b" is silent.
stroke	/strok/	one	CCCVC	The letter "e" doesn't represent any sound. We say the "e" is silent.

* Remember, you do not need to memorize the IPA. We use it as a tool to think more clearly about sounds, not letters. If you don't understand a symbol, look it up in the IPA chart at the back of this book.

Exercise 3: Syllables in Your Native Language

 Focus on syllable structure

Think of syllables and words in your language in terms of the consonant and vowel *sounds*, even if your language does not use an alphabet. Answer the following questions and discuss your responses with a partner.

In your language. . .

1. What are some single syllables? (Think of words, or parts of words.) Choose four examples, and write them here the way they sound in English. _____

2. Can you begin a word with a vowel sound (VC)?   YES   NO

   Give an example: _____

3. Can you end a word with a vowel sound (CV)?   YES   NO

   Give an example: _____

4. Can you end a word with a consonant sound?   YES   NO

   Give an example: _____

5. Can you end a word with any consonant sound, or can you use only certain consonant sounds to end a word?   **ANY CONSONANT/CERTAIN ONES**

   Give examples: _____

6. Can you begin a word with any combination of consonant sounds, or can you use only certain combinations of consonant sounds to begin a word?   **ANY CONSONANT/CERTAIN ONES**

   Give examples: _____

 Eye-Opener: A group of two or more consonant sounds (not letters) next to each other in a single syllable is called a consonant cluster. English allows consonant clusters at the beginning, at the end, or at both the beginning and the end of a syllable. Some other languages don't.

Journal

Every language has *borrowed words*. When a language borrows a word from another language, speakers change its pronunciation. People use the syllable structure of their own language to say the new word.

Has your language borrowed any words from English? Work with a partner in class to list borrowed words. How do speakers of your language say these words? Try to write down the syllable structure.

After class, interview English speakers to find out how they say these words. Take notes on their pronunciations and report back to your class. What did you learn about different syllable structures?

If you have trouble saying any of these words with correct English syllable structure, enter them into your logbook now.

Syllable Structure and Linked Sounds

Sound Concepts	Rhythm & Music	Grammar Sounds	Consonant & Vowel Sounds
Linked sounds Contracted sounds	Syllable structure	Regular past tense verb endings	/t/ and /d/

 Sound Concepts

Introduction to Linked Sounds

Preview

Is it difficult for you to understand native speakers when they talk? Why?

Diagnostic

 You will hear six sentences. On a separate piece of paper, write the sentences you hear.

After Listening

Your teacher will go over the diagnostic you just took. Use the checklist below to decode what you heard. What was difficult about this diagnostic?

> ### Three Steps to Decode What You Hear
>
> **1** What did you hear? Write it down.
>
> **2** Does it make sense? Reread what you wrote.
>
> **3** What was really said? Use the Three Kinds of Information (p. 7) to make sense of what you heard.

 Eye-Opener: Sometimes students think that native speakers speak too fast. But speed is not the problem. The problem is the linking between sounds.

What is linking?

Linking is connecting sounds in speech. In written English, there is space between words. But in everyday speech, there is no space or pause between words. Native speakers connect words like links in a chain.

We can link a consonant sound from the end of one word to a vowel sound at the beginning of another word. We call this consonant-to-vowel linking.

Example: What's up? $\xrightarrow{\text{sounds like}}$ Whatsup?

How do we mark linking in this book?

Mark the linked sounds like this to help you remember to connect them in speech.

    Example: What's up?

Why is linking important?

Linking is important for both listening and speaking. Practice linked sounds to make your speech smoother and to help you understand linked sounds.

USAGE NOTE: LINKING and PAUSES in SPEECH and WRITING

In writing, commas sometimes signal pauses. But when speaking, we sometimes link sounds over commas:

"Did your last English class focus on pronunciation?"

"Yes, it did, Amy. We did lots of drills, amazing activities, and some good exercises."

In normal connected speech:

We link sounds at comma 1, comma 3, and comma 4. These commas signal very small pauses, and we link sounds over them.

There's no linking at comma 2. There's a large pause at a comma before the name of the person you're talking to.

Practice Linked Sounds

With a partner, go back to the diagnostic on p. 35. Mark the sentences for consonant-to-vowel linking. Remember to link consonant and vowel *sounds*, not letters.

Journal

English speakers link sounds in conversation all the time. Linked speech is not informal or "bad" speech. It's everyday, connected speech. All languages connect some sounds and words in conversation. Write about when you link sounds in your own language. Be ready to share your ideas with a partner or small group.

Introduction to Contracted Sounds

Some words in English are contracted, or combined. You hear contractions all around you, in normal connected English. You might see contractions written like this, with an apostrophe mark ('):

    Example: there is   ⟶   there's

The apostrophe shows missing sounds or syllables. Use linked sounds with contractions. In speaking, contractions are always acceptable. They aren't informal or "bad" speech.

Exercise 1: Neighborhood Places

 Focus on consonant-to-vowel linking; contracted sounds

Use the contraction "there's" in the examples below to show that something exists or is present. Link the sounds in "there's a."

> Example: There's a restaurant across the street

1. Match the statements on the left to the responses on the right. Mark the sentences on the right for linking. Then practice the dialogue with a partner.

> Example: I need to get some gas. There's a gas station on the corner.

I need to. . .

_____	1. buy a stamp	**A.**	There's a news stand down the street.
_____	2. get a taxi	**B.**	There's a laundromat next door.
_____	3. get some cash	**C.**	There's a bank across the street.
_____	4. buy a newspaper	**D.**	There's an ATM inside the bank.
_____	5. get a cup of coffee	**E.**	There's a taxi stand near the bus stop.
_____	6. cash a check	**F.**	There's a post office on your right.
_____	7. do some laundry	**G.**	There's a coffee shop two doors down.

2. Use "there is" to write sentences about places in your neighborhood. Mark your sentences for linking. In a group, take turns reading your sentences aloud.

> Example: There's a police station on Harrison Street.

Exercise 2: Describing a Place

 Focus on consonant-to-vowel linking

1. Think of a favorite room. Write six sentences using "there is/there are" to describe your room to a partner. Be specific! Use some of these words and phrases to help you: next to, above, in front of, behind.

2. Have your teacher or partner check the grammar in your description. Then mark all examples of linking in your description and read it aloud to a partner.

> Example: There's a brown rug in front of the bed. There are two big windows next to my desk.

Exercise 3: Is it a _____?

 Focus on consonant-to-vowel linking

Think of an everyday object. In a small group, try to guess the object by asking yes/no questions and giving clues. Link sounds when you speak. Use the impersonal "you" (see next page) in your clues.

Consonant & Vowel Sounds

Introduction to the Sounds /t/ and /d/

What's the first letter of "time"? _____ What sound does it make? _____

This sound is the first and final sound in the word "tight." Practice saying it.

What's the first letter of "dime"? _____ What sound does it make? _____

This sound is the first and final sound in the word "did." Practice saying it.

What's the same about these sounds?

You don't change the position of your lips, tongue, and teeth for the sound /t/ and the sound /d/. For both sounds, you stop the flow of air.

What's different about these sounds?

In "time," your voicebox is off: /t/ is unvoiced. In "dime," your voicebox is on: /d/ is voiced.

Exercise 4: What's the final sound?

 Focus on /t/ and /d/   **Recycle voiced and unvoiced sounds**

What's the final *sound* of each word? Say the word aloud. (see the list of unvoiced sounds on p. 200.)

	Is the final sound /t/?	Is the final sound /d/?	Is the final sound unvoiced, but not /t/?	Is the final sound voiced, but not /d/?
1. wash	No	No	Yes	No
2. decide				
3. want				
4. fix				
5. name				
6. call				
7. ask				
8. drive				

Rhythm & Music

Syllable Structure

* Be sure you've completed the section on counting syllables in Getting Ready for Chapter 3. If not, turn back to p. 31 now!

When the syllable structure of your language doesn't match that of English, you may have problems saying English syllables. Here are some possible English syllables. Can you have a syllable like this in your language?

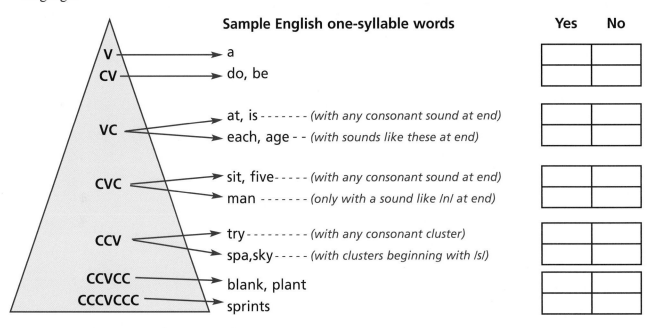

	Sample English one-syllable words	Yes	No
V	a		
CV	do, be		
VC	at, is - - - - - - - (with any consonant sound at end)		
	each, age - - (with sounds like these at end)		
CVC	sit, five - - - - - (with any consonant sound at end)		
	man - - - - - - - (only with a sound like /n/ at end)		
CCV	try - - - - - - - - (with any consonant cluster)		
	spa, sky - - - - - (with clusters beginning with /s/)		
CCVCC	blank, plant		
CCCVCCC	sprints		

 Eye-Opener: Why is syllable structure important for pronunciation?

If you checked any "No" boxes above, you may have a problem saying those syllables in English. It's natural to try to make difficult English syllables sound like syllables in your language. But it's like trying to put a square peg into a round hole: It doesn't work.

When syllable structures don't match:

- Speakers may add or delete sounds
- Listeners may misunderstand
- The rhythm of the sentence changes

 PRONUNCIATION GOAL

Reduce your accent by saying English syllables with the correct syllable structure. Don't add or delete sounds.

☑ CHECKLIST

Syllable Structure: Are you adding or deleting sounds?

Are you adding extra sounds?

If you add extra sounds to English syllables, there will be too many syllables in a word. Your listeners will be expecting fewer syllables, and they may be confused.

1. Are you adding sounds at the beginning of the word or syllable?

> Example: Saying "e-state" (two syllables) for "state" (one syllable)
> *Go to exercise 9.*

2. Are you adding sounds in the middle of a consonant cluster?

> Example: Saying "su-port" (two syllables) for "sport" (one syllable)
> *Read the logbook activity on page X.*

3. Are you adding sounds at the end of the word or syllable?

> Example: Saying "speech-ee" (two syllables) for "speech" (one syllable)
> *Go to exercise 8.*

Are you deleting sounds?

1. Are you deleting syllables in the middle of a word?

> Example: Saying "please" (one syllable) for "police" (two syllables)
> *Enter this into your log.*

2. Are you deleting the final consonants from the ends of a syllable?

> Example: Saying "wi" (CV) for "with" (CVC)
> *Go to exercise 8.*

3. Are you deleting syllables at the end of a word?

> Example: Saying "deparch" (two syllables) for "departure" (three syllables)
> *Go back to case study 1 in chapter 2.*

Exercise 5: Final Consonant Sounds

 Focus on syllable structure **Recycle counting syllables**

1. On your own, read the words in the chart aloud. Make sure not to add or delete sounds. Write down the final *sound* (not letter). For example, the final sound in "five" is /v/.

2. Work with a partner. Take turns reading the words aloud. Listen and write down the final sound and the number of syllables that your partner said. Do you and your partner agree?

Word	Final sound	Final sound your partner said	Number of syllables your partner said
1. piece			
2. Chinese			
3. front			
4. lunch			
5. judge			
6. dog			
7. back			
8. husband			
9. English			
10. teach			

Exercise 6: Initial Consonant Sounds

 Focus on syllable structure   **Recycle counting syllables**

On your own

1. Read the words in column 1 and add the correct indefinite article (a/an). Use "a" if the first sound of the next word is a consonant sound. Use "an" if the first sound of the next word is a vowel sound.

2. In column 2, write the number of syllables in the phrase.

    Example: an apple ⟶ 3

3. If there is linking in the phrase, check column 3 and mark it.

    Example: an apple

With a partner

4. Take turns reading aloud the phrases in column 1. When you listen, write the number of syllables your partner says in column 4.

5. Look at the number of syllables your partner recorded for your phrases. Do you agree?
   Use the checklist on the previous page to help solve any disagreements.

Phrase	Number of syllables in phrase	Is there linking?	Number of syllables partner says
1. _____ apple			
2. _____ state			
3. _____ escape			
4. _____ elbow			
5. _____ school			
6. _____ sport			
7. _____ skill			
8. _____ student			
9. _____ alphabet			
10. _____ vowel			
11. _____ consonant			
12. _____ syllable			
13. _____ speech			
14. _____ language			

 PRONUNCIATION GOAL

Don't add a sound at the beginning of English words that begin with the letter "s."

Look at the word "state." The first letter is "s." We say the name of this letter "es," but the sound of this letter is /s/.

What happens when you add an extra sound?

If you say "es" when you should say /s/, you add an extra syllable and change the rhythm of the sentence. Sometimes you also change the meaning of the word. If you say the first sound in "state" as "es," you make the word "estate."

| **state** | She lives in New York **State.** | one syllable |
| **estate** | Real **estate** brokers sell houses. | two syllables |

Reminder

 Use your log to identify and correct problems with syllables.

 The logbook on the next page shows two students' problems with syllable structure. Listen to the students explain their entries.

Student 1:

Word or phrase	How to say it	How did I say it?	What was my mistake?	Other examples
five	five (ends in /v/)	fi (no final consonant)	Syllable structure: CV instead of CVC; I left out the final consonant sound.	piece

Student 2:

Word or phrase	How to say it	How did I say it?	What was my mistake?	Other examples
brand	brand (1 syllable)	boo-ran-do (3 syllables)	Syllable structure: CV-CVC-CV instead of CCVCC; added a sound (and syllable) in a consonant cluster and at end.	stand

What are your biggest problems with English syllables? Look at the examples again, then enter the errors that you made in exercises 5 and 6 into your own logbook. Look at the checklist on syllable structure on page 40 for more help.

Sound Concepts

Consonant-to-Consonant Linking

When do we link consonant sounds to consonant sounds?

When the sounds are the same, even if the spelling isn't.

    Example: /s/ to /s/ in bus stop and /k/ to /k/ in take care

When the sounds are made in the same place, but one sound is voiced and the other is unvoiced.

    Example: /p/ to /b/ in clipboard (linking)

> **⚠ BE CAREFUL!** You must say both initial and final consonants. Otherwise, you won't be saying the sounds you need to link.

Test Yourself

Describe the two kinds of linking in this sentence. What time is it?

Discuss your answers with a partner.

Syllable Structure and Linked Sounds **43**

More Practice Linking

Go back to your description of a room in exercise 2. Mark examples of consonant-to-consonant linking. From now on, practice marking and saying both consonant-to-vowel and consonant-to-consonant linking.

 Eye-Opener: Linking is the first and most important Sound Concept. You must link sounds in order to practice the other Sound Concepts: reduced, deleted, altered, and contracted sounds. Linking also helps your overall fluency. You will be easier to understand, and your listeners will react more positively to your speech if you link sounds.

 PRONUNCIATION GOAL

Use linked sounds in everyday speech outside the classroom.

Grammar Sounds

Saying the Past Tense Ending "-ed"

Why is this ending important?

Even when you use "time" words like "yesterday," native speakers listen for the past tense ending ("-ed" on regular verbs) for tense and rhythm. If you don't say it,

- You sound ungrammatical
- Your listeners may be confused
- Your sentences may have the wrong rhythm

Use the following exercise to learn how to say the past tense ending correctly.

This ending is pronounced three different ways.

Exercise 7: Context for Practice–Language and Borrowings

 Focus on past tense endings   **Recycle linking**

1. Read the following passage to yourself. Then discuss the questions with a partner.

Many cultures have words for things that other cultures don't. Throughout history, when people **needed** a new word, they either **borrowed** or **created** one, or **invented** a new meaning for an old word. Meanings have also **changed** over time. A word's history is **called** its "etymology." The English word "nice" came from a Latin word, "nescium": "not knowing, ignorant." In Old French, it **started** meaning "silly." Middle English borrowed it in the thirteenth century with the meaning "foolish." Later it meant "shy," then "hard to please," and eventually "accurate." About 250 years ago, people **talked** about someone they **liked** as "nice," or pleasant. Although French **used** to use the word "nice" a lot, it hasn't **used** it for awhile. Today, there is still a city in France **named** Nice. The French city is **pronounced** "nees" (/nis/).

Adapted from *Who Talks Funny?* by Brenda S. Cox (North Haven, CT. Linnet Books, 1995), pp. 100-103

Think About It

Can you name some English words that were borrowed from other languages?

Did you know that words could change meaning over time? Can you think of any other examples of this?

Use the checklist below to complete the rest of this exercise (directions follow the checklist).

 **CHECKLIST**

How do you say the "-ed" ending on regular past tense verbs?

Look   Find the simple (root) form of a verb, without any endings.

Ask   What is the final sound (not letter)?

Is it   /t/ or /d/?

   If yes... ✔
      Add an extra syllable.
      → Say "-ed" as [Id].

   If no...

      Ask: Is the final sound unvoiced?

         If yes... ✔
            There is no extra syllable.
            → Say "-ed" as [t].

         If no...
            There is no extra syllable.
            → Say "-ed" as [d].

Are you having trouble finding the final sound of a word? Go back to exercise 4 (page 38) for help.

> **So, when saying the past tense ending:**
>
> 1. **Voiced** sounds use **voiced** endings, [d].
>
> 2. **Unvoiced** sounds use **unvoiced** endings, [t].
>
> 3. Sounds **/t/ or /d/** add an **extra syllable, [Id].**

 Eye-Opener: The verb "used" (past tense of "use") and the auxiliary "used" (in "used to") are both one-syllable words, but they're pronounced differently.

Example	Part of Speech	Sound of the Ending
I <u>used</u> a dictionary to look up a word.	verb	[d] (1 syllable)
I <u>used</u> to live in Toronto.	auxiliary	[t] (1 syllable)

1. Make a three-column chart like the one below. Label your chart with the three different pronunciations of the "-ed" ending.

[d]	[t]	[Id]
Extra syllable? yes no	Extra syllable? yes no	Extra syllable? yes no

2. Decide whether each ending is pronounced as an extra syllable. Circle the word *yes* or *no*.

3. Put each highlighted verb from the passage in the appropriate column.

4. Check your answers with a partner.

5. Write the sound of each "-ed" ending ([d], [t], or [Id]) above the highlighted verbs in the passage about borrowed words.

6. Mark the passage for linking.

7. Read the passage aloud to a partner, practicing linking and saying the endings correctly. Check your partner's pronunciation of the endings.

The Teacher-Student Partnership in Action

From now on, you are responsible for saying this ending correctly. Your teacher will correct you if you make a mistake with this ending. Your teacher will also tell you when you say it right (freeze-frame). Enter your mistakes with this ending into your log.

Exercise 8: Past Tense Endings and Syllables

 Focus on past tense endings   **Recycle counting syllables**

 Listen to the following past tense forms of regular verbs. How many syllables does each word have? Pay attention to the "-ed" ending. Put the ten words in two columns on a separate piece of paper.

One-Syllable Words	Two-Syllable Words

Classroom Language

The sentences below show several ways to say you are interested in something. One way uses a word with an "-ed" ending. Be sure to say the right number of syllables in each underlined word and the whole sentence. Practice clapping syllables with a partner until you say the right number.

	Number of syllables in underlined word	Number of syllables in sentence
I'm <u>interested</u> in biology.	3 or 4	9 or 10
I have an <u>interest</u> in biology.	2	10
I think biology is very <u>interesting</u>.	3 or 4	12 or 13

Exercise 9: Very Interesting!

recording.

 Focus on past tense endings   **Recycle counting syllables**

With a partner, take turns covering up the sentences and listening to your partner read. Which phrase did your partner say? Check the correct column. Check your answers with the sentences. Practice any difficult sentences. Remember to say all syllables.

	interested in	interest in	interesting
1. According to John, I'm an interesting person.			
2. I'm interested in meeting new people.			
3. I have an interest in meeting new people.			
4. My brother has an interest in cooking new dishes.			
5. My brother cooks interesting dishes.			
6. My brother is interested in cooking new dishes.			
7. I'm interested in taking an accounting class.			
8. I think accounting is an interesting class.			
9. I have an interest in taking an accounting class.			

Exercise 10: How do they feel?

 Focus on past tense endings   **Recycle linking and counting syllables**

We can use some of these "-ed" forms as adjectives to describe how people feel.

Part 1. Complete each sentence with an appropriate "-ed" form. Mark the sound of each ending [t], [d], or [Id]. Read your sentences aloud to a partner.

> ⚠️ **BE CAREFUL!**
> **For [t] or [d] "-ed" endings**—no extra syllable
> **For [Id] "-ed" endings**—keep the extra syllable
> **For all "-ed" endings**—remember to say the final consonant sound and link it

Example: Angela thought the film was interesting. She's <u>interested</u> in the topic.

Pronunciation of "-ed" ending: [Id]   Number of syllables in "-ed" word: 3 (or 4)

1. **A:** My roommate heard a fascinating lecture about the Navajo language.
    B: Yes, he's always been *fascinated* by the subject.
    Pronunciation of "-ed" ending: ____   Number of syllables in "-ed" word: ____

2. **A:** Jessica said the ending of her book was very surprising.
    B: Really? I didn't think she'd be *surprised* by the ending.
    Pronunciation of "-ed" ending: ____   Number of syllables in "-ed" word: ____

3. **A:** I was *amazed* to discover that there are more than 1,000 different languages spoken in the continent of Africa.
    B: Wow, that's amazing!
    Pronunciation of "-ed" ending: ____   Number of syllables in "-ed" word: ____

4. **A:** I was in a really boring class yesterday. Everyone was falling asleep.
    B: Wow, they must have really been *bored*.
    Pronunciation of "-ed" ending: ____   Number of syllables in "-ed" word: ____

5. **A:** There was a really frightening storm last night—my cat was very upset by it.
    B: Yeah, animals are often *frightened* by a storm.
    Pronunciation of "-ed" ending: ____   Number of syllables in "-ed" word: ____

6. **A:** There was a comedy show last night, but no one in the audience was *amused*.
    B: Yeah, I've seen that show before—it's not very amusing.
    Pronunciation of "-ed" ending: ____   Number of syllables in "-ed" word: ____

7. **A:** There's a soccer playoff tonight. It's going to be an exciting match.
    B: Yes, I'm very *excited* about it.
    Pronunciation of "-ed" ending: ____   Number of syllables in "-ed" word: ____

8. **A:** I was walking down the street with my friend when I tripped. It was very embarrassing.

    B: Oh, there's nothing to be _____ about—everyone's clumsy sometimes.

        Pronunciation of "-ed" ending: _____   Number of syllables in "-ed" word: _____

Part 2. Look at the photos on the right. What "-ed" adjectives would you use to describe their expressions? Discuss the photos with a classmate.

Part 3. With a partner, list other adjectives that end in "-ed." Write a sentence using each word, read your sentences aloud, and be sure to say the "-ed" ending correctly! Remember that vowel sounds are voiced sounds. If a present tense verb ends in a vowel SOUND, use the [d] ending.

    Example: worried   [d] I'm worried about my exam.   *no extra syllable*

                married   [d] He's a married man.   *no extra syllable*

Exercise 11: What We Did Yesterday—A Chain Story

 Focus on past tense endings

List five things you did yesterday, last week, last month, or last year. Try to use verbs with regular past tense endings. Mark the sound of the ending over each verb. In a small group, take turns reading aloud one of your sentences. Repeat your classmates' sentences, forming a chain.

    Example:

        John: [t] I watched TV.

        Mary: [t]   [t] John watched TV, and I walked the dog.

        Susan: [t]   [t]   [d] John watched TV, Mary walked the dog, and I used the dictionary.

Exercise 12: English Borrowings

 Focus on past tense endings

Look at the following English words borrowed from other languages. Look up any words you don't know. Make flashcards with these words. Take turns showing the cards to a partner and identifying the language.

    Example: hotel   French   "The word 'hotel' was borrowed from French."

 BE CAREFUL! Borrowed is a two-syllable word.

Word	Language
1. boss	Dutch
2. yankee	Dutch
3. cafeteria	Spanish
4. khaki	Urdu
5. pajamas	Hindi
6. karaoke	Japanese
7. cola	Temne (an African language)
8. kindergarten	German
9. banana	Wolof (an African language)
10. peak	French
11. dumb	German

PRONUNCIATION GOAL

By now, you should know the three pronunciations of the past tense endings. Use these pronunciations in everyday speech in and out of the classroom.

Exercise 13: The Navajo Code

 Focus on past tense endings   **Recycle linking**

Think About It

What's a code? When do people use codes? Did you ever make up or use a code? You are going to tell a story about the Navajo, a Native American nation. The Navajo have their own language, which very few non-Navajo know. At the time of WW II (say it "World War 2"), this language had never been written down. During the war, the U.S. government used the Navajo language for a secret military code.

For this activity, you need one group of eight volunteers to follow the steps below.

1. Look at the sentences on the next page. Each person is responsible for one sentence. Copy your sentence onto an index card. Mark your sentence for linking and the sounds of the past tense endings.

2. Close your book and memorize your sentence. Give your index card to your teacher (or group leader).

3. As a group, say your sentences aloud and try to put them in order to tell the story. Remember linking and the sounds of the "-ed" ending when you say your sentence aloud. When you think the sentences are in order, recite your sentences in order.

Directions for the rest of class

Small classes: Get together around a desk and spread out the index cards from volunteers. As a group, put the cards in order to tell a story. When everyone is finished, check the order of the sentences.

Large classes: Work with a partner to put the sentences in order. Make sure to read them aloud for linking and "-ed" endings.

All classes: Listen to the members of the small group. Are they saying the "-ed" endings correctly? For example, make sure "cracked" has only one syllable.

Sentences for Group Activity

a. _____ In 1942, they recruited twenty-nine Navajo speakers who developed a code based on their own language.

b. _____ No one ever cracked the Navajo code, which was kept classified until 1968.

c. _____ In 2001, the five who still survived were honored with Congressional gold medals.

d. _____ The Marines eventually trained about 400 Navajos to send messages by radio.

e. _____ During World War II, the U.S. Marines needed an unbreakable code to send and receive messages.

f. _____ These 400 participated in every Marine battle in the Pacific in World War II.

g. _____ In the 1990s, the Navajo "code-talkers" were finally recognized for their efforts.

h. _____ In one battle, over eight hundred accurate messages were transmitted and decoded in just two days.

Journal

Did you know the different endings of the past tense and the rule for when to use them before taking this course? Did you know why some people have problems with this ending? Explain this subject to someone—a friend, relative, or co-worker—who is not taking this course. Then listen to some native English speakers. Do you hear the three different past tense endings? Record some examples to show the class.

PRONUNCIATION GOAL

Say the names of the Sound Concepts correctly.

Look at the list of Sound Concepts on the inside back cover. List the five Sound Concepts here. Write the sound of each "-ed" ending next to each Sound Concept.

1. _____

2. _____

3. _____

4. _____

5. _____

Final Chapter Activity

 Recycle linking and past tense endings

1. Listen to this person talk about his experiences speaking other languages. Fill in the blanks with the words you hear. Each blank will contain two or three words.

In college I _____ language major, so I _____ lot of languages. I _____ Russian, and a little German, _____ high school I'd studied Spanish. After college, I _____ to go to Europe for the summer. I was really _____ my trip _____ getting to use my languages. First I _____ my friend in Spain, but _____ I realized I didn't know enough Spanish. Everyone _____ fast! I had _____ understanding anything, but at least my friend _____. After a _____ Spain, I took a train to France. On the train I _____ phrases in my French book. But when I _____ woman for directions to my hostel, she _____ my French, and I couldn't understand her—everyone sounded like they were swallowing the _____ their words. I was awfully _____ my accent. By the time I_____ Russia, I was getting really _____ everything I said. I _____ night on the train, and I was shocked when someone actually understood me _____!

2. Compare your answers with a partner. Do you agree? What makes sense in each blank? Remember, you can use the Three Kinds of Information to help you. (p. 7) Listen again and check your answers.

What did we do in this chapter?

 Circle any of the topics you still need more practice with. Enter them into your log.

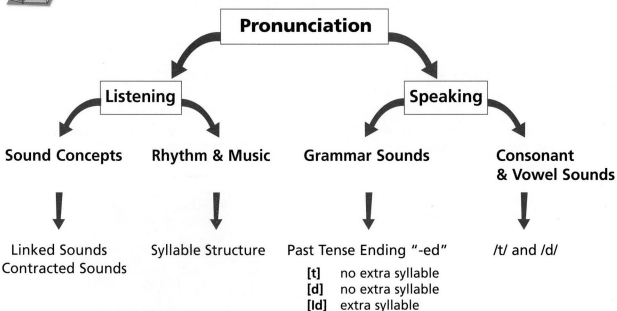

Look back at the first two chapters of this book. The following section answers some questions you might have. Talk about any other questions with a partner and your teacher.

Question 1: Why do some things we practiced in this book still feel strange? Why are they still difficult to say correctly?

Answer: Sometimes you may think that what you are saying still sounds wrong, even though your teacher says it is right (freeze-frame).

This is what you used to say: But this is what you say now: ♪

The new way feels strange because it is different. Your mind remembers the way you used to say it. The old way still *feels* right to you.

The new way doesn't match the sound memory in your mind. Don't worry—this feeling is normal. Everyone feels this way at first when they learn a new way to do something. With more practice, the new way will start to feel right.

Activity 1: Progress Report

Here are the sounds, patterns, and Sound Concepts that you've studied so far. Put a check next to any that still feel strange when you say them. Put a star next to your single biggest problem.

Sound Concepts	Rhythm & Music
☐ Sounds are linked	☐ Counting syllables
☐ Sounds are contracted	☐ Syllable structure
Grammar Sounds	**Consonant & Vowel Sounds**
☐ Regular past tense verb endings ("-ed")	☐ /θ/ ☐ /ð/ ☐ /t/ ☐ /d/

Journal

Do you remember feeling strange when you first learned to drive, to play a sport, or to do something else? Sometimes new skills feel strange because your body hasn't yet made a new *motor memory*. But when the new movements become a habit, they won't feel strange anymore. Write about a learning experience and how you overcame that strange feeling. Share your experience with a partner or small group. Can you give any advice to someone who's having the same experience?

What physical habit or motor memory is ▶ **the boy in the picture learning?**

Question 2: Do I really have to worry about all the things in this book when I speak? Are some things more important than others?

Answer: No, you do not have to worry about *all* the things in this book when you speak English. Yes, some things are more important than others. But how do you know which are more important?

Remember that pronunciation works both ways:

You can understand others.   Others can understand you.

Use the table below to understand which parts of pronunciation are most important.

Part of pronunciation	Why practice?	Practice in the classroom?	Use in everyday speech outside the classroom?	Importance for speaking	Importance for listening
Sound Concepts ONE WAY ▶	Necessary for listening (understanding others)	Yes	*Optional:* others will understand you without this	Low	Medium
Rhythm & Music ◀ ONE WAY ONE WAY ▶	Necessary for speaking and listening (understanding others and being understood)	Yes	Yes, always correct errors in this area	High	High
Grammar Sounds ◀ ONE WAY ONE WAY ▶	Necessary for speaking and listening (understanding others and being understood)	Yes	Yes, always correct errors in this area	High	High
Consonant & Vowel Sounds ◀ ONE WAY	Helpful for speaking	Yes	Yes, but others will probably understand you without this	Medium	Low

Activity 2: Pair Discussions

1. Look at the table above and the pronunciation pyramid on the inside of the back cover. Discuss with a partner: Why are Rhythm & Music and Grammar Sounds the most important parts to try to say correctly?

2. Read the following section and then talk with your partner again. What do you think about the two levels of pronunciation?

A New Way to Think About Pronunciation

Sound Concepts and Consonant & Vowel Sounds focus on specific sounds or parts of words called *segments*. Usually listeners can understand you even if you make mistakes with individual segments.

Rhythm & Music and Grammar Sounds focus on more than just individual segments: they focus on the *suprasegmental* level of pronunciation. This suprasegmental level is what a listener depends on to understand the speaker's message.

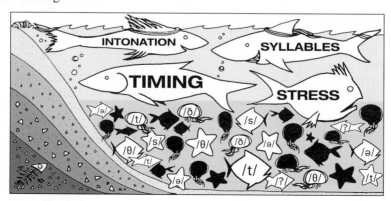

Eye-Opener: If a speaker makes mistakes with stress or syllables (the suprasegmentals), listeners will sometimes not have enough information to understand the message—even if all the individual sounds (the segmentals) are correct!

PRONUNCIATION GOAL

Use what you learn about Rhythm & Music and Grammar Sounds in everyday speech outside the classroom.

Question 3: If Rhythm & Music and Grammar Sounds are the most important, how do I solve my problems in these areas?

Answer: Your teacher, your logbook, and your classmates can help with these problems.

The Teacher-Student Partnership in Action

Who?	What?	Why?
Teacher	Error correction	To point out when you've made a mistake
Teacher	Freeze-frame	To let you know when you've corrected a mistake
You		To let your classmates know when they've corrected a mistake
You	Logbook	To remind yourself how to correct your own mistakes

Journal

Remember that level 2 of the Four Levels of Competence (conscious incompetence, p. 25) is when you know your mistakes, but you still make them. Are you getting better at labeling your mistakes and understanding how to correct them? Why or why not? Remember, if you're starting to understand your mistakes, you're making progress in this course.

What happens when people don't understand you or when your teacher corrects your mistakes? Do you think, "Oh, I know—I always make that mistake?" If you feel this way, then you're ready to move on to level 3, conscious competence. You need to try to begin correcting your frequent mistakes, both in and out of class.

Look back at your responses in the initial diagnostic, part 3: Thinking About Listening and Speaking, (p. 21). What did you know about your mistakes then? What do you know about them now? What can you do in the future to improve and move on to level 3, conscious competence?

Stress Patterns and Deleted Sounds

Sound Concepts	**Rhythm & Music**	**Grammar Sounds**	**Consonant & Vowel Sounds**
Deleted and reduced sounds	*Syllable patterns: Stress in words and phrases*	*Third-person singular verb endings*	*$/s/$ and $/z/$*

Sound Concepts

Introduction to Deleted Sounds

Diagnostic

You will hear six sentences. On a separate piece of paper, write the sentences you hear.

After Listening

With a partner or the whole class, use the checklist below to decode what you heard.

> **Three Steps to Decode What You Hear**
>
> **1** What did you hear?
>
> **2** Does it make sense?
>
> **3** What was really said?

> **Remember, you can use the three kinds of information to help you:**
>
> **1** Background information—what you know about the topic
>
> **2** Language information—what you know about English
>
> **3** Sound information—what you heard

What Sound Concepts do you recognize in these sentences? Did you have trouble hearing one of the sounds in these sentences? Which one?

Deleted /h/

How do we mark deleted /h/ in this book?

1. Put an X through it: Where is ~~h~~e?

2. If there is a linked consonant sound before the "h" word, mark linking from that consonant sound to the vowel in the "h" word: Where is ~~h~~e?

When do we use deleted /h/?

The sound /h/ is ONLY deleted in the words "he," "his," "him," and "her" when there is linking from the word before it.

    Example: The man put ~~h~~is coat in the closet.

Sometimes there is no linking before "he," "his," "him," and "her."

1. There is no linking when "he," "his," "him," or "her" follows a pause (usually shown in writing by a period or a comma). If you use these words at the beginning of a sentence or clause, /h/ is not deleted.

    Example: I really like my assistant. He's very efficient.

2. There is no linking when "he," "his," "him," or "her" makes a contrast. Stress the word that makes a contrast. If you stress "he," "his," "him," or "her," /h/ is not deleted.

    Example: No, I don't mean *him*, I mean *HIM!*

3. There is no linking when "he," "his," "him," or "her" is said in slow, careful speech. If you speak very carefully, /h/ is not deleted.

    Example: The news announcer said, "The president will deliver her speech at 8:00."

4. There is no linking when "his" comes at the end of a sentence or phrase.

    Example: That book is John's. It's his.

Remember, everyday speech is connected (linked) speech. If sounds are not linked, /h/ will not be deleted.

Practice Deleted /h/

With a partner, go back to the diagnostic on the previous page. Mark the sentences for deleted /h/.

Eye-Opener: The Silent "H"
Some words in English start with the letter "h" but not the sound /h/. We call this a silent "h." We do not say /h/ is deleted here because there is no /h/ sound in these words: "hour," "honest," "heir," "heiress," and "honor."

Exercise 1: Mystery Man

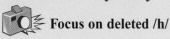 **Focus on deleted /h/**   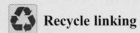 **Recycle linking**

Work in small groups. Take turns thinking of a famous man and guessing each other's "mystery man" using only yes or no questions. Write questions and mark them for deleted /h/ and linking.

> Example: Catharine is thinking about Gandhi.
>
> Jason: Is ~~h~~e alive?
>
> Catharine: No, ~~h~~e isn't.
>
> Jason: Did ~~h~~e live in Europe?
>
> Catharine: No, ~~h~~e didn't. . . .

USAGE NOTE: PUNCTUATION and DELETED /h/

Look at the linking in Catharine's answers. When we answer a question with yes or no, and then add more information in the same sentence, we usually link sounds across the comma.

 Eye-Opener: Sometimes English speakers delete the /ð/ sound made by the letters "th" in the word "them." So these two sentences may sound the same:

Tell him I'm ~~h~~ere.   Tell ~~th~~em I'm here.

Exercise 2: Phone Messages

 Focus on deleted /h/   **Recycle /ð/ and linking**

Role play taking telephone messages. Remember to use deleted /h/. Try to use deleted /ð/ too.

> Example: Mary / she left her coat at Susan's house
>
> **A:** Hi, is Mary there?
> **B:** No, she's not. Can I take a message?
> **A:** Sure. Can you tell ~~h~~er she left ~~h~~er coat at Susan's house?
> **B:** No problem. I'll tell ~~h~~er.

1. John / to call his doctor right away
2. Lucy / this is Jane, and I'll talk to her tomorrow
3. Alan / to meet me at school tomorrow at ten
4. Paul and Mike / their friend Laura called

Exercise 3: Learn About Lindbergh

 Focus on deleted /h/   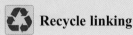 **Recycle linking**

Use the phrases in the box to complete the dialogue. Mark the text for linking and deleted /h/. In pairs, practice the dialogue.

Elena: "Hi, I was wondering if you could help me. I'm looking up Charles Lindbergh. Who _was he?_ "

Librarian: "Oh, he was a great pilot."
Elena: "Can you tell me more about him? Why _____ ?"

Librarian: "Well, he was the first to fly across the Atlantic."

Elena: "Where _____ ?"

Librarian: "Paris, France."

Elena: "So when _____ ?"

Librarian: "In 1927."

Elena: "How long _____ ?"

Librarian: "33 hours and 33 minutes."

Elena: "That's a long time! What _____ ?"

Librarian: "Supposedly, he had just five sandwiches and a bottle of water for the trip."

Elena: "One more thing: What _____ ?"

Librarian: "The Spirit of St. Louis. You can see it in the Smithsonian Museum in Washington, D.C."

did he land
did he cross the Atlantic
was he famous
did he eat
~~was he~~
was his flight
was the name of his plane

 Journal
Practice listening for deleted /h/ in everyday speech. Can you notice it? Write down what you observe and report back to the class. At the end of this chapter, repeat this exercise and compare your notes. Did you get better at hearing deleted /h/? Why do you think that is?

Rhythm & Music

Introduction to Stress

Strong and Weak Beats in English

 Like music, English speech has a rhythm. Where does this rhythm begin? Sentences have a rhythm. So do phrases. Even words have a rhythm. The rhythm starts with the syllable.

Remember, every syllable is a beat. But in English, not all syllables (beats) are equal: some are strong and some are weak. Strong and weak syllables give English its *own* rhythm. Strong syllables are *stressed* syllables, and weak syllables are *unstressed* syllables.

A stressed syllable in English always has a vowel sound (CV, VC, CVC, CVCC, etc.).

What is the sound of the vowel in a stressed syllable?

- A stressed syllable's vowel is LOUD er
- A stressed syllable's vowel is L - O - N - G er
- A stressed syllable's vowel is CLEAR er
- A stressed syllable's vowel is HIGH er

[handwritten: vowel sound- weak syllable |ə| |I| cons   strong —weak.]

What is the sound of the vowel in an unstressed syllable?

The spelling of an unstressed syllable does not matter. The vowel sound in most unstressed syllables sounds is like the vowel in "but" or in the first syllable of "about." Your mouth is relaxed when you say this vowel sound.

We write this sound: /ə/. Say it: "schwa." You need to recognize this symbol, but you do not have to write it.

Unstressed syllables can sometimes be difficult to hear.

How do we mark stressed and unstressed syllables?

- Use a curve ⌣ over the unstressed (weak) syllable.
- Use a stress mark ╱ over the stressed (strong) syllable.

> The message is in the music: Strong and weak syllables alternate.

Diagnostic 2

Can you hear unstressed syllables? Circle the sentence you hear.

1. A. They have to change plans.   B. They have a change of plans.

2. A. He has the right of way.   B. He has the right way.

Standard Stress Patterns

Stress in Two-Syllable Words

Two-syllable Words · Compound Nouns · Phrasal Verbs · Noun Phrases · Prepositional Phrases · Sentence-level Stress

We call the pattern of stressed and unstressed syllables in a word a *stress pattern*. Every two-syllable word has one of the two stress patterns shown below. But there's no way of predicting which words have which pattern. When you learn a new two-syllable word, learn its stress pattern at the same time.

strong-weak	weak-strong
╱ ⌣ teacher	⌣ ╱ ago
╱ ⌣ student	⌣ ╱ belong
╱ ⌣ person	⌣ ╱ percent

Exercise 4: Practice with Two-Syllable Word Stress Patterns

 Focus on stress in two-syllable words

1. Read the journal entry below. Look up any of the bolded words you don't know how to pronounce, and say them according to the dictionary's stress pattern. Which words are strong-weak? Which words are weak-strong? Put the bolded words in two columns and mark them to show their stress patterns. Read the list of words in each column aloud, using the correct stress pattern. Remember to make the vowel sound of the stressed syllable longer and clearer than the rest of the word.

When I **observe people talking** on the street **corner** or the **subway**, I **notice** that they stand **farther away** from each **other** than people in my **country**. In my country, you stand **very** close to **someone** when you talk to them, right **beside** them, but **English speakers** have a **little** more **distance between** them. I also **notice** that they **debate** and **argue** with each other—I saw two people **moving** their hands and **changing** their **facial** expressions a lot, but they **didn't** seem **really angry** or **upset**. In conversation, some English speakers make eye **contact** with each other—they look right at each other, not down or away. It's interesting to think **about** these differences.

2. Remember that most, but not all, unstressed vowels sound like /ə/. Which words in your columns have unstressed syllables that don't sound like /ə/? (Examples: country, subway) Circle them.

Journal

To use correct stress in a word, you first need to learn the word with the correct number of syllables. Some English words have two acceptable pronunciations, with different numbers of syllables.

       Example: family   **FAM**-i-ly: 3 syllables or **FAM**-ly: 2 syllables

Both pronunciations are correct.

Other examples: "camera," "interesting," "chocolate," and "interested."

Look these words up in two or more dictionaries and note the number of syllables. Ask some native English speakers to say these words in a sentence. How many syllables do they say? Report your findings to the class.

 Eye-Opener: Sometimes when you change the stress in a two-syllable word, you change the meaning of the word.

The message is in the music: Stress carries meaning.

Exercise 5: Stress in Noun-Verb Pairs

 Focus on stress in words

Some pairs of words have the same spelling, but different meanings and different stress patterns. Read the following sentences aloud. Mark the stressed syllables in each underlined verb. Write the part of speech (noun or verb) next to each sentence.

Example: **A.** Who is the <u>object</u> of your affection?   noun

B. They didn't <u>object</u> to the decision.   verb

1. **A.** The <u>conflict</u> in the Balkans is centuries old. _____

   B. Eating pork would <u>conflict</u> with our religion. _____

2. **A.** We don't <u>permit</u> that behavior around here. _____

   B. Do I need a <u>permit</u> to build an addition to my house? _____

3. **A.** The students' <u>conduct</u> made teaching difficult. _____

   B. At work, <u>conduct</u> yourself as a professional. _____

4. **A.** Actors must learn to <u>project</u> their voices. _____

   B. What's the topic of your research <u>project</u>? _____

What patterns do you see? _____

Standard Stress Patterns

Stress in Phrases

| Two-syllable Words | Compound Nouns | Phrasal Verbs | Noun Phrases | Prepositional Phrases | Sentence-level Stress |

Compound Nouns

Did everybody get the **handout**? (handout: strong-weak)

> **BE CAREFUL!** Some compound nouns may be written as two words.

Phrasal (Two-Word) Verbs

The teacher asked the student to **hand out** the papers. (hand out: strong-strong)

The student **handed** the papers **out**.

Exercise 6: Stress Changes Meaning in Phrases

 Focus on stress in phrases   ♻ Recycle deleted /h/ and linking

Mark the following questions and answers for stress, deleted /h/, and linking.

Practice asking and answering the questions with a partner.

1. **Q:** Did he work out at the gym?   **A:** Yes, he had a good workout today.

2. **Q:** Did he drop out of high school?   **A:** Sadly, he's a high school dropout now.

3. **Q:** Did he print out his research paper? **A:** Yes, he turned in his printout.

4. **Q:** Did he try out for the band?   **A:** No, but there's a tryout tomorrow.

5. **Q:** Did he play back the video?   **A:** No. Let's watch the playback now.

Standard Stress Patterns

Stress in Phrases

| Two-syllable Words | Compound Nouns | Phrasal Verbs | Noun Phrases | Prepositional Phrases | Sentence-level Stress |

Compound Noun

Teachers write on blackboards. (blackboards: strong-weak)

Noun Phrase

They built the doghouse with black boards. (black boards: weak-strong)

Exercise 7: Matching Columns

 Focus on stress in compound nouns and noun phrases

Mark the correct stress pattern in the compound nouns or noun phrases in the left-hand column. Match the two columns, then practice reading them aloud.

Compound nouns or noun phrases	Definitions
1. _____ greenhouse	A. where you develop photos
2. _____ green house	B. where the president lives
3. _____ White House	C. a house that's green
4. _____ white house	D. a room with no lights on
5. _____ darkroom	E. a house that's white
6. _____ dark room	F. where you grow plants

Standard Stress Patterns

Stress in Phrases

| Two-syllable Words | Compound Nouns | Phrasal Verbs | Noun Phrases | Prepositional Phrases | Sentence-level Stress |

English phrases have content words and function words. Content words give you the information (content) of the phrase. Usually the most important word in a phrase is the content word. Function words are grammatical words like prepositions (such as *in, on, at*) and articles (*the, a, an*) that connect content words to complete the phrase. Content words are usually stressed. Function words are usually unstressed.

Example: at the bank

at the ——————→ function words: unstressed

bank ——————→ content word: stressed

Stress in Sentences

| Two-syllable Words | Compound Nouns | Phrasal Verbs | Noun Phrases | Prepositional Phrases | Sentence-level Stress |

Stress the content words in a sentence, not the function words. This is neutral or standard sentence-level stress, the normal stress pattern in English.

Example: He leaves for work in the morning.

Exercise 8: Daily Activities and Prepositional Phrases

 Focus on unstressed function words: prepositions; standard sentence-level stress

Read the following sentences and mark their stress patterns. Write the three stressed content words at the right. Take turns reading the sentences aloud with a partner. Be sure to use standard sentence-level stress: stress the content words in your sentences.

Example: I wash my hands at the sink.   <u>wash</u>   <u>hands</u>   <u>sink</u>

Group A

1. I change my clothes at the gym.   _____   _____   _____

2. I catch my bus at the corner.   _____   _____   _____

Group B

3. I study English in Chicago.   _____   _____   _____

4. I borrow a book from the library.   _____   _____   _____

Group C

5. I deposit my paycheck at the ATM.   _____   _____   _____

6. I make a snack in the kitchen.   _____   _____   _____

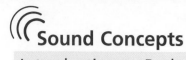# Sound Concepts

 ### Diagnostic 3

You will hear four sentences. On a separate piece of paper, write the sentences you hear.

After Listening

With a partner or the whole class, use the checklist to decode what you heard: What did you hear? Does it make sense? What was really said? Remember, you can use the three kinds of information to help you. What was difficult about listening to these sentences?

 Eye-Opener: In these sentences, the unstressed function word "can" is reduced. You didn't hear "can," you heard /kn/. There is no vowel sound, and it is very short.

Reduced Can: Can⟶ /kn/

When do we *not* reduce can?

- When it is negative ("cannot" or "can't")
- When "can" is the last word in a sentence
- When "can" is stressed

How do we mark *reduced can* in this book?

Put a slash through the vowel to help you remember to reduce it: c̸an

Practice *Reduced Can*

Go back to the diagnostic. Mark each example of **reduced can**.

# Sound Concepts

Contracted Not: Not ⟶ n't

 Eye-Opener: Contracted **not** is always acceptable in speech. It isn't too informal.

How do you say *contracted not?*

Sometimes **contracted not** is a separate syllable. Don't pause before it. Say it: /Int/

Examples:	didn't	isn't	wasn't	hadn't	haven't

Sometimes **contracted not** is *not* a separate syllable, as in these words:

can't	won't	don't

In these words, the /t/ sound is very hard to hear, but the vowel is clear.

Listen for the vowel sound in order to understand these words.

What's the difference between "can" and "can't"?

Both are one-syllable function words. But the vowel in "can" is reduced and the /t/ in "can't" is hard to hear (it's not released).

They look like this: can   can't

But they sound like this: /kn/   /kaen/

The difference is the vowel sound: "can't" has a longer, clearer vowel sound. Listen for the vowel sound (not the /t/) to tell the difference between "can" and "can't."

 Eye-Opener: The unstressed function word "can" (/kn/) is not the same as the noun (content word) "can." Don't reduce the content word.

Example: Would you like a can of soda? Căn I open it for you?

Exercise 9: You Căn Use It to. . .

 Focus on reduced can   **Recycle linking**

1. In groups, brainstorm things you can use a cell phone for and write sentences about them. Mark your sentences for **reduced can** and linked sounds, and read your list aloud. Here are a few sentences to get you started:

   You căn use it to find out the time.

   You căn use it to check your e-mail.

2. Imagine that you are inventors. In groups, decide on your latest invention. Try to sell it to the rest of your class by telling them the many things you can use it for. Use the form "You can use it to. . ." and say "can" as /kn/.

 **Consonant & Vowel Sounds**

Introduction to the Sound /s/

What is the sound?

This is the sound of the letter "s" at the beginning of words like "state." It's a sibilant sound (a hissing sound).

How do you spell it?

     state   hi**ss**ing   **c**ity   **s**cience   sen**se**   box

How do you form it?

The sound /s/ is an unvoiced sound.

Trouble Spots

Be careful of spelling—many different letters might make the sound /s/.

Introduction to the Sound /z/

What is the sound?
This is the sound of the letter "z" at the beginning of the name of the letter "z" (zee).

How do you spell it?

quiz   blizzard   is   these   scissors

How do you form it?
Form the sound /z/ in the same place in your mouth as the sound /s/. The two sounds are minimal pairs: the sound /s/ is unvoiced, and the /z/ is voiced.

Trouble Spots
Say the sound /z/ as a voiced sound. Otherwise you'll say a different sound, and sometimes a different word.

When you see the letter "z," you need to say the sound /z/. Not all languages use this sound. It can be difficult for some students to say. But you have already been using this sound in these words: "these," "words," "use," "was," and "is." You say these words this way: "theze," "wordz," "uze," "waz," and "iz."

Practice /z/
Try saying this tongue-twister with the sound /z/. Don't say the sound /s/. Mark the tongue-twister for deleted /h/ and linking. Practice saying it quickly!

Fuzzy Wuzzy was a bear.

Fuzzy Wuzzy had no hair.

Fuzzy Wuzzy wasn't fuzzy, was he?

 Eye-Opener: Minimal Pairs with the Sounds /s/ and /z/

The Sound /s/	The Sound /z/
sip	zip
C	Z
racing	raising
lacy	lazy
price	prize
niece	knees

When you see the letter "z," always say the sound /z/.
When you see the letters "s" or "c," sometimes you say the sound /s/. Sometimes these letters make another sound.

 Grammar Sounds

Third-Person Singular Present Tense Ending ("-s" or "-es")

Why is this ending important?
This ending carries a lot of information. It says that there is a singular subject—he, she, or it—and that the verb is in the present tense.

Native speakers listen for verb endings. They depend on the grammatical information in those endings, on the sound of the linking from the final "s," and sometimes on the extra syllable that the ending makes.

What happens if you don't say it?

- You sound ungrammatical
- Your listeners may be confused
- Your sentences may have the wrong rhythm

Use the following exercise to learn how to say the third-person singular ending correctly. This ending is pronounced three different ways.

Exercise 10: Trial by Jury

 Focus on third-person singular present tense endings ("-s" or "-es")

 Recycle linking and counting syllables

A. Read the following passage to yourself. Then discuss the questions with a partner.

The U.S. Constitution **guarantees** the right to a trial by jury. Over two hundred years later, the jury system **continues** to serve a vital role in our democracy. The court **views** jury duty as a duty and privilege of citizenship, and as a check against wrongly convicting the innocent.

In the United States, each state **notifies** its citizens that they must report for jury duty. If a person **wishes** to be excused for reasons of great hardship, she or he must ask the judge. In most states, a trial jury **consists** of 12 jurors plus 2 alternates who listen to evidence in a criminal or civil trial. A jury **concerns** itself only with the issues of a particular trial. A jury **meets** for as long as the trial **lasts**. A jury **examines** the evidence, **ignores** any outside information, and **remains** impartial (fair) during the trial. After each lawyer **presents** all the evidence, a jury **deliberates**. The jury **takes** directions from the judge: It **sorts** out the facts and **applies** the law as the judge **explains** it. If the prosecution **convinces** the jury of its case, the jury **finds** the defendant guilty. Otherwise, the jury **reaches** a verdict of not guilty. If the jury **decides** that the defendant is guilty, the judge **sentences** the criminal according to the law.

Adapted from http://www.state.ma.us/courts/jury

Think About It

Do you have juries in your country? What did you know about jury duty before reading this passage?

Some people are excited by jury duty, and others are bored by it. What do you think? How would you feel if you were asked to serve on a jury?

B. Use the checklist below to complete the rest of this exercise (directions follow the checklist).

☑CHECKLIST

How do you say the "-s" or "-es" on third-person singular present tense verbs?

Look   Find the simple (root) form of a verb, without any endings.

Ask   What is the final sound (not letter)?

Is it   /s/—the sound at the end of "box"?

   /z/—the sound at the end of "raise"?

   /sh/—the sound at the end of "wash"?

   /tch/—the sound at the end of "watch"?

   /j/—the sound at the end of "judge"?

These five sounds are called *sibilants*.
They hiss when you say them.

If yes... ✓

   Add an extra syllable. ⟶ Say "-s" or "-es" as [Iz].

If no...

   Ask: Is the final sound unvoiced?

      If yes... ✓
      There is no extra syllable. Say "-s" as [s].

      If no...
      There is no extra syllable. Say "-s" as [z].

Are you having trouble finding the final sound of a word?
Go back to exercise 4 in chapter 3 (page 38) for help.

> **So, when saying the third-person singular present tense ending:**
>
> 1. Voiced sounds use voiced endings, **[z]**
> 2. Unvoiced sounds use unvoiced endings, **[s]**
> 3. Hissing sounds (sibilants) add an extra syllable to the ending, **[Iz]**

---

1. Make a three-column chart like the one below. Label your chart with the three different pronunciations of the "s" or "es" ending.

[z]	[s]	[Iz]
Extra syllable? yes no	Extra syllable? yes no	Extra syllable? yes no

2. Decide whether the ending in each column is pronounced as an extra syllable.
   Circle the word yes or no.

3. Put each bolded verb from the passage in the appropriate column.

4. Check your answers with a partner.

5. Write the sound of each ending—[z], [s], or [Iz]—above the bolded verbs in the passage about trial by jury.

6. Mark the passage for linking and deleted /h/.

7. Read the passage aloud to a partner, remembering to practice linking, deleted /h/, and saying the endings correctly. Check your partner's pronunciation of the endings.

The Teacher-Student Partnership in Action

From now on, you are responsible for saying this ending correctly. Your teacher will correct you if you make a mistake with this ending. Your teacher will also tell you when you say it right (freeze-frame). Enter your mistakes with this ending into your log.

Exercise 11: More Daily Activities

 Focus on third-person singular endings, stress in sentences

 Recycle linking, deleted /h/, present tense endings; unstressed function words

Go back to exercise 8. With a partner, practice reading sentences based on the content words you wrote next to each line. This time, use the subject "He" for your sentences.

Remember to

- Say the third-person singular endings correctly

- Say linked sounds

- Use deleted /h/

- Use unstressed function words and stressed content words

Write the appropriate sound of the third-person singular ending next to each section (hint: the verbs in each group all take the same ending).

Example: He washes his hands at the sink.

Exercise 12: Your Classmates' Routines

 Focus on third-person singular present tense endings

 Recycle linking

1. Interview a classmate. Find out something he or she does *always*, *usually*, *sometimes*, or *never*. Write sentences about your classmate's activities and mark them for linking, verb endings, and stressed content words.

2. Sit in a circle with your class and take turns saying sentences about one another. When it's your turn, say one of your sentences, and then repeat the sentences of the students before you.

    Example

    Suzanne: "Howard always exercises [Iz] in the morning."

    Carol: "Francisco never eats [s] fish, and Howard always exercises [Iz] in the morning," etc.

Exercise 13: What Happens in an American Courtroom?

 Focus on third-person singular present tense endings

 Recycle linking, deleted /h/, stressed content words

Use the words in the box to complete the sentences. Add the third-person singular ending to every verb. Mark your sentences and read them aloud. Remember to stress the content words. Then, for each sentence, choose three stressed content words or phrases and write them in columns A–C at the right.

keep	~~hire~~	sentence	swear	call
defend	prove	reach	plead	try

		A	**B**	**C**
1.	A defendant hires [z] a lawyer.	defendant	hires	lawyer
2.	A defense attorney _____ his client.	_____	_____	_____
3.	A court _____ a case.	_____	_____	_____
4.	A defendant _____ not guilty.	_____	_____	_____
5.	A prosecuting attorney _____ a witness.	_____	_____	_____
6.	A court recorder _____ records.	_____	_____	_____
7.	A bailiff _____ in a witness.	_____	_____	_____
8.	A jury _____ a verdict.	_____	_____	_____
9.	A successful lawyer _____ her case.	_____	_____	_____
10.	A judge _____ the criminal.	_____	_____	_____

Test yourself!

How much have you learned about courtrooms and juries? Work with your partner. Use the verb phrase that is written in short form in columns B and C (*hires a lawyer*) to ask your partner a "Who" question: "Who hires a lawyer?" Be sure to say the correct third-person singular ending in your question. Your partner's answer should be the noun in column A (*a defendant*).

Exercise 14: Cities vs. Suburbs

 Focus on third-person singular present tense endings

 Recycle linking, deleted /h/, verb endings

1. Listen and fill in the missing word or words.

Zach works downtown, _____ the suburbs and commutes. He _____ city in lots of ways. Some _____, but it's not worth the trouble. There's too much _____ rush hour, and it's too expensive to _____ car. So he _____ bus _____ and _____ downtown. When he travels for _____ Monday, he _____ on Sunday because _____ airport in forty minutes. The same trip _____ Monday.

2. Complete the following story about Zach's business trip by writing the "-ed" forms of the verbs in parentheses. Read the story aloud with a partner, remembering to pronounce the "-ed" endings correctly and to distinguish between /s/ and "es" in words like "snow."

While Zach was sleeping, there was a snowstorm heading his way. But when he

_____ (open) his eyes, the sky was sunny. He _____ (turn) on the radio,
        1   2

and _____ (listen) to the forecast. When he _____ (learn) it might snow,
            3   4

he _____ (look) out the window again. He _____ (notice) it was a little
        5   6

cloudy. While he was in the shower, it _____ (start) to flurry. When he got
                                                7

_____ (dress) and looked out the window again, there was a foot of snow on the
        8

ground. He was staring out the window when the phone rang. When he _____
                                                                              9

(answer) it, he _____ (discover) that his meeting was _____ (cancel)
                      10   11

because of the storm.

Exercise 15: Discussing Newspaper Articles

 Focus on third-person singular present tense endings

Find an article about a current trial. Write a summary of your article, mark it for deleted h and linking, and read it aloud to a partner. Use the simple present tense to talk about *movies, books, poems,* and *articles.* Use other tenses as necessary to talk about events mentioned in an article or book.

Possible sentence starters:

- This article talks about...   • This article discusses...   • The crime happened...

Journal

Go back to the sample journal entry in exercise 4. The student wrote about English speakers' body language and conversational styles. Body language, eye contact, and facial expressions help speakers around the world express their intent—their meaning. For example, someone who rolls his or her eyes and shrugs while speaking might be sarcastic, not sincere. Noticing these signals helps you understand English speakers better. Communicating with facial expressions and body language of your own helps other people understand you.

What do you think about the observations in exercise 4? Do you agree? Have you ever noticed cultural differences in body language? Talk about your observations with a partner.

Recycle linking, past tense endings, deleted /h/, unstressed function words

Context for Practice: The Trial of the Century

1. Listen to the following account of a famous 20th century trial. Fill in the blanks with the words you hear.

Charles Lindbergh was the first person to fly across the Atlantic Ocean, in a plane _____ Spirit of St. Louis. In 1932, his baby son _____: he was _____ crib. They had _____ at 8:00, _____ fine, but by 10:00 _____ gone. The kidnapper _____ homemade ladder to _____ room. The Lindberghs _____ ransom note, and _____ money, but three months later, the baby's body was _____ woods. The police _____ crime was _____ the ransom money was _____ New York by a man _____ Bruno Hauptmann. When they _____ ransom money _____ wallet, they _____ house and found another $10,000. His trial _____ several months, and _____ trial he _____ innocence. He was convicted by a jury and _____ judge. Hauptmann's trial _____ "trial of the century" because so many people _____ with the Lindberghs and _____ the case.

2. Discuss your answers with a partner.

Remember, you can use the Three Kinds of Information to help you:
1 Background information—what you know about the topic
2 Language information—what you know about English
3 Sound information—what you heard

3. Listen to the passage again and check your answers.

What did we do in this chapter?

 If you are still having trouble with Rhythm & Music or Grammar Sounds, circle the difficult topics on the chart below and enter them in your logbook.

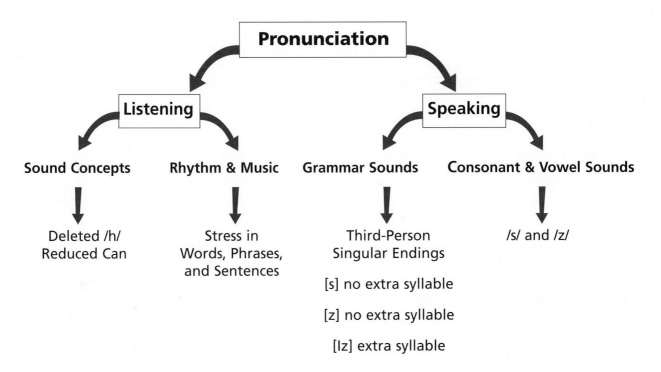

Assessment Section 1: Unit 1 (Chapters 1–4)

Part 1: Listening

Listen to the lecture on sign language for overall comprehension.

When you are finished listening, work with a partner or in a small group on the following activities. Your teacher may ask you to concentrate on one or more of the activities at a time. Your teacher may also ask you to listen to the lecture again. Write your answers on a separate piece of paper.

ACTIVITY 1: Listening Strategies

A   What words or phrases jumped out at you when you were listening?

B   Check with a partner or a group: did other students hear the same phrases? With your group, try to remember what was said about each of the words or phrases. Which are more important than others in the context of the lecture? Why?

C   Talk with a group: What strategies did you use while listening? What are the three kinds of information, and how did they help you here? What should you do if you didn't understand a part of the lecture?

ACTIVITY 2: Sound Concepts

How many of the Sound Concepts did you notice in this lecture? Write down each Sound Concept and an example that you heard.

ACTIVITY 3: Grammar Sounds

Write down every word you heard with a third-person singular present tense ending. Discuss the context of each word with a partner.

ACTIVITY 4: Grammar Sounds

Write down every word you heard with an "-ed" ending. Discuss the context of each word with a partner.

ACTIVITY 5: Consonant & Vowel Sounds

Below is a list of words from the lecture with the sounds /θ/ and /ð/. Which sound is voiced and which is unvoiced? Put the words in two columns, labeled with the appropriate sound. Read them aloud, making sure not to say other sounds. Did you hear them in the lecture?

thought	that	the	throughout	this	their
other	with	either	theory	three	whether
	birth	those	themselves		

Part 2: Speaking

ACTIVITY 1: Read Aloud

Turn to the audio script at the back of this book (p.209). Read part or all of the lecture to a partner. Your teacher may ask you to record yourself. You should focus on three things:

1. Verb endings: past tense and third-person singular present
   Examples: exposed, used, called, produces, allows, helps

2. Syllable structure: don't add or delete sounds or syllables.
   Examples: worldwide, speech, language, states

3. Word-level stress in two-syllable words: Look up the stress patterns of any words you don't know.
   Examples: percent; person

ACTIVITY 2: Focus Sounds

In the box below, list the consonant and vowel sounds from this unit.

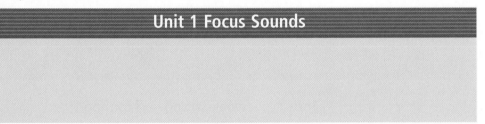

Unit 1 Focus Sounds

Go back to the speaking diagnostic on p. 21. With a partner, circle every word with one of the focus sounds listed in the box. Practice reading the diagnostic aloud. Are you saying the focus sounds correctly?

Part 3: Thinking About Listening and Speaking

ACTIVITY 1: Write and Reflect

Where are your biggest pronunciation problems (Sound Concepts, Rhythm & Music, Grammar Sounds, or Consonant & Vowel Sounds) right now? Be specific: make a list of your three biggest problems and give examples. What do you need to work on to try to solve your problems?

ACTIVITY 2: Quiz Yourself

1. What are sibilants?

2. What kinds of syllables does English allow?

3. What are content words and function words?

4. What is standard stress in sentences?

5. Why are Grammar Sounds so important?

6. Why are Consonant & Vowel Sounds not so important?

7. What are the pronunciations of the past tense verb ending?

8. What are the pronunciations of the third-person singular verb ending?

9. Why is it important to know the difference between voiced and unvoiced sounds?

Getting Ready for Chapter 5

What You Need to Know About Stress in Longer Words

| Two-Syllable Words | **Three-Syllable Words** | Four-Syllable Words | Five-Syllable Words |

Stress in Three-Syllable Words

Stressed and unstressed syllables usually alternate. There is no way to predict the stress pattern of a new word. In words of three or more syllables, it's possible to have two weak syllables next to each other.

How do we write stress patterns for three-syllable words?

Write the number of syllables in the word and the number of the syllable that gets the stress.

> **Example:** piano pi-AN-o 3-2
>
> 3 syllables   stress on the 2nd syllable

The chart below shows the possible stress patterns for three-syllable words. After you study the examples, use the words in exercise 1 below to complete the chart.

Model Word	Number of Syllables	Stressed Syllable	Stress Pattern	Frequency	Other Examples
piano pi-AN-o	3	2nd	3-2 weak-strong-weak	common	
piccolo PIC-co-lo	3	1st	3-1 strong-weak-weak	common	
violin vi-o-LIN	3	3rd	3-3 weak-weak-strong	rare	

Exercise 1: Understanding Stress in Three-Syllable Words

 Focus on word-level stress

1. Look at the words below. Use a dictionary to find each word's stress pattern. Write the word in the correct row above.

specific   comedy   attitude   committee

integrate   component   reproduce   adjective

2. Write your own example for each pattern. Choose a word that you use often and will remember. Use these words as model words for three-syllable word stress patterns.

   3-2 _____   3-1 _____   3-3 _____

When you learn a new word, learn its stress pattern along with its definition and part of speech.

Eye-Opener: Words borrowed from another language may keep the stress pattern of their original language instead of having an English stress pattern.

| Two-Syllable Words | Three-Syllable Words | Four-Syllable Words | Five-Syllable Words |

Stress in Four-Syllable Words

Four-syllable words may have more than one stressed syllable. One syllable receives *primary* stress. It is the loudest, longest, clearest, and highest syllable in the word. Another syllable receives *secondary* stress. It is also stressed, but not as much—not as loud, long, clear, or high—as the primary stressed syllable.

Strategies for using correct stress in words with four or more syllables:

1. Stressed and unstressed syllables alternate. Syllables with primary stress and secondary stress have one or more unstressed syllables between them.

2. Words never end on a primary stressed syllable. They end on an unstressed or secondary-stressed syllable.

3. Words almost never begin with a primary stressed syllable.

How do we write stress patterns for four-syllable words?

Write the number of syllables in the word, the number of the syllable that gets primary stress, and the number of the syllable that gets secondary stress.

Example: economize   e-CON-o-*mize*   4-2-4

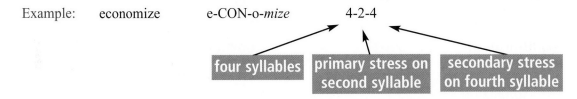

four syllables   primary stress on second syllable   secondary stress on fourth syllable

The chart below shows the possible stress patterns for four-syllable words. After you study the examples, use the words in exercise 2 to complete the chart.

Model Word	Number of Syllables	Syllable with Primary Stress	Syllable with Secondary Stress	Stress Pattern	Frequency	Other Examples
economy majority	4	2nd	none	4-2	very common	
economize personify	4	2nd	4th	4-2-4	common	
economics celebration	4	3rd	1st	4-3-1	common	
categorize personalize	4	1st	variable	4-1	rare	

Exercise 2: Understanding Stress in Four-Syllable Words

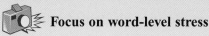 **Focus on word-level stress**

1. Look at the words below. Use a dictionary to find each word's stress pattern. Write the word in the correct row above.

    hypothesis   methodical   analysis   variable   graduation   appreciate

2. Write your own example for each pattern. Choose a word that you use often and will remember. Use these words as model words for four-syllable word stress patterns.

    4-2 _____   4-2-4 _____

    4-3-1 _____   4-1 _____

| Two-Syllable Words | Three-Syllable Words | Four-Syllable Words | Five-Syllable Words |

Stress in Five-Syllable Words

Mark the stress patterns for five- (and six-) syllable words the same way you marked the patterns for four-syllable words.

The chart below shows the possible stress patterns for five-syllable words. Look up other five-syllable words to complete the chart.

Model Word	Stress Pattern	Frequency	Other Examples
personality	5-3-1	very common	
pronunciation	5-4-2	common	
gratification	5-4-1	common	
vocabulary	5-2	less common	
personalizing	5-1	rare	

LANGUAGE STRATEGY: Using Correct Stress in Longer Words

1. Remember that stressed and unstressed syllables alternate.

2. Slow down: count the number of syllables in the word and don't omit unstressed syllables. Remember to say unstressed prefixes (additions like "il-" or "un-" at the beginning of a word: "illogical," "unreasonable").

3. Use your dictionary to find the stress pattern. In some dictionaries you need to know the root (the word without prefixes and suffixes) in order to look it up. Your dictionary may not have stress information for every word.

4. Use suffixes (endings like "-ic," "-ically," "-ion," "-ate," etc.) to help decide which syllable to stress. Different suffixes have their own stress patterns. You will learn some of these patterns in later chapters.

5. Use the checklist on the next page.

✓ CHECKLIST

Determining the Stress Pattern of a New Word

How many syllables does the word have?

> If 2 syllables. . .
>
>> Is it a compound (*blackboard*)?
>>
>>> If **yes...** ✓ strong-strong (see chapter 4)
>>>
>>> If **no...**   two possibilities: strong–weak or weak–strong (see chapter 4)
>>> Look up the word, ask someone, or guess.
>
> If 3 syllables… three possibilities: 3-2, 3-1, 3-3 (see exercise 1)
>
>> Remember that vowel sounds may change from shorter root words.
>>
>>> Look up the word, ask someone, or guess.
>
> If 4 or more syllables… (see exercise 2)
>
>> Words almost never begin with primary stress.
>>
>> Words almost never end with primary stress.
>>
>>> Look up the word, ask someone, or guess.

USAGE NOTE: WORD-LEVEL STRESS

It's always acceptable to ask your teacher or a helpful native speaker about word-level stress. Use one of the following questions:

LANGUAGE STRATEGY: Avoiding Communication Breakdown

Remember that successful communication works on two levels:

You can understand others.

Others can understand you.

When others don't understand you, communication begins to break down.

You can be more active in avoiding communication breakdowns. If you pay attention to these signs, you'll be able to check for and repair a breakdown in communication:

Look for puzzled stares, tilted heads, frowns

Listen for requests for repetition, requests for clarification, answers that don't make sense

Which photo shows successful communication? Which photo shows a communication breakdown? Discuss the body language and facial expressions of the people in the photos.

When you notice signs of communication breakdown, think about what's causing the problem. Is it word-level stress? Remember, stress carries meaning.

The person makes a difference.

The % make a difference?

Journal

Before doing this activity, think about how you will mark primary and secondary stress in your log entries. Remember that dictionaries mark stress in different ways. What does your dictionary do? Does it mark stress before, on top of, or after the stressed syllable? How does it show primary and secondary stress?

1. List ten words you use a lot, such as names of courses you're taking, items you use at work or home, and place names. Remember to check your spelling: misspellings often accompany mispronunciations.

2. Mark the stress patterns of these words as you say them now.

3. Use each word in a sentence ("I'm taking microeconomics this semester"). When you say your sentence to a native speaker, check for signs of communication breakdowns.

4. Look up the stress pattern of each word, or ask a native speaker about proper nouns such as street or place names.

5. If you've been saying these words with incorrect stress patterns, enter them into your log. Practice saying the word with the correct stress pattern and number of syllables.

Stress in Sentences and Reduced Sounds

Sound Concepts	Rhythm & Music	Grammar Sounds	Consonant & Vowel Sounds
Reduced sounds: and, of	*Stress in sentences; thought groups; stress with "–ation" suffixes*	*Regular plural noun endings*	*/b/, /v/, /y/, /ʃ/ /I/, /iʸ/ and /aI/ (it, eat, eye)*

Sound Concepts

Reduced Sounds

Diagnostic

You will hear five sentences. On a separate piece of paper, write the sentences you hear.

After Listening

With a partner or the whole class, use the checklist (Three Steps, p. 8) to decode what you heard. What Sound Concepts do you recognize in these sentences?

Did you have trouble hearing some of the unstressed function words in these sentences?
If so, which ones?

Reduced And *and* Of

In connected speech, "and" and "of" are reduced. Each word is still a syllable—a rhythmic beat—but the final consonant in each word disappears. The vowel "a" in "and" is also reduced, as in **reduced can**.

Say them: and ——————▶ /n/ of ——————▶ /ə/

Remember, the sound /ə/ is the first syllable in the word "about." We call this symbol schwa.

When do we use *reduced and* and *reduced of*?

We reduce "and" and "of " in regular connected speech.

However, *don't* reduce them if the next word starts with a vowel sound (not letter). Instead, link the sounds:

Example: Have you seen Allison and Elaine? Link the /d/.

  They were supposed to buy a carton of eggs. Link the /v/.

How do we mark *reduced and* and *reduced of* in this book?

Draw a slash through the reduced letters to help remember to reduce them.

  cup o̸f coffee soap a̸n̸d water

Practice Reduced Sounds

With a partner, go back to the diagnostic on p. 81. Mark the sentences for **reduced and** and **reduced of**.

USAGE NOTE: SIGNS and *REDUCED AND*

Sometimes, especially on signs, people write **reduced and** the following ways:

'n'	**+**	**&**
	(say it: "plus sign")	(say it: "ampersand")

Treat these symbols just like the word "and." Say them /n/ in connected speech.

Read the following signs aloud. Say **reduced and** as /n/.

FISH 'N' CHIPS
ON FRIDAYS!

Coffee
+
Pastries

Sold Here

Try Our

Black & White
Cookies!

Find more signs or advertisements that use &, +, or 'n' instead of the word "and," and share them with your classmates.

Exercise 1: Grocery Shopping

 Focus on *reduced of*

Match the columns to make a grocery list. Mark it for **reduced of**. Read your list aloud to a partner. Make up more examples, and add them to your list.

head	butter	**1.** <u>head of lettuce</u>
six-pack	lettuce	**2.** _____
pound	carrots	**3.** _____
bunch	soup	**4.** _____
carton	soda	**5.** _____
can	milk	**6.** _____

Exercise 2: Fixed Phrases with "And"

 Focus on *reduced and*   **Recycle** *reduced can*

Match the columns.

1.	You can use them to season your food.	**A.**	cream and sugar
2.	You can drink them.	**B.**	half and half
3.	You can eat them for dessert.	**C.**	milk and honey
4.	You can put them in your tea.	**D.**	apples and orange
5.	You can eat it with dinner.	**E.**	salt and pepper
6.	You can't compare them.	**F.**	tea and coffee
7.	You can put it in your coffee.	**G.**	cake and ice cream
8.	You can put them in your coffee or tea.	**H.**	bread and butter

Can you think of any other fixed phrases with "and"? Here are two more to get you started: "room and board" and "sick and tired." What do they mean?

Exercise 3: Everyday Habits

 Focus on *reduced and* **and** *reduced of*   **Recycle sentence-level stress, third-person singular present tense endings**

Make sentences from the phrases below and read them aloud to a partner. Mark your sentences for **reduced and** and **reduced of**.

You will need to

- Add a subject ("he," "she," or a name) at the beginning of the sentence
- Add a third-person singular present tense ending onto the verb
- Add a preposition ("with" or "at") between the phrases

Remember to

- Stress the content words
- Say the correct third-person singular present tense ending
- Link sounds

1.	wash the dishes	**A.**	soap and water
2.	start new classes	**B.**	the beginning of the semester
3.	come to class	**C.**	a pen and paper
4.	drink coffee	**D.**	cream and sugar
5.	pay bills	**E.**	the end of the month

Consonant & Vowel Sounds

English has only five vowel letters, but fifteen vowel sounds. Spelling won't help you keep track of these sounds. Different books use their own symbols to represent these sounds. Use the chart in the back of this book for reference (see p. 200).

Introduction to the Sound /aɪ/

What is the sound?

Say it: "eye"   Say the symbol /aɪ/ as "eye."

How do you spell it?

I	m**y**	**eye**
p**ie**	l**igh**t	**ei**ther (some pronunciations)

How do you form it?

The sound /aɪ/ is a vowel sound, so it's unblocked and voiced. It's a long sound. This sound is a dipthong, a combination of two vowel sounds. When you say this sound, your jaw drops and your tongue moves forward. The movement of your jaw, tongue, and mouth produces a slight change in pitch for this sound.

At the beginning of the sound: mouth relaxed: open but not rounded

At the end of the sound: mouth tense: partially closed, smiling

Trouble Spots

This is a long sound with two parts. Don't make it too short. Don't be confused by the spelling of this sound.

Eye-Opener: The sound /aɪ/ is extra long before a voiced consonant.

Before unvoiced consonants: (normal /aɪ/ sound)	Before voiced consonants: (longer /aɪ/ sound)
bright	bride
right/write	ride
light	lied

Practice /aɪ/

Use the words below to make sentences. Can you think of other one-syllable /aɪ/ words?

bike	rice	five	write
right	hike	like	ice
Psych	I	pie	sky
my	fry	Mike	ride
fried	buy	nice	strike

Introduction to the Sound /iʸ/

What is the sound?

The sound /iʸ/ is the sound in the word "feet." Say the symbol /iʸ/ as "E."

How do you spell it?

m**ea**t	s**ee**n	m**e**te	m**e**
rec**ei**ve	bel**ie**ve	p**eo**ple	p**i**zza

How do you form it?

The sound /iʸ/ is a vowel sound, so it's unblocked and voiced. This sound is a long sound. When you say this sound, your jaw muscles are tense, and your mouth should be slightly open, smiling. The small "y" after the main symbol helps remind us that this is a tense vowel sound.

Trouble Spots

This sound is written /iʸ/, but it is pronounced "E," like the name of the letter. Other languages pronounce the letter "E" differently. Don't be confused by the spelling of this sound.

Introduction to the Sound /I/

What is the sound?

This is the sound in the second syllable of "pencil," "until," and "needed." It's the vowel sound in the [Id] pronunciation of the past tense ending "-ed." Say the symbol /I/ as "capital I."

How do you spell it?

it	pr**e**tty	w**o**men	b**u**sy	b**ui**lt	g**y**m	b**ee**n

How do you form it?

The sound /I/ is a vowel sound, so it's unblocked and voiced. This sound is a short sound. It is lax, not tense. When you say it, your mouth should be open and relaxed; don't smile.

Trouble Spots

1. Don't say /iʸ/ for /I/. If you stretch out the short /I/ sound and make your mouth tense, then you will say the long /iʸ/ sound. Sometimes the sounds /I/ and /iʸ/ are the only difference between two words.

2. Don't worry if saying a relaxed, short /I/ sound feels strange to you. That's normal. Your teacher will tell you when you say it correctly. Try to remember how your mouth feels and what position your jaw is in when that happens. "Freeze-frame" the correct position so that you remember.

Practice /I/ and /iʸ/

Look at the following minimal pairs. The only difference between each pair of words is the vowel sound.

/I/ + longer length + tenseness ⟶ /iʸ/

hit ⟶ heat		rich ⟶ reach	
sit ⟶ seat		fill ⟶ feel	
it ⟶ eat		live ⟶ leave	

 Eye-Opener: Sometimes the sounds /I/ and /iʸ/ occur in the same word, as in "needed," /niydId/. When you say "needed," your mouth moves from the long tense /iʸ/ to the short relaxed /I/. Your jaw drops, and your mouth relaxes. Practice saying "needed" aloud to a partner, paying attention to the movement between the first and second syllable.

Exercise 4: Same or Different

 Focus on the sounds /I/ and /iʸ/

You will hear ten pairs of words. On a separate piece of paper, write "S" if you hear the same word twice and "D" if you hear two different words.

Exercise 5: Minimal Pairs

 Focus on the sounds /I/ and /iʸ/

1. Copy the words below onto index cards. Work in small groups. One person shuffles his or her cards and makes a pile of them, face down. The other group members spread their cards on their desks, face up. The person with the pile draws a card at random and reads it aloud. The rest of the group holds up the card that matches what they heard. If the cards don't match, set them aside to go over with the teacher or entire class.

did	sit	fill	hip	hit	heat
deed	seat	feel	heap	rich	reach
live	it	rid	lip	chip	cheap
leave	eat	read	leap	dip	deep

2. Make sentences using each of the words. With a partner, take turns drawing cards and reading aloud the word from one of the cards at random. Respond to your partner's word with the matching sentence. If the word and sentence don't match, set them aside to go over with the teacher or entire class.

Introduction to the Sounds /b/ and /v/

What are the sounds?
The sound /b/ is the sound of the letter "B," and the sound /v/ is the sound of the letter "V." These are different sounds.

How do you spell them?
Write the sound /b/ as "b" and /v/ as "v." Pronounce the letter "b" as /b/ and the letter "v" as /v/ in every position in a word.

How do you form them?

	/b/	**/v/**
Place	lips together	top teeth touching bottom lip
Manner	stop (air is stopped)	continuant (air continues)
Voicing	voiced	voiced

Trouble Spots
1. Don't pronounce the English letter "v" like /b/.

   This causes problems in minimal pairs like boat/vote and berry/very. If you're having trouble saying the sounds /b/ and /v/, use the Language Strategy for Commonly Confused Consonants in appendix 1.

2. Don't pronounce the letter "v" like /f/.

Introduction to the Sound /ʝ/

What is the sound?
Look at the word "judge." The word begins and ends with the same sound, /ʝ/. If you can pronounce "judge," you already know the sound /ʝ/—the sound of the letter "j."

How do you spell it?

June	gra**d**ual	**judg**e	pa**g**e

 Eye-Opener: The letter "j" is always pronounced /ʝ/. There are no exceptions.

How do you form it?
This sound is a combined consonant sound. It's a voiced sound made up of a stop and a continuant. With a continuant, the sound continues—there's friction. To form this sound, you need two different positions for your mouth. First, form the sound /d/, with your tongue touching the ridge behind your top teeth. Then move your tongue back a little.

Trouble Spots
Don't be confused by the spelling of this sound.

Introduction to the Sound /y/

What is the sound?
Say the word "busy." The sound at the end of "busy" is the vowel sound /iʸ/. Think about the position of your mouth when you say that sound: freeze-frame. This is the position to begin forming the sound /y/.

Say the sentence: "It's been a busy year." Your mouth should stay in the same position for the last two syllables. If you do this, you are saying the sound /y/.

How do you spell it?

you	con**v**en**i**ent	**u**seful	fe**w**

How do you form it?
The sound /y/ is a voiced, vowel-like sound. The air is not blocked, and there is no friction.

Trouble Spots
Don't confuse the sounds /ʝ/ and /y/. The chart below shows their differences.

	/ʝ/	/y/
Place	beginning: tongue touching ridge at back of top teeth end: lips slightly rounded, more relaxed	lips more tense, slightly smiling
Manner	air continues, with friction	air unblocked, no friction
Voicing	voiced	voiced

Violence Chicago story.

Exercise 6: Same or Different?

 Focus on the sounds /b/, /v/, /y/, and /j/

 Now that you've practiced saying these sounds, find out if you can hear them better. Remember, what you say affects what you hear. You will hear ten pairs of words. On a separate piece of paper, write "S" if you hear the same word twice and "D" if you hear two different words.

Exercise 7: Key Words

 Focus on the sounds /b/, /v/, /y/, and /j/

Take turns reading the words in the left column to a partner. Your partner responds with the matching key word or phrase.

Word	Key Word or Phrase
Yale	military leader
yellow	Ivy League college
jail	participate in elections
major	government leader
Jello	ship
boat	prison
vote	gelatin dessert
mayor	color

Exercise 8: Minimal Pair Sentences

 Focus on the sounds /b/, /v/, /y/, /j/, /aI/, /iʸ/, and /I/

Take turns reading a sentence from the column on the left to a partner. Your partner responds with the matching reply from the other column.

1. She has problems with the mayor.
2. She has problems with the major.
3. She went to Yale.
4. She went to jail.
5. I want her to live.
6. I want her to leave.
7. Did you get much use out of that?
8. Did you get much juice out of that?
9. Did he heat it?
10. Did he hit it?
11. On Tuesday she'll register to vote.
12. On Tuesday she'll register her boat.
13. Yello is my favorite.

A. City government can be difficult to deal with.
B. She should talk to her commanding officer.
C. Really? How wonderful!
D. Oh no! What did she do?
E. So do I. I care about her a lot.
F. I don't—I really want her to stay.
G. No, it broke before I even got to use it twice.
H. Yes, it's a really juicy orange.
I. No, he ate it cold.
J. Yes, he hit it out of the baseball park.
K. That's great—the elections are next month.
L. Really? I didn't know she knew how to sail.
M. Personally, I prefer blue.

Grammar Sounds

Regular Plural Count Noun Endings ("-s" or "-es")

Why is this ending important?

This ending tells you that a noun is countable and plural. Native speakers listen for this noun ending. They depend on the grammatical information, on the sound of the linking from the final "s," and on the extra syllable that the ending sometimes makes.

If you don't say it,

- You sound ungrammatical

- Your listeners may be confused

- Your sentences may have the wrong rhythm

Use the following exercise to learn how to say the regular plural count noun ending correctly. This ending is pronounced three different ways.

Exercise 9: Context for Practice–Ben and Jerry's Ice Cream

 Focus on regular plural count noun endings ("-s" or "-es")

 Recycle linking, *reduced and*, and *reduced of*

USAGE NOTE: READING DOLLAR AMOUNTS

Read dollar amounts written with numbers exactly like words.
Say *ten thousand dollars* the same way you say *$10,000*.

A.   Read the following passage to yourself. Then discuss the questions with a partner.

Based in the state of Vermont, the ice cream company Ben & Jerry's Homemade, Inc. was founded in 1978. Ben Cohen and Jerry Greenfield were childhood **friends** from junior high school **classes.** The two friends started their company in an old gas station with just **$12,000.** They soon became popular for their innovative **flavors,** made from fresh Vermont dairy **products.** The company currently sells ice **creams** and frozen **yogurts** in **countries** around the world. You can find their ice cream in **supermarkets**, grocery **stores**, and **restaurants**, and Ben & Jerry's **franchises** (small, privately owned ice cream **shops**). But Ben & Jerry's does more than just make frozen **desserts**: The company also believes in supporting local **charities** and community **projects**, as well as global, environmental **causes**.

www.benjerry.com/our_company/about_us/our_history

Think About It

Have you heard of Ben & Jerry's ice cream? Did you know that the company gives so much money to charities and to environmental causes?

Do you think successful businesses should support various good causes in their community or around the world? Why or why not?

B. Use the checklist below to complete the rest of this exercise (directions follow the checklist).

✓CHECKLIST

How do you say the "-s" or "-es" on regular count noun plurals?

Look   Find the root (singular) form of a noun, without any endings.

Ask   What is the final sound (not letter)?

Is it   **/s/**   the sound at the end of "box"?

   /z/   the sound at the end of "raise"?

   /sh/   the sound at the end of "wash"?

   /tch/ the sound at the end of "watch"?

   /j/   the sound at the end of "judge"?

These five sounds are called sibilants.

They hiss when you say them.

> **So, when saying the third-person singular present tense ending:**
>
> **1.** Voiced sounds use voiced endings, **[z]**
>
> **2.** Unvoiced sounds use unvoiced endings, **[s]**
>
> **3.** Hissing sounds (sibilants) add an extra syllable to the ending, **[Iz]**

If **yes**... ✓

   Add an extra syllable ⟶ Say "-s" or "-es" as [Iz].

If **no**...

   Ask   Is the final sound unvoiced?

      If **yes**... ✓

      There is no extra syllable ⟶ Say "-s" as [s].

      If **no**...

      There is no extra syllable ⟶ Say "-s" as [z].

Are you having trouble finding the final sound of a word?
Go back to exercise 4 in chapter 3 (page 38) for help.

---

1. Make a three-column chart like the one below. Label your chart with the three different pronunciations of the regular count noun plural ending ("-s" or "-es").

[z]	[s]	[Iz]
Extra syllable? yes no	Extra syllable? yes no	Extra syllable? yes no

2. Decide whether the ending in each column is pronounced as an extra syllable. Circle the word "yes" or "no."

3. Put each highlighted word from the passage in the appropriate column.

4. Check your answers with a partner.

5. Write the sound of each ending—[z], [s], or [Iz]—above the highlighted words in the passage.

6. Mark the passage for linking and for **reduced and** and **reduced of.**

7. Read the passage aloud to a partner, practicing linking, reduced sounds, and plural endings. Check your partner's pronunciation of the endings.

Eye-Opener: The three pronunciations of the plural noun ending are the same as the three pronunciations of the third-person singular present tense verb ending. Use the same rules to remember how to say these endings.

The Teacher-Student Partnership in Action

From now on, you are responsible for saying this ending correctly. Your teacher will correct you if you make a mistake with this ending. Your teacher will also tell you when you say it right (freeze-frame). Enter your mistakes with this ending into your log.

 ## Rhythm & Music

Thought Groups

When we speak or read aloud, we take words within a single sentence that go together and group them together. But how do you *know* which words go together? Words in a preposition phrase, like "in the morning" or "at the bank" go together. The words in a noun phrase or a verb phrase also go together. Sometimes in a very short sentence, the whole sentence is just one group. We call these groups of words thought groups. Each thought group has one thought or idea. We pause at the end of a thought group when we speak or read aloud.

How do you know where to pause for a thought group?

Thought groups are generally 3–8 words long. Use clues from punctuation, grammar, and stressed content words to help recognize thought groups.

1. **Punctuation Clues**

   The following punctuation marks may indicate the end of a thought group in a longer sentence:

, comma	smallest pause or no pause
; semi-colon	slightly bigger pause
: colon	slightly bigger pause

   In general, pause when you see one of these punctuation marks.

2. **Grammar Clues**

   You may know the grammatical term "clause" from studying dependent clauses, relative clauses, or other kinds of clauses.

   A clause is a group of words with a verb in it, but not necessarily a complete sentence.

   Each clause is usually its own thought group. Pause at the beginning of a new clause.

3. **Clues from Stressed Content Words**

   Each thought group has at least one stressed word. Remember that content words are usually stressed, and function words are usually unstressed. Use the content words in a sentence to identify thought groups.

   Example

sentence:	He	washes	his	hands	at	the	sink.
three stressed content words:		**washes**		**hands**			**sink**
three small thought groups:	[He washes]		[his hands]		[at the sink.]		

How do we mark thought groups?

Draw brackets around each thought group to remember to pause slightly.

PRONUNCIATION GOAL

Practice dividing sentences into thought groups so you pause in the right places when speaking or reading aloud.

Thought Groups and Linking

In longer sentences, and with bigger thought groups, we generally have longer pauses.

Sometimes, when a sentence has very small thought groups, the pauses between thought groups are also very small. When the pauses between thought groups are very small, we still link sounds across thought groups and delete the sound /h/:

[He washes] [his hands] [at the sink.]

When you add more phrases to a sentence, you have more thought groups.

[Every morning,] [he washes] [his hands] [at the sink.]

[Every morning,] [he washes] [his hands] [at the sink] [before he goes to work.]

Exercise 10: Who Did What When?

 Focus on thought groups   **Recycle linking, past tense endings, stress**

Think about a business you know, or research a company or organization. Write a paragraph about how it began. Mark your sentences for thought groups.

> Example: [As a young man,] [Bill Gates started a business] [in his garage.]

Read your paragraph to a partner. Be sure to say the past tense endings correctly.

Does your partner agree with the thought groups you marked? Why or why not?

Journal

Find an English poem you like and bring a copy of it to class. Where do you think you should pause when you read the poem aloud? Mark your poem for thought groups and for linking within thought groups. Practice reading aloud your poem, and recite it for a small group.

Write a paragraph about why you like your poem. Mark your paragraph for thought groups and for linking within thought groups. Read your paragraph to the group.

Rhythm & Music

Stress with "–ation" Suffixes

Basic rule: Stress the first syllable of the suffix (the "A" in -A-tion). The suffix "-ation" changes a verb into a noun.

verb		noun
cancel + "-ation"	⟶	can-cel-**LA**-tion
alter + "-ation"	⟶	alt-er-**A**-tion

Advanced rules for secondary stress: Secondary stress in "-ation" words depends on the stress pattern of the original verb.

1. When verbs end in a weak syllable, the stressed syllable in the original verb receives secondary stress in the "-ation" noun.

CAN-cel	strong-weak	⟶	*can*-cel-LA-tion	(4-3-1)
JUS-ti-fy	3-1	⟶	*jus*-ti-fi-CA-tion	(5-4-1)

2. When verbs end in a strong syllable, the stressed syllable in the original verb receives no stress in the new "-ation" word. Remember that stressed and unstressed syllables alternate: two stressed syllables are never next to each other. Instead, move the secondary stress one syllable to the left.

in-FORM	weak-strong	⟶	*in*-for-MA-tion	(4-3-1)

 Eye-Opener: If you know the stress pattern of the original verb and the rule for "-ation" primary stress, you know the stress patterns of these nouns.

USAGE NOTE: SPELLING and "-ation" NOUNS

Sometimes you have to change the spelling in order to form an "-ation" noun.

converse	⟶	converSAtion
justify	⟶	justifiCAtion
cancel	⟶	cancelLAtion

These spelling changes are not always predictable, so you may need to use a dictionary.

Exercise 11: Practice with "-ation" Words

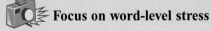 **Focus on word-level stress**

For each word below, find the root verb, look it up in a dictionary, and mark its primary stress. Then mark primary stress on the "-ation" words in the chart. Practice saying these words with a partner.

3-syllable words	4-syllable words	5-syllable words
formation	education	recommendation
frustration	concentration	appreciation
	expectation	pronunciation
		evacuation

Exercise 12: Using "-ation" Words in Context

 Focus on word-level stress

Work with a partner to match the columns. Practice reading the sentences and phrases aloud to practice the stress patterns in context.

1. Thank you so much! It's so kind of you!   A. Congratulations!

2. Well done! Good job!   B. Please submit an application.

3. No eating, drinking, or smoking.   C. I'd like to express my appreciation!

4. Many people would like to apply for this job.   D. There are too many rules and regulations.

Which photo shows someone expressing congratulations? Which photo shows frustration?

Journal

Listen to the news for "-ation" words. Write down the words you hear. Listen for the stress patterns in these words and their context. Use these words to write a summary of the news report, and then read the summary aloud to your classmates. Be sure to use correct stress patterns.

Grammar Sounds

Exercise 13: Generalizations with Plurals

 Focus on plural noun endings

With a partner, brainstorm count noun plurals for each of the categories below. List your words on a separate piece of paper. Then make up two more categories of your own. Read your lists aloud to another student pair to see if you thought of any items others did not. Remember to say the plural endings correctly. If you have trouble with any words, enter them into your log.

Example

Desserts: cakes, cookies, pies, puddings, tarts, souffles…

articles of clothing	jobs	tools	things in bedrooms
things in classrooms	utensils	kinds of dogs	zoo animals

Recycle linking, thought groups, *reduced and* and *reduced of,* /b/ and /v/, /y/ and /ʝ/

Write the sentences that you hear, dividing each one into its major thought groups (marked for you below). Put all of the words in one thought group together.

1. [_____ ,]

   [_____ .]

2. [_____] [_____ .]

3. [_____ ,] [_____ .]

4. [_____ .]

5. [_____] [_____ ,]

   [_____ .]

What did we do in this chapter?

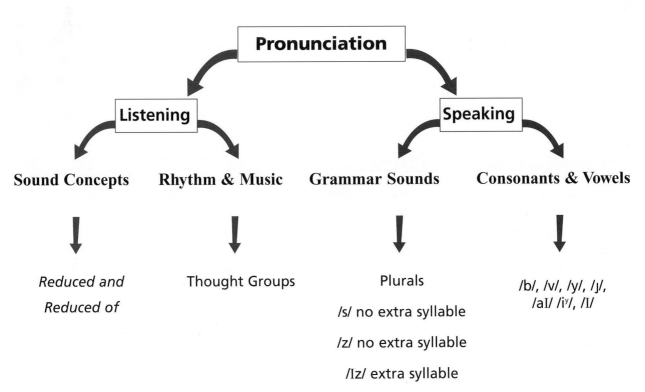

Pronunciation

Listening → Speaking

Sound Concepts   Rhythm & Music   Grammar Sounds   Consonants & Vowels

Reduced and   Thought Groups   Plurals   /b/, /v/, /y/, /ʝ/,
Reduced of   /aɪ/ /iʸ/, /ɪ/

                                        /s/ no extra syllable

                                        /z/ no extra syllable

                                        /ɪz/ extra syllable

Think About It

Students often want to "improve" their pronunciation. What do you think it means to improve? How will you know when you've improved?

 Eye-Opener: Improving your pronunciation means making changes.

When you start to make changes to your pronunciation, you might have one of the following reactions:

1. I know what my mistakes are, but I'm used to saying things my own way.

2. I don't like the way I sound to myself when I correct my pronunciation—I just sound wrong.

3. I've studied English for a long time. People seem to understand me—I manage to get along.

Discuss these reactions with a partner:

> Why might learners feel this way? Have you ever felt this way when working on your pronunciation? How can these feelings interfere with improvement?

 Eye-Opener: All three reactions lead to the same problem—no change in a learner's pronunciation. But not making changes in pronunciation can have serious consequences.

Activity 1: Progress Report

 Look through your logbook. Do your entries focus on one or two of the areas of pronunciation (Sound Concepts, Rhythm & Music, Grammar Sounds, Consonant & Vowel Sounds)? Which is the most difficult area for you?

Think about what happens when you make a pronunciation mistake. Can you correct yourself right away, or do you need to look at your logbook and checklists? Either way, you're making progress: you're moving toward level 3, conscious competence (page 25).

If you can't correct your mistakes, why do you think that is?

What problems are you still having?

Case Study 1: The Engineer

A software engineer in an ESL pronunciation course thought that English Grammar Sounds were unimportant and unnecessary. He argued that since English has words like "yesterday," "last week," or "many" to show tense or number, he didn't need to use noun and verb endings. The engineer was a member of a project team. When the team had a big project with a quick deadline, the other team members decided they didn't have time to include the software engineer in the project.

Discuss the following questions with a partner:

1. What's the problem here? Why do you think the team members had this reaction?

2. What might be difficult or time-consuming about talking to the engineer?

3. What happens if someone doesn't say noun and verb endings? List all the aspects of pronunciation that are affected by these missing endings.

4. Do you know anyone who's been excluded from a group or conversation because of their pronunciation? Describe the situation.

 Eye-Opener: The engineer took the pronunciation course because he thought he wanted to improve, but he didn't really want to change his pronunciation. Look at the next case study for another example of a student who wanted to improve.

Case Study 2: Motivation to Improve

An ESL student was working as a dishwasher. The manager promised to promote the student to a better job with higher pay when her pronunciation improved. The student was motivated and asked her teacher for extra help.

During class, the student's pronunciation improved, but she wasn't sure she wanted to speak that way outside class. She had one of the reactions above: "I don't like the way I sound to myself when I correct my pronunciation—I just sound *wrong*."

Discuss the following questions with a partner:

1. What does the student need to do?

2. Should she change her pronunciation even if it feels wrong? Or should she stay in the lower-paying job?

3. Do you think her reactions to her new pronunciation will eventually change? Why or why not?

4. Brainstorm with a partner everything the student can do to improve her pronunciation.

 Eye-Opener: Studying pronunciation helps you learn more about pronunciation. This is how you become conscious of your errors and move from level 1 to level 2. But studying *about* pronunciation is not enough to improve.

Speaking more English outside class is also a good goal, but if you still make the same mistakes when you speak, then you're not improving. If you change your speech in classroom exercises and outside the classroom (at home, work, and school), then you will improve. Improving pronunciation means making changes all the time—not just during class.

Why should you change your pronunciation?

Some students feel that they don't need to make changes because they're getting along all right in English: other people understand them. But what may be happening is that the students' listeners are doing all the work:

Communication should be balanced.
Don't make your listeners do all the work of trying to understand you—you also need to work on being understood.

Remember the team members who stopped working with the software engineer in case study 1? They were tired of doing all the work in conversations with him.

Consciousness, Competence, and Change

Where Are You Now?

At the beginning of this course, you were asked to list your pronunciation problems. By now, you probably have a better idea of your problems. You're more *conscious* of your repeated errors, but being conscious of them isn't enough. To become *competent*, you need to make changes in your pronunciation.

Think about why you took this course. You probably wanted to improve your pronunciation. Improving doesn't mean learning new information *about* pronunciation; it means making changes *in* your pronunciation.

You may feel that some exercises in this book focus on things you already know. However, if you *know* an ending or sound but don't *pronounce* it correctly, there's still a problem—you need to change your pronunciation.

> **Journal**
> **1.** Why did you decide to take this course? What's been the most difficult area for you? How do you feel when you notice changes in your pronunciation? Why? What specific sounds or concepts will you try to improve (change) in the future?
> **2.** Go back to the diagnostic, section C. (page 23) Reread your responses. Would you answer any questions differently now? Why?

Discussion of Case Studies

1. **The Engineer** The group members knew that talking to the engineer took a lot of time. They always had to ask, "What do you mean?" "What did you say?" They also had to keep explaining themselves to him, which also took a lot of time. When the engineer left off noun and verb endings, he created problems in these other areas of his speech: linked sounds, number of syllables, sentence-level rhythm and music. Sometimes his team had to ask, "When did this happen?" if they weren't sure whether the engineer was talking about the present or past.

   The team met their deadline without the engineer's expertise. However, the final project wasn't acceptable to the customer because of a serious design flaw. The engineer would have solved the problem if he'd been included in the project. The company lost money and almost lost their customer.

2. **Motivation to Improve** The student really wanted to make changes to her pronunciation, even though it felt strange to her. She worked on her pronunciation in class and outside class. The student's supervisor noticed the changes in her speech and promoted her.

   Motivation to change is the first step, but improvement only happens with the actual pronunciation change.

Contrastive Stress and Altered Sounds

Sound Concepts	**Rhythm & Music**	**Grammar Sounds**	**Consonant & Vowel Sounds**
Altered sounds (you, do, to, have to, gonna)	*Contrastive stress*	*Possessive noun endings*	*/sh/, /tch/, /zh/, /h/*

 Sound Concepts

Introduction to Altered Sounds

Preview

What do you think is the most difficult word in the English language? Why?

Diagnostic

You will hear six statements or questions. On a separate piece of paper, write the statements or questions you hear.

After Listening

With a partner or the whole class, use the checklist (Three Steps, p. 8) to decode what you heard. What was difficult about this diagnostic?

 Eye-Opener: Did you notice that each example had the word "you" in it? "You" may seem like an easy word, but it can be difficult to hear. "You" is a function word, and function words are usually unstressed. The unstressed word "you" (/yu/) in connected speech almost never sounds like /yu/. In these examples, the word "you" was altered. It sounded like /yə/.

Altered You: you ⟶ /yə/

What is *altered you*?

In connected speech, the vowel sound in the unstressed word "you" changes from the tense, round vowel /u/ to the lax, unrounded vowel /ə/ (schwa).

tense ⟶ lax

How do we mark *altered you* in this book?

Cross out the vowels in "you," and write the schwa symbol (ə) over it, like this: y̶o̶u̶ ə

When do we use *altered you*?

Use **altered you** in connected speech.

Two exceptions:

1. When "you" is used to make a contrast: No, I don't mean you, I mean YOU!

2. When "you" comes at the end of a sentence or question: Thank you!

Practice *Altered You*

With a partner, go back to the diagnostic on p. 99. Mark the sentences for **altered you**.

Exercise 1: Poll Your Classmates!

 Focus on *altered you*   **Recycle sentence-level stress**

Write a list of yes/no questions to ask your classmates. Underline the stressed content words and mark your questions for **altered you**. Ask your classmates the questions and note their answers. Be sure to use **altered you** in your questions. Later in this chapter you'll have a chance to report your findings to the class.

Examples:
1. Have you <u>lived</u> here for <u>more</u> than a <u>year</u>?

2. Do you <u>like</u> the <u>neighborhood</u>?

3. Are you <u>planning</u> on <u>moving</u>?

Exercise 2: Impersonal You

 Focus on *altered you*

With a partner, write five questions you might ask when trying to get information at each of the following places. Mark your questions for **altered you** and practice asking them.

Examples: hardware store   How do you fix a broken pipe?

post office   How do you mail a package to China?

Department of Motor Vehicles   How do you take a road test?

USAGE NOTE: IDIOMS WITH *ALTERED YOU*

"Yóu know…" is a casual form of "Do you know. . ."
Use it to start a conversation, join one, or shift to a new topic.

"Yóu know what I mean?" is a casual form of "Do you know what I mean?"
Use it to check your listeners' comprehension or ask for agreement.

 Journal

1. English speakers almost always use **altered you** in conversation. Choose a place where you can listen to English speakers in conversation. Listen for **altered you**. Write down as many examples as you can. Discuss your results with the class.

2. Some English idioms use **altered you**, such as "Are you all set?" You may hear this idiom in restaurants when a waiter asks if you need anything else, or in many other situations. Listen for "Are you all set?" and record the circumstances in which you heard it.

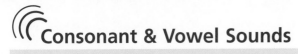

Consonant & Vowel Sounds

Introduction to the Sound /sh/

What is the sound?

This is the sound people say when they want someone to be quiet: "Shhh!" Say it: "sh."

How do you spell it?

ocean   sugar   confession   anxious   machine (very rare)

How do you form it?

The sound /sh/ is an unvoiced consonant sound. Say "Shhh!" and notice where your lips are. This is the position for the sound /sh/.

Trouble Spots

Don't let spelling confuse you. If a word contains the letters "sh," always say the sound /sh/.

Introduction to the Sound /tch/

What is the sound?

This is the sound at the end of the words "much" and "match." Say it: "tch."

How do you spell it?

teacher   match   picture   question

How do you form it?

The sound /tch/ is an unvoiced consonant sound. It has two parts. Start by putting your mouth in the position to say /t/. This position blocks air. Now say the sound /t/ and the sound /sh/. Be sure to stop the air before you say the /sh/ sound.

Trouble Spots

Don't let spelling confuse you.

When you see the letters "ch," say the sound /tch/.	When you see the letters "sh," say the sound /sh/.
Example: chocolate	Example: shoe
There are very few exceptions. (Chicago, machine)	There are no exceptions.

Introduction to the Sound /zh/

What is the sound?

This is the voiced version of the sound /sh/.

How do you spell it?

massage   vision   usual   equation

How do you form it?

Form this sound by saying /sh/ and letting your vocal cords vibrate. It's a voiced sound.

Trouble Spots

Use your voicebox to say this sound. Don't say /z/ or /s/.

Introduction to the Sound /h/

What is the sound?

The sound /h/ is the consonant sound in the middle of "ahead" and "behind," and at the beginning of "hello."

How do you spell it?

hello   **wh**o

How do you form it?

The sound /h/ is the unvoiced sound of air escaping your mouth. Your vocal cords are not vibrating, so the space between the cords—your glottis—is open (see diagram, appendix 1).

When you say a word that begins with /h/, there will be an unvoiced sound before the vowel. You can imagine this sound as the sound of breathing out loud.

Trouble Spots

Don't drop the /h/ sound. Some languages don't have the /h/ sound, and some students find it difficult to say. Remember that the sound /h/ is the *unvoiced* sound of air escaping from your vocal cords *before* you say a voiced sound like a vowel. Try taking a deep breath and being ready to exhale before you say /h/.

English speakers expect you to say /h/. Sometimes the /h/ sound is the difference between two words:

high vs. **eye**	a high-level course / an eye-level picture
hate vs. **eight / ate**	I hate it. / I ate it.
how vs. **ow**	How are you? / Ow! I hurt myself!

Always say the /h/ sound, except in these few cases:

- Deleted /h/ in unstressed "his," "her," "he," "him"
- Silent "h" in words like "herb," "heir," "honest," "vehicle," "hour"

Exercise 3: H-Phrases

 Focus on the sound /h/

If you have trouble saying the /h/ sound, circle the "h" in the words below to help you remember to pronounce it. Take turns reading the phrases aloud to a partner. Check the box next to each phrase if your partner says the /h/ sound. If any boxes are unchecked, review how to form /h/.

1. a helpful person ☐
2. a half-day meeting ☐
3. a high-level course ☐
4. a house in the country ☐
5. a hot summer day ☐
6. a hand-delivered message ☐

Rhythm & Music

Introduction to Contrastive Stress

Preview

Remember that in general content words are stressed and function words are unstressed. This is standard sentence-level stress. It's neutral—there's no extra meaning. In English, you can also stress *any* word in a sentence that you want, depending on the meaning (intent) you want to convey.

Diagnostic

Imagine that you are shopping with a friend for clothes. Your friend can't decide which shirt to buy. Underline each word you would stress if you were having this conversation.

    A: "Should I get the shirt with buttons or without buttons?"

    B: "How about with the buttons?"

    A: "Well, should I get the short-sleeved one or the long-sleeved?"

    B: "Well, I like short-sleeved shirts."

    A: "Okay, do you like the blue or the white?"

    B: "I like the yellow. Can we go now?"

 Now listen to the dialogue. Circle the words that the speakers stress. Remember that a stressed word is louder, longer, clearer, and higher than the rest of the sentence.

After Listening

With a partner, compare your responses. Do you agree? Why or why not? Listen to the dialogue again. Make a list of the stressed words you heard. Which of the stressed words are content words and which are function words? What's unusual about this?

Standard Sentence-Level Stress: When a speaker says, "I like short-sleeved shirts" with standard stress, there's no extra stress on "short." The speaker stresses the content words. There's no extra meaning, and we don't know anything about the context. The sentence is neutral.	**Contrastive Stress:** When a speaker says, "I like *short*-sleeved shirts" with extra stress on "*short*," the speaker is making a contrast: *short*-sleeved, not *long*-sleeved. There is extra meaning, and we know something about the context. The sentence is not neutral; it's contrastive.

The message is in the music: Stress carries meaning.

What is contrastive stress?

Contrastive stress is extra stress placed on the stressed syllable of a word in order to make a contrast. The word-level stress pattern doesn't change. The strong syllable is still strong, and the weak syllable is still weak.

How do we mark contrastive stress in this book?

Underline or circle contrastively stressed words.

 Eye-Opener: Not all stressed syllables are equal. Stressed syllables are louder, longer, clearer, and higher, but contrastive stress is *extra* stress.

word-level secondary stress	word-level primary stress	standard sentence-level stress (content words)	contrastive stress

LANGUAGE STRATEGY: Visualizing Stress in Syllables

An unstressed syllable is like a person standing still; a stressed syllable is like a person stretching.
An unstressed syllable is like a coiled spring; a stressed syllable is like an uncoiled spring.
An unstressed syllable is like a folded-up ladder; a stressed syllable is like an extended ladder.

Can you think of more images for stressed syllables?

Try acting out stress in the following ways:

- Stand up for stressed words; sit down for unstressed words.

- Stretch your arms up for stressed words; leave them down for unstressed words.

Practice Contrastive Stress

Practice the diagnostic dialogue with a partner until your stress matches the speakers' stress on the recording. Perform your dialogue for the class or a small group. Which pair had the best contrastive stress?

 Eye-Opener: Contrastive stress calls attention to the important (contrastive) word. Show contrastive stress in writing with *italics* (or sometimes <u>underlining</u>).

Exercise 4: Report Your Findings

 Focus on contrastive stress

Go back to your notes from exercise 1, the poll of your classmates. Report your findings to the class. Use contrastive stress where appropriate in your statements.

>   Examples: *Jeremy* wears a watch, but *Mary* doesn't.
>
>   *John* has lived here for *two* years, but *Susan* for *four*.

USAGE NOTE: IMPLICIT and EXPLICIT CONTRASTS

In the sentence "*Jeremy* wears a watch, but *Mary* doesn't," both points of contrast (Jeremy and Mary) are stated. Both points of contrast are explicit.

In the sentence "*I* didn't do that," only one point of contrast (I) is stated. The other point of contrast (someone else who is not mentioned) is suggested, or implicit.

USAGE NOTE: USE CONTRASTIVE STRESS to BE MORE CONCISE

These two sentences have the same meaning, but the second sentence is more concise.

1. Even though you think I did that, I'm not the person who did it; it was someone else who did it. (with standard sentence-level stress)

2. *I* didn't do that. (with contrastive stress on "I")

Contrastive stress is economical—you can use it to express the same meaning in fewer words.

Exercise 5: What Did the Doctor Do?

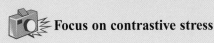 **Focus on contrastive stress**

Imagine that you go to your doctor's office for your test results. The doctor's assistant speaks to you. You could hear many different versions of the assistant's message. Use the italics (written indications of contrastive stress) below to understand the meaning of the message. Match the columns.

1. The *doctor* didn't read your X-rays yet.

2. The doctor didn't *read* your X-rays yet.

3. The doctor didn't read *your* X-rays yet.

4. The doctor didn't read your *X-rays* yet.

5. The doctor didn't read your X-rays *yet*.

A. But she will soon.

B. But someone else did

C. But she put them in your file.

D. But she read the other patients' x-rays.

E. But she read your lab test results.

 Eye-Opener: The *content* of each sentence you heard in exercise 4 was the same, but the *intent* of each sentence was different. Contrastive stress makes the difference: stress carries meaning.

USAGE NOTE: CONTRASTIVE STRESS and NUMBERS

Use contrastive stress to contrast two numbers that end in "-teen," such as "fourteen" and "fifteen." Stress the first syllable: the number (the contrast).

Exercise 6: These, Not Those

 Focus on contrastive stress

With a partner, take turns reading the noun phrases below. When it's your turn to read, decide which content word you want to stress. Don't let your partner know which word you choose, but underline the word to remind yourself to stress it. Your partner will choose the appropriate implication.

Example: three *CDs* (implies) ⟶ CDs, not videotapes

three CDs (implies) ⟶ three, not four

Noun phrases	**Implications**
1. four bags	four, not fourteen / bags, not boxes
2. sixty days	sixty, not six / days, not weeks
3. a large desk	large, not small / desk, not chair
4. my coat	mine, not yours / coat, not hat
5. fifteen years	fifteen, not fourteen / years, not months
6. three cities	three, not four / cities, not states

Are you saying and hearing contrastive stress?

Are you stressing the word you intend?

If not, practice more in exercises 5 and 6.

Are you stressing only the vowel sound in the strong syllable in that word?

If not, practice word-level stress in chapter 3.

Are you able to recognize stressed words when you hear them?

If not, practice saying the explicit contrasts in exercise 3.

Test your progress by listening to the contrastive words in exercise 4.

Exercise 7: Past Activities and Contrasts

 Focus on contrastive stress

Write three sentences about what you did last week, month, or year. For each sentence, choose a word you want to stress based on a contrast you want to imply. Underline that word. Take turns reading your sentences aloud to a partner. Use contrastive stress on the strong syllable of your chosen word. Your partner responds by stating your implication.

Example   **A:** "I went to the *supermarket* yesterday."

B: "You went to the supermarket and not somewhere else. You wanted to go somewhere else instead."

USAGE NOTE: STANDARD SENTENCE-LEVEL STRESS

When asking for help in a store or other situation, use standard sentence-level stress.

1. **Standard stress:** "Can you help me?" (content-word stress on "help")
   Meaning: Can you help me?

2. **Contrastive stress:** "Can *you* help me?"
   Implied meaning: Can you, and not someone else, help me?

3. **Contrastive stress:** "Can you help *me*?"
   Implied meaning: Can you help me, and not someone else?

4. **Contrastive stress:** "Can you *help* me?"
   Implied meaning: Can you help me, instead of ignoring me?

Questions **2**, **3**, and **4** could sound rude. In question **2**, you're implying that someone else didn't or wouldn't help you. In question **3**, you're implying that you need help more than someone else. In question **4**, you're implying that the person wasn't doing his or her job. All three questions imply that you're unhappy with the service.

The next time you're in a store or another place where people ask for help, listen to how English speakers ask this question.

Eye-Opener: Contrastive stress provides background information (one of the Three Kinds of Information) about a speaker's implications. If you hear contrastive stress, use the background information to make sense of the speaker's meaning. Contrastive stress carries meaning.

Exercise 8: Standard or Contrastive?

 Focus on contrastive stress   **Recycle standard sentence-level stress**

 A. Listen to the following questions. Which questions use standard stress? Which use contrastive stress? Check the box and compare your choices with a partner.

Question	Standard Stress	Contrastive Stress
1. Do you know today's date?	☐	☑
2. Do I need extra postage for this?	☐	☐
3. Is there any research on this topic?	☐	☐
4. Do you know today's date?	☐	☐
5. Can I have that pizza with pepperoni?	☐	☐
6. Do I need extra postage for this?	☐	☐
7. Is there any research on this topic?	☐	☐
8. Can I have that pizza with pepperoni?	☐	☐

B. Listen to the implied background information one student imagined for the first question in part A. Can you imagine other possibilities? Discuss them with a partner. For each question with contrastive stress, explain the implications (the background information) with a partner. Why would a speaker stress that word? What does the stress tell you about the context or situation?

 Journal

People often use body language to accompany contrastive stress. Pointed fingers or gesturing hands, raised eyebrows, and shrugged shoulders all help to signal a speaker's intent. Many television comedies, or sitcoms, use contrastive stress for humor. Comedic actors exaggerate the gestures and expressions that go with contrastive stress, just as they exaggerate their own stress patterns.

Watch a sitcom in English; if possible, record it so you can watch it again. Use the actors' gestures and expressions, as well as the audience's laughter, to help you find examples of contrastive stress. Describe the gestures and expressions that accompanied your examples. What does each example of contrastive stress imply? Share your findings with the class.

Exercise 9: Who Did What to My What?

 Focus on contrastive stress

Use the information in the second and third columns to decide if the sentence in the first column should have standard sentence-level stress or contrastive stress. If a sentence has contrastive stress, underline the stressed word. If a sentence has standard stress, do nothing. With a partner, read each line as a three-part dialogue. Use contrastive stress on your underlined words. Be ready to explain your choices.

Student A says…	**Student B asks…**	**Student A responds…**
1. The teacher didn't grade your exam.	Who did?	The TA did.
2. The teacher didn't grade your exam.	Why not?	He was too busy.
3. The teacher didn't grade your exam.	What did he do to it, then?	He looked it over, but didn't grade it yet.
4. The teacher didn't grade your exam.	Whose exam did he grade?	Sean's. Yours is next.
5. The teacher didn't grade your exam.	What did he grade?	Just the homework.

Journal

The answer to "thank you" is usually "you're welcome," but sometimes both people have reasons to thank the other. You may hear the following exchange:

> Person 1: Thank you! (normal sentence-level stress)
> Person 2: Thank *you!* (contrastive stress: you, not me)

Listen to a radio or TV talk show. At the end of the interview, the guest and host may thank each other. The guest thanks the host for being invited to be on the show. The host thanks the guest for accepting the invitation and appearing on the show. Listen for this exchange and report your findings to the class.

What are other situations in which this happens? Listen for this exchange in banks, stores, and other places. Take notes on what you hear and report your findings to the class.

Sound Concepts

More Altered Sounds

Diagnostic 2

You will hear four sentences. On a separate piece of paper, write the statements or questions you hear.

After Listening

With a partner or the whole class, use the checklist (Three Steps, p. 8) to decode what you heard. What was difficult about this diagnostic?

 Eye-Opener: Each of these sentences had the word "have," but the word "have" didn't always sound the same. In numbers I and 3, you heard the word "have" as "have." The content word "have" is the main verb. In numbers 2 and 4, you heard the words "have to" as /haftə/. The function words "have to" are not the main verb.

(((Sound Concepts

Altered Sounds: Have to ——→/haftə/

How do we mark *altered have to* in this book?

Cross out the "v" and write an "f" above the word to remind yourself to say /haftə/.

Exercise 10: Making Plans

Focus on *altered have to*

Each sentence below describes a group project. For each sentence below, list five things the group members have to do to plan their project. Mark your sentences for **altered have to**. Read your sentences aloud.

Example: A group of students is planning an oral report.

First, they haᵛⁱe to decide on a topic. Then they haᵛⁱe to choose a group leader. Next, ...

1. The members of a professional sports team are planning a new strategy.

2. The members of a Neighborhood Watch group are planning a local festival.

3. _____ are planning _____

Exercise 11: Listening for *Altered Have to*

Focus on *altered have to*

You will hear six sentences. Do you hear **have** or **altered have to**? Check the appropriate box.

	have	/haftə/			have	/haftə/
1.	☐	☐	4.		☐	☐
2.	☐	☐	5.		☐	☐
3.	☐	☐	6.		☐	☐

Exercise 12: Parents and Children

Focus on *altered have to*   **Recycle plural count nouns**

Listen to a short talk and fill in each blank with the two-word, two-syllable phrase you hear.

Parents around the world _____ similar hope for their children. Usually they want their children to _____ connection to their culture. Some parents feel that their children _____ be musical or _____ succeed academically. Some sociologists and psychologists _____ theory about how children develop in relation to these goals. According to the theory, children _____ feel accepted by their friends. As a result, children may _____ different perspective on life than their parents.

Rhythm & Music

Stress with "-ment" and "-mental" Suffixes

Look at the word "develop." What part of speech is it? (Hint: use it in a sentence if you're not sure) What words can you think of that are related to "develop"? (Hint: try adding suffixes)

In "-mental" adjectives, the primary stress goes on the first suffix syllable, -MENT. The stressed syllable in the original noun receives secondary stress.

Verb ⟶	Noun ⟶	Adjective
de-VE-lop	de-VE-lop-ment	de-*ve*-lop-MENT-al
3-2	4-2 (no stress change)	5-4-2 (stress change)

Other words have the same pattern. However, some words don't exist in all possible forms (parts of speech). Look at the chart below:

Verb ⟶	Noun ⟶	Adjective
require	requirement	(no adjective form)
judge	judgment	judgmental
(no verb form)	environment	environmental

Mark primary stress on the words above. Practice saying each word with correct stress.

Stress with "-al" and "-ical" Suffixes

What part of speech are words with "-al" and "-ical" suffixes? (Hint: examples include "cultural," "personal," and "musical")

Noun ⟶	Adjective
CUL-ture	CUL-tur-al (no stress change)

If you know the stress pattern of the following root nouns, you also know the stress pattern of these adjectives. Be careful! Sometimes a vowel sound in the stressed syllable will change.

Noun ⟶	Adjective	Stress change?	Sound change?
culture	cultural	no	no
person	personal	no	no
nation	national	no	yes

(first vowel sound: /e^y/)   (first vowel sound: /ae/)

Some verbs also turn into adjectives that end in "-al":

Verb ⟶	Adjective	Stress change?	Sound change?
survive	survival	no	no
arrive	arrival	no	no

Can you think of other nouns or verbs with this pattern?

Consonant & Vowel Sounds

Introduction to the Sound /uʷ/

What is the sound?

This is the vowel sound in "who." Say it: "oo."

How do you spell it?

who	food	you	tune	
new	blue	through	suit	neutral

How do you form it?

Round your lips and form the sound /uʷ/ in the upper part of the back of your mouth.

Trouble Spots

Be sure not to confuse /uʷ/ with other vowel sounds.

Introduction to the Sound /ʌ/

What is the sound?

This is the vowel sound in "but" or "up." Say the symbol /ʌ/ as "inverted v."

How do you spell it?

up   love   does

How do you form it?

This sound is formed in the middle of your mouth, with your lips relaxed and unrounded. This is the same sound as /ə/, but /ə/ is used to show this sound in unstressed syllables (such as the first syllable of "about" and many unstressed function words). Use the symbol /ʌ/ to show this sound in stressed syllables.

Trouble Spots

Be careful not to say a different vowel sound, one that's lower in your mouth. Make sure your lips aren't spread when you say this vowel.

USAGE NOTE: CONTRASTIVE STRESS with *ALTERED YOU*

In conversation, we sometimes shift between *altered you* and contrastive (stressed) "you."

Teacher: "Good morning, class. Have yǝu done your homework?" (*altered you*)

   (The teacher is asking the entire class if they did their homework.)

Teacher: "How about *you*, Louis? Have *you* done your homework?" (**not altered**)

   (The teacher is asking one specific person in the class if he did his homework.)

When "you" is contrastively stressed, it's not altered:

Student 1: "Do yǝu like the neighborhood?" (*altered you*)

Student 2: "Yes, I do. How about *you*?" (**contrastive**)

Sound Concepts

Altered Sounds

 Diagnostic 3

You will hear three questions. On a separate piece of paper, write the questions you hear.

After Listening

With a partner or the whole class, use the checklist (Three Steps, p. 8) to decode what you heard. What was difficult about this diagnostic?

 Eye-Opener: In addition to **altered you**, these questions contained two other altered unstressed function words.

Altered Do: do ⟶ /də/; Altered To: to ⟶ /tə/

How do we mark *altered do* and *altered to*?

Put a line through the "o" and a /ə/ over the word. Remember, there's still a syllable there, but it's unstressed and its vowel is different.

When do we not alter functional "do" and "to"?

1. Don't alter "do" and "to" before a vowel sound:

   I wanted to accept your invitation.   When do I take the test?

2. Don't alter "do" at the beginning or end of a sentence or question:

   I do.   What should he do?   Do they need a ride?

                                                  /də/ /yə/
   Exception: Do + **altered you** = D'ya   Dø you have the time?

USAGE NOTE: *ALTERED DO* and *ALTERED TO*

Altered do: /duʷ/ ⟶ /də/
FUNCTION WORD

Where dø you live? *(auxiliary verb)*

Altered to: /tuʷ/ ⟶ /tə/
FUNCTION WORD

I'm going **to** the store. *(preposition)*

I need **to** go now. *(infinitive marker)*

Unaltered: /duʷ/
CONTENT WORD

I **do** my homework at night. *(main verb)*

Your essay is **due** tomorrow. *(adjective)*

Unaltered: /tuʷ/
CONTENT WORD

I'm going **two** blocks away. *(number)*

I'm going **too**. *(adverb)*

Eye-Opener: Altered *do*, *to*, and **you** don't rhyme with "blue."

Dictionaries say these words sound the same, but in connected speech, they don't.

Example: I'd like to show you the one in blue. Do you have time?

altered **do**	/də/
altered **to**	/tə/
altered **you**	/yə/
blue	/bluʷ/

Altered Going to: Going to ⟶ Gonna

Going to
- three syllables

Gonna
- two syllables
- no full "–ing" ending
- no /t/ sound in "to"
- altered vowel in "to" (/ə/)

Practice "gonna" to be better at understanding it when you hear it. You do not have to use "gonna" in everyday speech. However, "gonna" is always acceptable in conversation. Always use the full form in writing.

USAGE NOTE: CONTENT WORDS in "WH-" QUESTIONS

In "wh-" questions, the "wh" word is the focus of the question. It's a content word with normal sentence-level stress.

Exercise 13: Content Word or Function Word?

 Focus on *altered do* and *altered to*   Recycle standard sentence-level stress

1. Read each sentence below and decide whether each "do" and "to" is a function word (altered) or content word (unaltered). Mark all altered sounds.

2. For each sentence, decide which two or three content words receive standard sentence-level stress. Circle each stressed content word.

3. Read the sentences aloud to a partner. Practice **altered do**, **altered to**, and standard sentence-level stress.

Example: I (do) my (home)work every (night.)

1. What do you plan to do next?

2. I plan to study economics.

3. What do you think about that?

4. When are you going to school?

5. I'd like to buy a ticket.

6. Where do you live?

Exercise 14: Planning a Trip

 Focus on *altered do/to/you*   **Recycle linked sounds**

1. Plan an imaginary trip. Interview a partner about his or her plans for the trip. Use the following questions as a guide. Be sure to use **altered do, to,** and **you.** Remember to link sounds.

ə ə **What dø you...**	ə ə **How dø you...**	ə ə **When dø you...**
need to pack?	plan to get there?	leave?
plan to do?		get back?

2. Take turns giving each other advice about what to do before you leave. Remind your partner of things to do around the house or for school before the trip.

/ə/ **Make sure tø...**	/ə/ **Don't forget tø...**	/ə/ **You'll need tø...**

> **Journal**
>
> Some idioms in English use **altered to:**
>
>   a to-do list   about to (do something)   according to (a person or text)
>
> Look up these phrases in an idiom dictionary. Ask English speakers how they would use these phrases. Use each phrase in a sentence. Mark your sentences for as many Sound Concepts as you can. Share your sentences with a partner.

USAGE NOTE: *ALTERED YOU*

Don't exaggerate **altered you** in everyday conversation.

If you link sounds, stress content words, and try to pause at thought groups, you will probably begin to say unstressed, altered function words like "you" without noticing.

Practice **altered you** in order to hear it better.

Exercise 15: Listening for *Altered Do*

 Focus on *altered do*

 You will hear four sentences. Write "C" for content word if you heard unaltered "do". Write "F" for function word if you heard **altered do.**

Exercise 16: Listening for *Altered To*

Focus on *altered to*

 You will hear four sentences. Write "C" for content word if you heard unaltered "two" or "too." Write "F" for function word if you heard **altered to.**

(Hint: use all three kinds of information here, including language information, because function word "to" is very hard to hear. Think about where function word "to" might appear in a sentence.)

Grammar Sounds

Introduction to Possessive Noun Endings: -'s and -s'

The possessive noun ending has three different pronunciations. Fill out the last line of the chart below for *your* name.

Name	Final Sound	Possessive Form	Sound of the Ending
Pat	/t/, unvoiced	Pat's	[s] no extra syllable
Tom	/m/, voiced	Tom's	[z] no extra syllable
Charles	/z/, sibilant	Charles's	[Iz] extra syllable
_____	_____	_____	_____

 Eye-Opener: If you know how to say plural noun endings, you know how to say possessive noun endings. Look at the checklists for saying third-person singular verb endings and plural noun endings for detailed steps (pp. 68 and 90).

Exercise 17: Context for Practice–Parents, Children, and Peers

 Focus on possessive noun endings   **Recycle plural noun endings**

Preview Vocabulary

soak up–(verb phrase) to take in

immune to–(adjective phrase) not affected by something

tactics–(plural count noun) strategies

naggings–(plural count noun form of verb "to nag") annoying repeated complaints and requests

A. Read the passage. Then follow the directions below to practice possessive noun endings.

> If you grew up in a different part of the world from your **parents'** childhood home, consider this question: do you sound like your parents, or like the people you grew up with? What about the way you dress, or the music you listen to, or the way you spend your free time?
>
> Consider the same question about your children, or your **friends'** children, if they grew up in a different part of the world from where you grew up—or for that matter, even if they didn't. In almost every case, people model themselves after their **peers'** behavior, not their **parents'**.
>
> This is **Harris's** Group Socialization theory…. To some extent, children are immune to their **parents'** expectations. Even if children go along with their **parents'** rewards, punishments, examples, and naggings for the time being, **children's** personalities are not likely to be shaped by their **parents'** tactics…. Children learn what it takes to gain status among their peers and to be accepted by their friends.
>
> For example, **people's** accents almost always resemble their childhood **peers'** accents, rather than the accents of their parents. An **immigrant's** children acquire their adopted **homeland's** language perfectly, without a foreign accent, as long as they have access to native speaking peers. Children of immigrants soak up not just their adopted homeland's language, but its culture as well.

Stephen Pinker, *The Blank Slate: The Modern Denial of Human Nature.* Viking/Penguin, 2002

*Do you want to read more about parent-child interactions and culture? Go to your local library and use your **branch's** resources to help you.*

B. Make a three-column chart like the one below. Label your chart with the three pronunciations of the possessive noun ending.

[z]	[s]	[Iz]
No extra syllable	**No extra syllable**	**Extra syllable**
people's	immigrant's	Harris's

1. Put each highlighted word from the passage in the appropriate column.

2. Write the sound of the possessive ending above each underlined word.

3. Mark the passage for linking, and read it aloud to a partner.

Final Chapter Activity

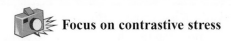 **Focus on contrastive stress**

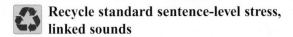 **Recycle standard sentence-level stress, linked sounds**

The following activity contains four two-person dialogues. Work in groups of eight students. Number the students in your group from 1 to 8 and copy your corresponding sentence onto a separate piece of paper. For example, student 1 copies sentence 1.

Mark your sentence for linked, deleted, reduced, and altered sounds. Mark your sentence for standard sentence-level stress or contrastive stress if appropriate. Memorize your sentence and be ready to say it aloud to your group. Your goal is to find a student whose sentence completes your dialogue.

1. Here are the pants that you brought in. That'll be $4.

2. I'm not looking for men's coats, I'm looking for *women's* coats.

3. I didn't stay in room #12, I stayed in room *#11*.

4. I didn't bring in pants, I brought in *shirts*.

5. The flight to Dulles International Airport leaves from Gate 32B.

6. Room no. 12 made some long-distance calls. That'll be $72.

7. Men's coats are on the third floor.

8. I'm not going to Dulles, I'm going to *Dallas*.

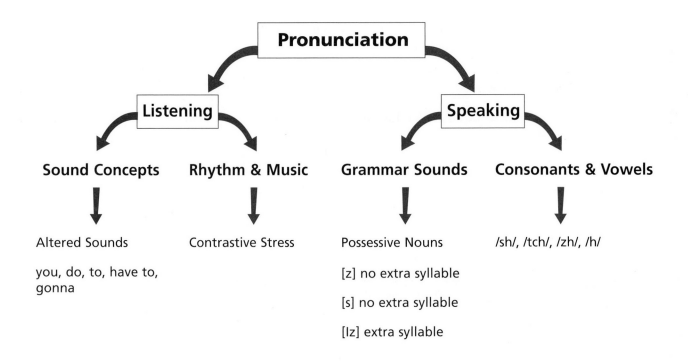

Getting Ready for Chapter 7
What You Need to Know About Stress and Sentence Rhythm

Preview

Have you ever had the experience of only catching a few words in a sentence? This is normal. If there's background noise, you may not be able to hear every word. You may hear only the stressed words: words that are louder, longer, clearer, and easier to hear than others.

Diagnostic

Listen to the following dialogue. The speakers are in a crowded room, so you won't be able to hear all of their conversation. Listen for the stressed content words (two, three, or even four in each sentence). Write the stressed words you hear.

After Listening

Compare your list of stressed content words with a partner. Use the Three Kinds of Information and your combined lists to reconstruct the dialogue. What do you think was said? Connect the content words to make a conversation that makes sense. Use your knowledge of sentence structure to add function words to make complete sentences.

Listen to the dialogue again. Did you understand more of what the speakers said? Use the checklist to decode what you heard (Three Steps, p.8). What was difficult about this diagnostic?

 Eye-Opener: When you hear stressed content words, you're hearing the standard rhythm of English sentences.

Exercise 1: Sentence Creation

 Focus on standard sentence-level stress

Work with a partner or small group. For each group of stressed content words below, add the necessary function words to create as many sentences as you can. Take turns reading the sentences aloud to your group. Stress the three content words no matter how many function words (unstressed syllables) are in the rest of the sentence.

| Example: | movie | Friday | Boston |

I went to a **movie** last **Friday** in **Boston**. She'll see a **movie** next **Friday** in **Boston**.

1. book   library   Tuesday

2. drove   country   weekend

3. when   friends   visit

Journal

Go to a noisy place where you can listen to English speakers. Listen for five minutes and write down as many words as you hear. What do you notice about the words you heard? Report to the class. Did you hear more content words than function words? Why or why not?

7

Informational Stress and Altered Sounds

Sound Concepts
Altered /t/, hesitations, contractions

Rhythm & Music
Informational stress patterns, introduction to intonation

Grammar Sounds
Recycle endings (past tense, plural nouns, third-person singular present tense)

Consonant & Vowel Sounds
/r/, /l/, /ʊ/

Sound Concepts

Introduction to Altered /t/

Preview

Try this free-association activity before doing the diagnostic below. Free association means saying the first word or words that come into your head. For example, if you see the word "doctor," what do you think of? Listen to three words and free associate.

Diagnostic

You will hear seven sentences. On a separate piece of paper, write the sentences you hear.

After Listening

Use the checklist (Three Steps, p. 8) to decode what you heard.
What was difficult about this diagnostic?

 Eye-Opener: Even though the words and sentences you heard have the letter "t," none of them have the /t/ sound.

Altered /t/: /t/ ⟶ /D/

What is altered /t/?

The sounds /t/ and /d/ are formed in the same place in your mouth: /t/ is unvoiced and /d/ is voiced. When /t/ is altered, it makes a sound between a /t/ and a /d/. Think of altered /t/ as a short, quick /d/ sound. Your tongue makes a quick tap or flap. It's a shorter sound than /d/. Your tongue just makes a quick tap or flap. Sometimes altered /t/ is called flapped /t/.

How do we mark altered /t/ in this book?

Write a capital "D" above the altered /t/ to help you remember.

Where do we use altered /t/?

The sound /t/ is altered to /D/ in these situations:

1. In the middle of a single word between vowel sounds: better, letter, meter

2. Between two linked words with vowel sounds: out of, right away

3. Between two linked words with deleted /h/:   bet her, let her, meet her

 Eye-Opener: In connected speech, "let her" = letter.

You heard the same sounds in the free association and diagnostic activity.

Practice Altered /t/

With a partner, go back to sentences you wrote in the diagnostic activity. Mark the sentences for altered /t/.

Exercise 1: Preparing for a Trip

 Focus on altered /t/   **Recycle linked sounds**

Imagine that you and a friend are going on a trip. Make sure you haven't forgotten anything. Complete your answers to your friend's questions, and mark your answers for altered /t/ and linking. Practice your conversations with a partner.

Did you. . .   **Yes, I've already**. . .

1. fill up the tank with gas?   _filled it up_

2. look up the address?   _____

3. look over the map?   _____

4. turn off the light?   _____

5. clean out the refrigerator?   _____

6. put out the trash?   _____

7. lock up the house?   _____

Exercise 2: Fixed Phrases with "Out of"

 Focus on altered /t/   **Recycle linked sounds**

Many English idioms and phrases begin with the words "out of." Match the columns to complete the sentences. Mark each sentence for altered /t/, linked sounds, **reduced of,** and deleted /h/.

1. My boss is   **A.** out of time.

2. The soda machine is   **B.** out of the office.

3. That pen is   **C.** out of gas.

4. During the test I ran   **D.** out of order.

5. My car ran   **E.** out of ink.

Consonant & Vowel Sounds

Introduction to the Sound /r/

What is the sound?

Start by saying the name of this letter: "R." Say it the same as this word: "are."

Now add a consonant sound before it, as in "car," "far," and "bar." The sound at the end of these words is the sound /r/.

How do you spell it?

red   a**rr**ive   **wr**ong   **rh**ythm

How do you form it?

When you say the sound /r/, your tongue is curved. The back of your tongue is higher than the front, but the tip of your tongue curls up just a little. This can be hard to imagine, but think of a slide at a playground.

The tip of your tongue shouldn't touch your teeth or any other part of your mouth.

Trouble Spots

Don't omit the sound /r/, especially when it follows a vowel sound. Think of the words "car" and "far": Say them as CVC syllables—don't omit the final consonant sound /r/. You should feel movement in your mouth when you finish saying the /r/ sound. Your lower jaw should move up slightly at the end of the word. Your mouth needs to be tense in order to say the /r/ sound. If your jaw is too relaxed, you'll have difficulty forming the sound.

 Eye-Opener: Why is the sound /r/ important?

Use the sound /r/ to distinguish between minimal pairs like hot/hurt.

Without the sound /r/ at the end of words like "far" and "car" your English sounds incomplete.

You can't link the word to the next vowel sound, and you're not saying CVC syllables.

Exercise 3: Linking with /r/

 Focus on the sound /r   **Recycle linking**

1. Mark the consonant-to-vowel (/r/) linking in the following sentence and read it aloud.

> He lives far away from school, so he takes the car all day.

2. Mark /r/ linking in the following phrases and read them aloud.

     A. dancer in the show   **C.** actor on the stage

     B. teacher of the year   **D.** author of the book

3. Mark /r/ linking within the following words and contractions and read them aloud.

     A. during   **C.** aren't

     B. boring   **D.** weren't

Exercise 4: Practice /r/

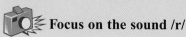 **Focus on the sound /r/**

Circle all the /r/ sounds in the following passage. Read it aloud to a partner.

Every semester, more and more students turn to the World Wide Web—the Internet—on

a daily basis to help them learn English. Use a computer at your local library or school

computer room. Use a search engine to find resources to practice English or learn new

words. You can even burn a CD with grammar exercises to listen to and practice with later.

 Journal

Use the Internet as described in the exercise above. Write about your experiences. Tell your class about any useful resources you found.

Introduction to the Sound /l/

What is the sound?

Say the name of the letter "L." You are making the sound /l/. This is the sound at the end of the words "tell," "bell," "well," and "yell."

How do you spell it?

light   yellow

How do you form it?

When you say the sound /l/, the tip of your tongue makes contact with the roof of your mouth, just behind your top front teeth. You should be able to feel air on either side of your tongue.

Trouble Spots

1. Don't confuse the sounds /l/ and /r/. In English, these are different sounds. You need to say /r/ and /l/ correctly in order to distinguish between certain words, such as "arrive" and "alive." If you confuse /l/ and /r/, use the language strategy on p. 205 to help match the right sound to the right letters.

2. Don't say the sound /l/ when the letter "l" is silent. There is no /l/ sound in the word "would." Say it "wood." These words sound the same: "wood" and "would."

Introduction to the Sound /ʊ/

What is the sound?

Say the symbol as "upsilon." It's hard to discuss the sound /ʊ/ because spelling doesn't help you, and the sound is very similar to another vowel sound (the sound /uʷ/ in the words "boot" and "food." Think about the sound /ʊ/ in contrast to the sound /uʷ/ (p. 111). Look at the chart below:

Sound:	/uʷ/		/ʊ/
Examples:	boot	≠	book
	food	≠	foot

The sound /ʊ/ is the sound of the vowel in the words "book," "foot," and "put." It is *not* the same as the vowel sound /uʷ/ in "boot" and "food."

How do you spell it?

book   put   could   woman

How do you form it?

The sound upsilon is a high back vowel. Your lips are slightly rounded when you say it, but the muscles in your face are relaxed (not tense).

Trouble Spots

If the muscles in your face are too tense, and your lips are too rounded, the vowel will sound more like /uʷ/ (in the word "two") than /ʊ/ (in the word "put").

Exercise 5: Rhyming Words

 Focus on the sound /ʊ/

1. Which of the following words rhyme (end with the same sound) with "should"? Circle every word that rhymes. Compare answers with a partner.

   stood   cold   could   gold   cooled

   would   bold   good   wood   fooled

2. Circle the /ʊ/ sounds in the following sentences. Write two more sentences with at least two /ʊ/ sounds in each. Practice saying your sentences with a partner.

   1. You should be good.

   2. I would if I could.

   3. You could if you stood on a footstool.

 # Sound Concepts

More Contracted Sounds

 **Diagnostic 2**

You will hear six sentences. Circle the form you hear in each sentence.

1. I'd OR I   4. I'd OR I

2. I'd OR I   5. I'd OR I

3. I'd OR I   6. I'd OR I

After Listening

Use the checklist to decode what you heard (Three Steps, p. 8).
What was difficult about this diagnostic?

Eye-Opener: You may have trouble telling the difference between "I" and "I'd." Some contractions are difficult to hear and to say, especially since they're usually unstressed. Sometimes you can use clues from the rest of the sentence to help you decide what was said.

PRONUNCIATION GOAL

Practice saying "I'd" and other contractions so that you'll be better at hearing them and using them in your everyday speech. They have different meanings, so be careful which one you say. If you don't say them, your listeners lose valuable information, and you might sound ungrammatical.

 Eye-Opener: Only ten English words can be contracted.

Three forms of "be": **am, is, are**	as in *I'm, it's, you're*	
Three forms of "have": **have, has, had**	as in *they've, it's, I'd*	in any person
Two modals: **will, would**	as in *I'll, I'd*	
One negative word: **not**	as in *can't, won't, don't, couldn't, hasn't, isn't*	
One pronoun: **us**	as in *Let's*	

USAGE NOTE: CONTRACTIONS with NOUNS and PRONOUNS

1. When you see a contraction, pronounce the whole contraction. Remember to say the sounds after the apostrophe, and don't say the uncontracted words. For example, if you see "I'm going," *don't* say "I going" or say "I am going."

2. **Contractions with pronouns,** such as "he's," "I'll," "let's," and other examples in the box above, usually just add a consonant sound (not a syllable).
   Exception: "it'd" (two syllables) Say it: /It-Id/.
   These contractions with pronouns are acceptable in all levels of English speech. They are not "wrong" or too casual. These forms are also common in writing.

3. **Contractions with nouns** are sometimes pronounced as a single syllable.
   These contractions are sometimes used in writing: *Mary's done her homework.*
   Some contractions with nouns are pronounced with an extra syllable: *John'll meet him*. These contractions are less common in writing.

Exercise 6: You Need to. . .

 Focus on contractions and contrastive stress

Make a list of things your friend needs to do. Practice the following conversation with your partner for each item on your list. Remember to pronounce the contracted form "I've" and to use contrastive stress.

A: You need to do the dishes.

B: I've already *done* that.

 Eye-Opener: "You" is never altered in contractions. Use *unaltered* "you" in the following exercise.

Exercise 7: Things I Hate

 Focus on contractions   **Recycle "should"** and *altered to*

With a partner, match each cause in column A with its effect in column B. Then read the dialogue below, and practice dialogues of your own with the words from the columns.

	A		B
1.	practice	**A.**	get in shape
2.	study	**B.**	lose weight
3.	exercise	**C.**	pass the exam
4.	try	**D.**	improve
5.	diet	**E.**	succeed

A: I hate to practice.

B: Yes, but if you practice, you'll improve.

A: You're right, I really should practice.

Exercise 8: Minimal Pairs

 Focus on contractions and /r/

1. Work with a partner. Take turns reading aloud from the first column; your partner responds appropriately from the second column.

1.	I'm worried you'll get hot.	**A.**	I work in an office.
2.	Where do you walk?	**B.**	Right, I shouldn't wear that jacket.
3.	I'm worried you'll get hurt.	**C.**	I walk in the park.
4.	That's really a hot spot.	**D.**	Right, I shouldn't climb that tree.
5.	Where do you work?	**E.**	Yes, it's a popular place.
6.	That's really a hot sport.	**F.**	Yes, soccer is the world's most popular sport.

2. Make up a sentence using "hot" or "hurt" for each photo. Begin your sentences with the word "It." Read your sentences aloud to a partner.

Which sentence uses the contraction "It's" ? Which sentence uses "It" + verb? Why?

> **Journal**
>
> If someone has trouble saying /r/ but uses correct grammar, the sentence "It hurts" is understandable, even if it sounds like "It hots." Listeners use their knowledge of the language to make sense of this. Write about a time when you used your knowledge of the language to make sense of someone else's pronunciation.

Exercise 9: Listening for Contractions

 Focus on contractions

 Listen to John describe how he spent the week. Check the correct box for each item John mentions.

		already done	doing now	will do in the future
1.	file the reports	❑	❑	❑
2.	update the database	❑	❑	❑
3.	contact the customers	❑	❑	❑
4.	talk to the salespeople	❑	❑	❑
5.	plan the next conference	❑	❑	❑
6.	set up a new meeting	❑	❑	❑
7.	reprogram the database	❑	❑	❑
8.	like to talk to you more	❑	❑	❑

 **Rhythm & Music**

Sentence-Level Stress

Exercise 10: Listening for Stress

 Recycle standard sentence-level stress and contrastive stress

 Listen to the following six-line dialogue. On a separate piece of paper, write the stressed word in each sentence. Remember, stressed words are louder, longer, clearer, and higher. When you are finished, compare your responses with a partner.

Introduction to Informational Stress

The most important word in every phrase or sentence receives the most stress. But how do you recognize the most important word(s)? In chapter 5, you learned about contrastive stress:

Do your homework!   standard content-word stress on "homework"

I've already *done* my homework!   contrastive stress on "done"

In addition to contrastive stress, there are other reasons to stress a word. In general, new information in a sentence is more important than old information, so the new information gets more stress. Something that's new information in one sentence becomes old information when you refer to it again in the next sentence. Stress on the new information in a sentence is called informational stress.

> Example
>
> **A:** Do your homework! (standard sentence-level stress: content word)
>
> **B:** Which homework? (informational stress: "which" is new information)
>
> **A:** Your math homework. (informational stress: "math" is new information)
>
> **B:** I've already *done* my math homework! (contrastive stress on "done")

 Eye-Opener: Conversations use both contrastive stress and informational stress, sometimes even in the same sentence!

 When do you use informational stress?

Read the text below as you listen to the dialogue from exercise 10 again.

A: **Where's the book?**

The content word "book" is the most important word in this question. It receives standard sentence-level stress.

B: **The book's on the counter.**

The word "book" is now old information, so the content word "counter"—the new piece of information—is stressed (informational stress).

A: **Next to the paper?**

The content word "paper" is the most important word in this question. It's new information. Notice that the stressed words in all the examples so far have been content words. Usually the most important word in a sentence is a content word. However, this isn't always the case.

B: **No, *under* the paper.**

Here, the most important word is the preposition "under" (a function word) because it's a new piece of information and because it contrasts with "next to."

A: **I've already looked under the paper.**

The content word "looked" is the new piece of information. "Looked" receives informational stress.

B: **Well, look *again*.**

Now the word "look" is old information. The word "again" is stressed because it is the new piece of information and it's contrastive.

Exercise 11: What Did You Lose?

 Focus on informational stress   Recycle standard sentence-level stress and contrastive stress

1. Read the following dialogue through once. Decide which word will receive the most stress in each sentence, and why. Underline the stressed word. Then write the reason (standard, informational, or contrastive) next to each line. In line 10, choose one stressed word for each sentence.

		Kind of Stress
1.	**A:** I lost something.	standard
2.	**B:** What did you lose?	_____
3.	**A:** I lost my book.	_____
4.	**B:** What kind of book?	_____
5.	**A:** My school book.	_____
6.	**B:** Which school book?	_____
7.	**A:** My chemistry book.	_____
8.	**B:** Look in your backpack.	_____
9.	**A:** I've already looked in my backpack.	_____
10.	**B:** Look! It's over there! It's on your desk!	_____ _____ _____

2. Compare your work with a partner. Read the dialogue aloud with your partner. Practice stressing the most important word in each line.

Exercise 12: More Practice with Informational Stress

 Focus on informational stress

Read the following dialogue silently and decide which word in each sentence receives sentence-level stress. Underline the stressed words, and practice reading the dialogue aloud with a partner.

1. **A:** I think I need new glasses.
2. **B:** What's wrong with the glasses you have?
3. **A:** I can't see out of them.
4. **B:** Maybe you need a new prescription.
5. **A:** I just got a new prescription.
6. **B:** I know why you can't see. Your glasses are dirty!

Exercise 13: Informational Stress Dialogues

 Focus on informational stress

Make up a dialogue of your own, using the two exercises above as examples. Mark your dialogue for stressed words and practice reading it aloud. Remember to notice what is old and new information in each sentence.

Exercise 14: Reported Speech

 Focus on contractions and contrastive/informational stress

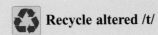 **Recycle altered /t/**

1. Listen to the following sentences and fill in the blanks with the words that you hear.

    1. John said _____ car and _____ dinner.

    2. Paul's having a party _____ apartment _____.

    3. _____ office after work.

    4. Bill _____ loan _____ lecture notes.

2. For each sentence in part 1, write a response using the hint and the example below. With a partner, take turns reading sentences and responses aloud. Remember to delete /h/ in the original sentence. Use full, not deleted, /h/ in the contrastively stressed words in the response.

    1. (Hint: you know that his car's in the shop.) Response: He said he'd take *his* car? His car's in the shop!

    2. (Hint: you know that his apartment's too small.)

    3. (Hint: you know that his office is too far away.)

    4. (Hint: you know that his lecture notes are too messy.)

Exercise 15: Who Said Who Went Where How?

Focus on contrastive stress, informational stress

For this activity, you will need a group of eight people to follow these steps:

1. Look at the sentences and questions below. Each person in your group is responsible for one sentence or question. Copy your sentence or question onto an index card.

    1. John said Mary went to Florida by *bus.*   5. Did John say Mary went to *Canada* by bus?

    2. *John* said Mary went to Florida by bus.   6. Did *Paul* say Mary went to Florida by bus?

    3. John said *Mary* went to Florida by bus.   7. Did John say Mary went to Florida by *train?*

    4. John said Mary went to *Florida* by bus.   8. Did John say *Susan* went to Florida by bus?

2. Close your book and memorize your sentence or question. Give your index card to your teacher (or group leader).

3. As a group, say your sentences and questions aloud and try to match them. Remember to use correct sentence-level stress. When you have matched each question with its answer, recite your questions and answers for the class.

For small classes: Get together around a desk and spread out the index cards from the group of volunteers. As a group, match the cards. When everyone is finished, check the volunteers' dialogues.

For large classes: Work with a partner to match the sentences and questions below. Make sure to read them aloud with correct sentence-level stress.

For all classes: Listen to the members of the small group. Are they using sentence-level stress to convey their meaning?

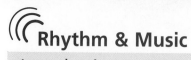

Rhythm & Music

Introduction to Intonation

Preview

Do you sing or play a musical instrument? Have you ever heard of pitch in the context of music?

Have you ever thought of pitch, or intonation, in the context of a language? Do you use intonation in your native language? If so, how?

What is intonation?

Intonation is the melody of a language. Words, sentences, and questions can rise ↗ or fall ↘ in pitch. This means your voice gets higher ↗ or lower ↘, just like notes in music. The intonation (or pitch contour) of a given word or sentence can rise, fall, and then rise again.

English sentences have standard sentence-level stress. This is the basic stress pattern (content words are stressed, function words are unstressed), without any added meaning.

English sentences also have standard sentence-level intonation. In normal declarative sentences, such as "He washes his hands at the sink," intonation rises slightly on each stressed word (washes, hands, sink) and drops slightly at the end of the sentence.

How do we mark intonation in this book?

You may have seen sentences marked with a wavy line to show the sentence's intonation, or pitch. In this book, we only mark intonation on single (stressed) words.

Draw an arrow pointing up and to the right when intonation rises: ↗

Draw an arrow pointing down and to the right when intonation falls: ↘

 Eye-Opener: Sentence-level intonation may not be completely new to you. If you already use standard sentence-level stress, and if you try to pause at thought groups, you may already be starting to use intonation correctly.

Remember that stressed words are louder, longer, clearer, and higher. Higher means higher in pitch—stressed words generally have rising intonation.

The message is in the music: Intonation accompanies stress.

Exercise 16: A Very Messy Room

 Focus on standard intonation

Your friend has a very messy room. You're visiting to look for a book you need. But your friend's room is *so* messy that it's hard to tell what things are! You point to something and ask, "What's that?"

Every time you ask, your friend answers you in grammatical sentences with standard intonation and standard stress. Here are your friend's responses. Circle the stressed content word in each sentence and practice saying the sentences.

1. That's some medicine.
2. That's some money.
3. That's some shampoo.
4. That's some paper.
5. That's some mail.
6. That's some homework.

 Eye-Opener: Imagine that you finally see the book you want under your friend's bed. You hold up the book, and your friend says, with extra stress and rising intonation on the word "some": That's *some ↗* book.

With extra stress and rising intonation on the word *some*, this is an acceptable sentence, even though the word *some* is used to modify a singular count noun. In this case, the word *some* has a special meaning: it does more than identify the book. It also makes a statement about the book—the speaker is saying that there is something distinctive about this book.

The message is in the music: Intonation overrides grammar.

INTONATION

GRAMMAR

USAGE NOTE: LENGTHENING STRESSED WORDS

The word "*some*" in "That's *some ↗* book" is much longer than the word "some" in a sentence like "That's some mail."

Practice saying "That's *some ↗* book." Use the strategy on p. 104 for lengthening stressed words. Stressed words are louder, longer, clearer, and higher. The longer length of a stressed word gives you time to make your voice rise or fall in pitch and then return to normal for the rest of the sentence.

Functions of Intonation: Use rising and falling intonation to express positive and negative emotions.

Some single words can be an entire message:

| oh | great | so | sure | hm |
| uh-huh | no | yes | well | uh-uh |

These words can be questions, statements, exclamations, or pause-fillers. We can say these words with different intonations that change the meaning of the message.

Example: 1. Great! ↗   2. Great. ↘

In message 1, the speaker is happy. The speaker's intonation goes up.

In message 2, the speaker isn't happy. The speaker's intonation goes down.

 PRONUNCIATION GOAL

Paralinguistic features (body language and facial expressions) often accompany a change in intonation. Watch for body language when listening for changing intonation.

USAGE NOTE: PUNCTUATION and INTONATION

Sometimes written punctuation helps us understand the intended intonation and emotion of a message.

Oh?	curiosity/interest	(↗ rising intonation: rise-fall-rise)
Oh.	boredom/disrespect	(↘ falling intonation)
Oh!	surprise/shock/happiness	(↗ rising intonation: rise-fall)

Exercise 17: Good News, Bad News

 Focus on two kinds of rising intonation

1. Your friend says: "Remember that really hard exam I was worried about? I passed it!" What emotions do you feel about your friend's good news?
   List them here: _____

   You might say any of the following to express your emotions:

   Great! ↗   Wow! ↗   Yes! ↗   Oh! ↗

   Practice saying these one-word responses with rising intonation to show your positive emotions. Notice the exclamation marks next to these words. What kind of body language and facial expressions would accompany your rising intonation and positive emotions?

   Role-play this conversation with a classmate. Make your intonation rise and fall on your single-word message. Make the word long enough to allow this change in pitch. Your response to your friend is a statement: it tells your friend how you feel.

2. Your friend says: "Well, I also have some bad news…" He hesitates, and you want him to continue talking. What emotions do you feel when you know someone is about to tell you bad news?
   List them here:_____

   To prompt your friend to tell you more, say:

   Oh? ↗   or   Yes? ↗

   Role-play this part of the conversation with a classmate. Make your intonation rise, fall, and then rise again on your single-word message. Make the word long enough to allow this change in pitch. Your one-word response to your friend is a question: it expresses curiosity or anxiety and asks for more information.

3. You remember that you loaned your friend your car to drive to his exam. Your friend finally tells you the bad news: "While driving back from the test, I accidentally ran a red light and crashed your car. I'm fine, but the car isn't." What emotions do you feel about your friend's bad news?
   List them here: _____

   In response to your friend's bad news, you might say:

   Great. ↘   or   Oh. ↘

Role-play this part of the conversation with a classmate. Make your intonation fall on your single-word message. Make the word long enough to allow this change in pitch. Your one-word response to your friend is a statement: it tells your friend how you feel.

The word "great" has a positive meaning, but you can use it to express negative emotions if you change your intonation. In part 1, you are sincere: you are really happy, and you really think your friend's news is great. In part 3, you are sarcastic. You don't *really* think it's great that your friend crashed your car.

The message is in the music: Intonation overrides word meaning.

Practice the entire conversation (1–3) with a partner.

Exercise 18: Listening for Rising Intonation

 Focus on rising intonation

You will hear six sentences. For each sentence, decide which intonation you hear—standard or rising.

Standard Intonation: "some" identifies a non-count noun

Rising Intonation: *"some"* comments on a count or non-count noun

After listening, discuss the meaning of each sentence with a partner.

Journal

Different languages use intonation in different ways. Some languages (such as Chinese) use intonation, or pitch changes, to distinguish between different words. English uses intonation to distinguish between different meanings of the *same* word, phrase, or sentence. Compare intonation in English and your native language. Describe any problems that you have ever had saying or listening to English intonation.

Rhythm & Music

Stress with Suffixes

What part of speech do you think words with the ending "-ogy" or "-ity" are? _____

What part of speech do you think words with the suffix "-ical" are? _____

What part of speech do you think words with the suffix "-ist" are? _____

Stress with "-ogy" and "-ogist" Suffixes

Words that end with "-ogy" are nouns (ideas/areas) with primary stress on the syllable before "-ogy ."

Words that end with "-ogist" are nouns (people/professions) with primary stress on the syllable before "-ogist."

psy CHOL ogy	psy CHOL ogist	soci OL ogy	soci OL ogist
anthro POL ogy	anthro POL ogist	bi OL ogy	bi OL ogist

Practice "-ogy" and "-ogist" Suffixes

Say the following words with correct stress:

psychiatrist	analogy	technology	ecologist

Stress with "-ical" Suffixes

Words that end with "-ical" are adjectives with primary stress on the syllable before "-ical."

Noun		Adjective
psyCHOlogy	⟶	psychoLOGical
METHod	⟶	methODical

 BE CAREFUL! There might be spelling changes as well as stress changes.

Practice "-ical" Suffixes

What part of speech are the following words? Say them with correct stress.

philosophical   method   economical   methodical

economy   periodical   philosophy   period

Do you use any "-ical" words at work or school? List them here and practice them.

Stress with "-ity" Suffixes

Words that end with "-ity" are nouns with primary stress on the syllable before "-ity."

possiBILity   reALity   morTALity

Look up each root word (adjective) and discuss the stress changes that accompany "-ity."

Grammar Sounds

LANGUAGE STRATEGY: Listening Effectively to Lectures

1. Listen for stressed content words that signal important ideas.
2. Listen for transitional and signaling words and key phrases. (function words) (see Key Phrases at right)
3. Listen for contrastive stress, pauses, and thought groups as clues for meaning.
4. Take notes of important ideas and events, in outline form.
5. Recognize hesitation words and sounds. (see Eye-Opener below)

Key Phrases	
• first of all	• the point is
• next	• it turns out that
• overall	• what he's saying is

 Eye-Opener: How to Hesitate

Speakers hesitate if they are nervous, planning their next sentence or phrase, or trying to remember something. Here are some common English hesitations. You may hear some of them in the lecture.

    • let me see   • let's see   • um   • uh   • er   • well   • hmmm

Final Chapter Activity

  Recycle past tense, plural noun, and third-person singular endings; linked, deleted, reduced, altered, and contracted sounds; thought groups, contrastive stress, and /r/ sounds

Recycle Past Tense, Plural Noun, and Third-Person Singular Endings

Discuss the following questions with a partner:

1. What do you think the basic emotions are? Do you think they're universal—that all people feel them the same way? Why?

2. What are some strategies you use when listening to a lecture? How do you manage to understand and remember the main points?

Listen for Content

Listen to a lecture on human emotions. Use the Language Strategy on the previous page to help you listen for the main idea. Don't worry if you don't understand every word. Use the sample lecture outline below and add your own notes to it as you listen.

Lecture Outline	Notes
1. Universality of human emotions	
A. Dr. Paul Ekman, UCSF Medical School	
B. background	
C. number of different emotions	
D. facial muscles	
2. Debate between science and anthropology	
A. Charles Darwin	
B. Margaret Mead	
C. experiment to try to solve the debate	
i. Part 1–different countries	
ii. Part 2–Papua New Guinea	
3. Implications of the theory	
A. emotions from the inside out–real and fake smiles	
B. emotional balance–Dalai Lama, Buddhists	
C. computer graphics and animation	

Self-Assessment

How well did you understand the lecture? Rate yourself on each of the following factors:

		Very good	Good	Need to Improve
1.	Identifying and understanding main ideas (overall comprehension)	☐	☐	☐
2.	Using an outline to follow along and take additional notes	☐	☐	☐
3.	Listening for and noticing transition/signal words	☐	☐	☐
4.	Noticing hesitation words and sounds	☐	☐	☐
5.	Noticing contrastive stress	☐	☐	☐

Listening for Sounds and Sound Concepts

Listen to the lecture again while you read the transcript below. Fill in the missing words and phrases as you listen. You may need to use more than one word or contraction to fill each blank.

Okay, today _____ talk about the universality of human emotions. _____, let me say that this theory is attributed to Paul Ekman, a professor of psychology _____ known as "the _____ most famous face reader." Dr. Ekman's based at the University of California Medical School at San Francisco, _____ done research _____ the world. Dr. Ekman _____ always been _____ emotions, ever since he was a teenager. And, being a photographer _____ was twelve, he just naturally _____ look at facial expressions. In Ekman's view, it _____ seven basic human emotions: anger, sadness, fear, surprise, disgust, contempt, and happiness. _____ these emotions have clear facial signals. _____ actually _____ facial muscles that combine to reveal these emotions.

Ekman's theory _____ resolve a debate between evolutionary science and anthropology—_____, scientists who follow the ideas of Charles Darwin've always _____ human facial expressions were universal. _____ anthropologists like Margaret Mead thought the opposite. So, _____, Ekman _____ investigate this. The first _____ was to show pictures of facial expressions to people _____ different countries, including _____, Japan, Argentina, Chile, and Brazil. It _____ everyone _____ expressions in the same way—everyone thought the happy face was happy, etcetera. It seemed _____ proved _____ point—human emotions are universal. However, it _____ argued that all _____ the _____ studied had been influenced by Western _____ television. So, Ekman needed _____ group of "visually isolated people." In other words, what he _____ was people _____ never seen _____ modern media.

Ekman _____ group of subjects in Papua New Guinea—a remote island _____ South Pacific. It just so happened that Papua New Guinea was the ideal place _____ this _____ investigation: it's very isolated, and had people who, _____ Ekman

visited, hadn't been exposed to the modern world. Ekman did two things in New Guinea:

_____ showed his subjects the same photos of facial expressions _____ the earlier

groups, and _____ they were judged exactly the same way. Next, he _____ people

in New Guinea to pose with expressions of the seven different emotions _____ and he

recorded them, and later _____ to people in the West. Americans _____ Westerners

perfectly understood the facial expressions and emotions _____ from Papua New

Guinea. Therefore, not only did they identify correctly the Western _____ emotions, but

Westerners correctly _____ their expressions. Ekman had the _____ needed.

Ekman's theories have implications for different aspects _____ lives. First of all,

_____ that, _____, "emotions work from the _____, as well as the inside out."

_____ saying is _____ you really manage to arrange _____ your facial muscles

into the expression _____ happiness or anger, then _____ actually feel that emotion

to a certain degree. This _____ easy _____, though, because for instance, with smil-

ing, _____ show happiness, _____ certain muscle around your eyes that must be

_____ order to truly feel happy — and, if you're just _____ smile, you're probably

not moving that muscle. So, Ekman believes _____ learn _____ difference between

a real smile, and a fake smile. On the other hand, _____ disgust are easier emotions to

experience merely by arranging your face into the right expressions.

Another thing _____ to do _____ theories is to help improve the emotional bal-

ance of schoolteachers _____ people in high-pressure _____. In fact, he _____

$50,000 grant from the Dalai Lama to investigate this. Dr. Ekman says that meeting the Dalai

Lama and working _____ has led _____ to study the emotions of Buddhist monks.

In addition, _____ sharpened _____ own ideas by contrasting _____ with

Buddhist beliefs.

One final application of _____ theories is to _____ computer generated graphics.

Dr. _____ been _____ be a consultant with animators in the technology departments

_____ several movie studios that use high-tech computer graphics to create realistic

emotions _____ their _____.

Overall, Ekman's theory _____ universality _____ seven human emotions, and

the facial expressions that reveal _____, is an important one for modern

psychology and sociology, with many useful _____ for education _____ science.

Journal

Think about the facial expressions that accompany intonation. Observe some English speakers and take notes on their facial expressions and intonation. Report back to your class.

Which photo matches which message?   1. Great! ↗   2. Great. ↘

What did we do in this chapter?

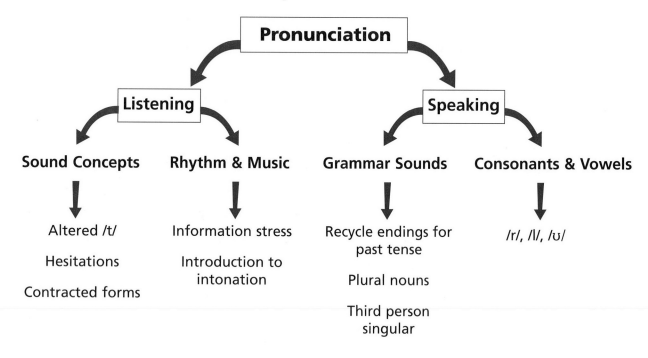

Pronunciation

Listening

Speaking

Sound Concepts

Rhythm & Music

Grammar Sounds

Consonants & Vowels

Altered /t/

Hesitations

Contracted forms

Information stress

Introduction to intonation

Recycle endings for past tense

Plural nouns

Third person singular

/r/, /l/, /ʊ/

Assessment Section 2: Unit 2 (Chapters 5–7)

Part 1: Listening and Thinking About Listening and Speaking

Listen to the following lecture on language problems and airplane pilots for overall comprehension.

When you are finished listening, work with a partner or in a small group on the following activities. Your teacher may ask you to concentrate on one or more of the activities at a time.

ACTIVITY 1: Listening Strategies

What words or phrases jumped out at you when you were listening?

Check with a partner or a group: did other students hear the same phrases? With your group, try to remember what was said about each of the words or phrases. Which are more important than others in the context of the lecture? Why?

ACTIVITY 2: Sound Concepts

How many of the Sound Concepts did you notice in this lecture? Write down each Sound Concept and an example that you heard.

ACTIVITY 3: Grammar Sounds

The four noun and verb endings we have studied are

1. _____   3. _____

2. _____   4. _____

Write examples of each of these endings from the lecture and discuss them with a partner.

Part 2: Speaking

ACTIVITY 1: Read Aloud

Turn to the audio script at the back of this book (p. 213). Read part or all of the lecture to a partner. Your teacher may ask you to record yourself. You should focus on three things:

1. Noun and verb endings (plurals, possessives, third-person singular, and past tense)

2. Standard and contrastive stress

3. Individual consonant and vowel sounds you've studied so far

ACTIVITY 2: Context for Practice–Air Traffic Controllers

In small groups, work on one of the following case studies from *Fatal Words* by Steven Cushing. Be ready to explain to the class what was *said*, as opposed to what was *heard,* and why. You'll need to use contrastive stress to make your points clear to the class. You'll also need to understand which pronunciation mistakes (Sound Concepts, stress, verb endings, etc.) caused the problem. Your teacher may grade your group on how well you can explain your case study using the terms from this book.

Case Study 1

Air traffic controller says: "Descent in four miles." (Meaning: the pilot shouldn't begin landing for another four miles.)

Pilot hears: "Descend to four." (He thinks that he should immediately begin descending to four thousand feet.)

Case Study 2

Air traffic controller says: "Descend two four zero zero." (Meaning: the pilot should descend to 2,400 feet above the ground.)

Pilot hears: "Descend to four zero zero." (She thinks that she should descend to just 400 feet above the ground.)

Case Study 3

Air traffic controller says: "Remain clear of the runway." (Meaning: it's not yet safe to land.)

Pilot hears: "Cleared." (She thinks that she was given permission to land.)

Case Study 4

Air traffic controller says: "Cross at sixty south." (Meaning: the pilot should cross a flight path sixty feet south of it.)

Pilot hears: "Cross at sixteen south." (He thinks that he should cross the flight path only sixteen feet south of it.)

ACTIVITY 3: Individual Consonant and Vowel Sounds

List the individual consonant and vowel sounds from this unit in the box.

Circle any sounds that you're still having trouble with.

Unit 2 Focus Sounds

Part 3: Thinking About Listening and Speaking

ACTIVITY 1: Reflect

Think about one of your problems with individual consonant and vowel sounds.

Do you have trouble *forming* the sound or *matching* the right sound to the right letters or words? Why is this a problem for you, and what are you doing to try to solve it?

ACTIVITY 2: Quiz Yourself

1. What is standard sentence-level stress?
2. What is contrastive stress? What does it have to do with the idea of implication?
3. What are the different pronunciations of plural and possessive noun endings?
4. What strategies should you use when listening to lectures?
5. What clues can you gather from facial expressions and body language?
6. What are thought groups? Why are they important for listening and speaking?

Getting Ready for Chapter 8
What You Need to Know About Reductions: Or and Are

Listening for Rhythm & Music

Diagnostic

You will hear eight questions. On a separate piece of paper, write the number of syllables in each question. Compare your results with a partner. Did you both hear the same number of syllables? Remember that some syllables are harder to hear than others.

Listening for Sound Concepts

Listen to the questions again and fill in the blanks. Each blank may represent one or more words.

1. Coffee _____?
2. _____ plastic?
3. For here _____?
4. _____ salad?

5. How _____ doing?
6. _____ you _____?
7. _____ you _____?
8. _____ your plans?

 Eye-Opener: Questions 1–4 all share the word _____. Questions 5–8 all share the word _____. Both of these words are reduced, unstressed function words that can be difficult to hear. When these words are reduced, they sound the same.

Sound Concepts

Reduced Sounds

$$\left.\begin{array}{l} \text{are} \\ \text{or} \end{array}\right\} \longrightarrow /ə^r/$$

What is the sound of *reduced are* and *reduced or*?

Say **reduced are** and **reduced or** the same as the syllable "er" in the words "dancer," "teller, " and "better": /ə^r/ *sounds like* schwa (unstressed vowel sound) with lips slightly rounded to say the sound /r/.

How do we mark *reduced are* and *reduced or* in this book?

Draw a line through the vowel letters in the words. Mark linking from consonant sounds to **reduced are** and **reduced or**:

Example: Where ar̶e̶ you going?   Paper o̶r plastic?

Trouble spots

Don't omit **reduced are** and **reduced or.** Reduced function words are still a syllable, a rhythmic beat. Your listeners need to hear you say them.

Practice *Reduced Are* and *Reduced Or*

With a partner, mark the questions above for **reduced are** and **reduced or.** Read them aloud.

Exercise 1: Fixed Phrases with *Reduced Or*

 Focus on *reduced or*   **Recycle linking**

Mark the phrases below for **reduced or** and practice saying them. When might you hear these phrases? Write sentences with these phrases and read them aloud to a small group.

black or white	better or worse	right or wrong	now or never
sooner or later	more or less	win or lose	rain or shine

Exercise 2: Interview

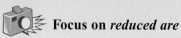 Focus on *reduced are*

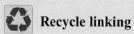 Recycle linking

Part 1. Work in groups of three. Choose a famous person that everyone knows. As a group, write ten questions to ask this person in an interview. Make sure your questions are grammatically correct and include **reduced are**. Practice your questions aloud: don't omit **reduced are**. Mark them for **reduced are** and linking.

Examples: What are your biggest successes?   How are you enjoying your fame?

               Where are you planning to be next year?

PRONUNCIATION GOAL

Use **reduced are** (a rhythmic beat) in "wh-" questions.

Best	**Good**	**Incorrect**
Saying reduced "are"	Saying unreduced "are"	Not saying "are"

Part 2. Choose roles from the following list. Switch roles after a few questions.

Interviewer: Interview the famous person, using your group's ten questions.

Famous Person: Answer questions from your interviewer.

Monitor: During the role-play, listen to the interviewer's questions and fill out the chart below. Check under the heading that describes how the interviewer said **reduced are** in each of the questions. Later, discuss your results with your group.

INTERVIEWER 1

	BEST Reduced "are"	**GOOD** Unreduced "are"	**INCORRECT** Missing "are"
1.			
2.			
3.			
4.			
5.			
6.			
7.			
8.			
9.			
10.			

INTERVIEWER 2

	BEST Reduced "are"	**GOOD** Unreduced "are"	**INCORRECT** Missing "are"
1.			
2.			
3.			
4.			
5.			
6.			
7.			
8.			
9.			
10.			

Journal

You probably knew how to form "wh-" questions before this lesson. However, you may not always have pronounced **reduced are** in these questions. Write a paragraph in which you reflect on this issue. What do you hear in the speech of English speakers around you? Have you been overlooking **reduced are**? Is it easier to hear now?

8 Functional Intonation and Reduced Sounds

Sound Concepts
Reduced have; altered you, your

Rhythm & Music
Overview of intonation and holding intonation

Grammar Sounds
Recycle regular past tense verb endings

Consonant & Vowel Sounds
/w/, /æ/, /ɛ/, /eʸ/ (pat, pet, bait)

Sound Concepts

Altered Sounds

Preview

Remember: you ——————▶ /yə/   Example: Do you̇ like it here?

> **Eye-Opener:** your ——————▶ /yəʳ/
>
> **Example:**   Do yoủʳ friends like it here?
> Usually "your" rhymes with "door," "four," and "more." When the vowel in "your" is altered, "your" rhymes with the second syllable of these words: "fixture," "mixture," and "future."

Diagnostic

You will hear nine sentences or questions. On a separate piece of paper, write the sentences or questions you hear.

After Listening

What was difficult about this diagnostic? What sounds did you hear at the beginning of the words "you" and "your" ?

Altered /y/

y ——————▶ /tch/ after /t/   Example: Put your. . .
y ——————▶ /j/ after /d/   Example: Did you. . .

When do we use altered /y/?

Alter /y/ after /t/ or /d/ in linked speech. Don't alter /y/ when it is not linked to /t/ or /d/.

Example: Diḋ yoủ do yoủʳ homework?

How do we mark *altered you* and *altered your*?

If the final sound of the word before "you" or "your" is /t/ or /d/, write /t/ or /d/ over the word. Draw a circle connecting the /t/ or /d/ and the letter "y."

Example: I washeḋ yoủʳ car.

Practice Altered /y/

Go back to the sentences and questions above. What is the final sound (not letter) of the word before "you" or "your"? Mark the sentences and questions for altered /y/ and the altered vowel sound in "you" and "your." To summarize, when we alter "you" and "your," we make two changes:

1. _____   2. _____

USAGE NOTE: PRONOUNCING *ALTERED YOU* and *ALTERED YOUR*

In everyday speech, **altered you** and **altered your** may have different pronunciations, depending on whether we:

1. **Alter the vowel sound.**

2. **Alter the /y/ sound.**

3. **Alter both sounds.**

	Vowel unaltered	Vowel altered
/y/ unaltered	did you let you	did yoͧu let yoͧu
/y/ altered	di(d y)ou le(t y)ou	di(d y)oͧu le(t y)oͧu

 PRONUNCIATION GOAL

Alter the sound /y/ in unstressed "you" and "your" after /t/ or /d/. Alter the sound /y/ in unstressed words like "yet" and "year" after /t/ or /d/.

USAGE NOTE: TAG QUESTIONS and *ALTERED YOU*

Use tag questions to make small talk, check assumptions, or get information in a polite way. Chapter 9 focuses on the intonation of tag questions. Check with your teacher or a grammar book if you don't understand tag questions. For now, focus on producing the "tag" with **altered you.**

Example: You've heard of tag questions, haven(t y)oͧu?

Exercise 1: Tag Questions with *Altered You*

Focus on *altered you*

Complete the tag questions below. Mark them for **altered you** and **altered your.** Read them aloud to a partner.

1. You can come over now.   (can't)   You ca(n) come over now, can(t y)oͧu?

2. You didn't like her.   (did)

3. You'll be there.   (won't)

4. You shouldn't do that.   (should)

5. You did that last year.   (didn't)

6. You're ready.   (aren't)

7. You didn't do that yet.   (did)

8. You couldn't help us.   (could)

Consonant & Vowel Sounds

Introduction to the Sound /w/

What is the sound?

The sound /w/ is the sound at the beginning of the word "window."

How do you spell it?

window	**wh**ere	**o**ne	lang**u**age

How do you form it?

The sound /w/ is a voiced sound. Your lips are tightly rounded but not tense. Don't let your teeth touch your lip.

Trouble Spots

1. Don't say /v/ instead of /w/. These are different sounds. The letter "v" is never pronounced /w/, and the letter "w" is never pronounced /v/.

2. Don't say /g/ or /gw/ instead of /w/ at the beginning of words like "would."

3. Don't omit /w/ at the beginning of words like "woman."

4. Don't omit /w/ after a consonant sound like /k/ or /g/ in words like "question" or "language."

 Eye-Opener: If you don't say the sound /w/ at the beginning of the word "wood" (or "would"), you change the syllable structure of these words. "Would" is a CVC word: /wʊd/. Listeners expect to hear a voiced consonant sound before the vowel.

USAGE NOTE: ASKING PERMISSION and REQUESTING

Many polite questions begin, "Would you mind. . . ?" Use **altered you** in these questions.

To make a request of someone else: "Would you mind + (gerund)?"

To ask permission to do something: "Would you mind + if I (past tense)?"

These questions are yes or no questions.

> **To answer "yes," say:** "Sure" or "No problem."
>
> **To answer "no," say:** "Sorry, but + (reason)" or "No, + (reason)."

Exercise 2: Would You Mind. . . ?

 Focus on the sound /w/, altered /y/

Work with a partner. Take turns asking and answering request and permission questions with "Would you mind?" Pronounce the /w/ sound at the beginning of "would." Use responses from the usage note above.

Request	Permission
lending me your notes	if I borrowed your notes
giving me directions	if I asked for directions
advising me on something	if I got your advice on something

Exercise 3: What Would You Do if. . . ?

 Focus on *altered you* and *altered your*, the sound /w/

Read the following questions to yourself and mark them for **altered you** and **altered your.** Discuss the questions with a partner or small group. Use the impersonal "you" in your answers to these hypothetical questions.

> Example: What would you do if a friend asked you to do him a favor you don't really want to do?
>
> "Well, you could tell your friend the truth, or you could just do the favor.
>
> It would depend on how much you liked your friend. . ."

1. What would you do if your friend who's a terrible driver offered to drive you to work?
2. What would you do if you got an unexpected day off from work?
3. What would you do if uninvited guests showed up at your house?
4. What would you do if you and your boss exchanged places for a day?

> **PRONUNCIATION GOAL**
>
> Try to say the sound /w/ correctly in the word "would." If you're still having trouble, use a contracted form to avoid saying "would." Contracting "I'd" instead of mispronouncing "I would" makes your English easier to understand.
>
> Example: I would like to get your advice. ⟶ I'd like to get your advice.

Introduction to the Sound /æ/

What is the sound?

This is the vowel sound in "have," "has," or "had." Say the symbol: "ash."

How do you spell it?

> had   la**ugh**

How do you form it?

The sound /æ/ is a low front vowel. Your lips are spread when you say it, and your jaw is low. If you can say the verb "have," you can say this sound.

Trouble Spots

Don't say any other vowel sounds for the sound /æ/.

Introduction to the Sound /eʸ/

What is the sound?

This is the second vowel sound in: "OK" (or "okay"). It's the vowel sound in the words "day," "pay," and "say." Say the symbol: "A." Do not say this symbol "E."

How do you spell it?

> s**ay**   s**a**me   p**ai**n   gr**ea**t   th**ey**   n**ei**ghbor

How do you form it?

Say this sound in the front of your mouth. Your mouth is a little bit open, and your tongue is a little bit rounded.

Trouble Spots

Don't let the symbol or the spelling confuse you. Remember, this sound is the same as the name of the letter "A." It's the sound in the words "same" and "name."

Introduction to the Sound /ɛ/

What is the sound?

This is the vowel sound in the words "when" and "then." It's also the vowel sound in the name of the letter "L." Say the symbol "epsilon."(3 syllables)

If you can say the abbreviation for Los Angeles (LA), you can say the sound /ɛ/ (the vowel sound in the letter "L"), and the sound /eʸ/ (the sound of the name of the letter "A"). These sounds are different.

How do you spell it?

yes	we**a**ther	s**ai**d	gu**e**ss	fr**ie**nd	m**a**ny

How do you form it?

This is a short, pure vowel sound: it doesn't glide, and it's not tense. Your tongue is low in your mouth.

Trouble Spots

Don't say the sound /eʸ/ for /ɛ/. Remember, spelling might not help you.

Exercise 4: Words with the Sound /eʸ/

 Focus on the sound /eʸ/

Circle all the words below that have the sound /eʸ/.

yes	says	days	said	say	many
they	weight	friend	great	later	tell

What vowel sound do all the uncircled words have in common? _____

Eye-Opener: "Said" does not rhyme with "stayed." "Says" does not rhyme with "days." These vowel sounds are difficult for many students. Be careful!

Exercise 5: Vowel Game

 Focus on the sounds /æ/, /eʸ/, and /ɛ/

1. Write a story using as many words as possible with the three vowel sounds /æ/, /eʸ/, and /ɛ/. Underline each of these focus words.

2. Make a chart like the one below. Put the focus words from your story into the correct columns. Keep the order the same, as in the chart below.

Words with /ae/	Words with /eʸ/	Words with /ɛ/
have	say	yes

3. Exchange stories and charts with another student. Does your partner's chart list all the focus words from his or her story? If not, underline the word in the story and add it to your partner's chart. Are any of the focus words in the incorrect columns on your partner's chart? If so, circle the word.

4. Talk with your partner about each other's charts. If you or your partner put any of the focus words in the wrong column, decide on the correct column for each word.

5. Practice reading your own story, making sure to pronounce the focus words correctly. Use your chart to help you. When you are ready, give your chart to your partner and read your story aloud.

6. While your partner is reading his or her story aloud, check off the focus words on his or her chart. Circle any words your partner mispronounces. Be careful: your partner might list a word in the correct column, but still mispronounce it.

7. Discuss any problems with your partner. Did you pronounce all of the focus words correctly? If not, add any problem words to your log for future practice.

Sound Concepts

Reduced Sounds

Diagnostic 2

Listen to the following passage and fill in the blanks with the word or words you hear.

He _____ listened to the weather forecast last night. If he'd listened, he

_____ taken his umbrella, and he _____ walked to work

today. He _____ taken his car, and his shoes _____

gotten wet. He _____ caught a cold, and he _____ saved

himself a lot of trouble.

Compare your responses with a partner. What word did all seven blank spaces have in common?

Introduction to Reduced Have

auxiliary "have" ⟶ /əv/

auxiliary "have" ⟶ /əv/ ⟶ /ə/

What is *reduced have?*

Auxiliary (function word) "have" is reduced, but it still has a syllabic beat.

Reduced have is very common in speech. It sounds like the end of the contraction "could've," but it's usually not written as one.

Two pronunciations of *reduced have:*

1. /əv/, like the sound of "of" — no /h/ at the beginning

2. /ə/, like the sound of **reduced of** — no /h/ at the beginning and no /v/ at the end

English speakers use **reduced have** without thinking about it. They probably don't notice whether they say /əv/ or /ə/ when they speak.

How do we mark *reduced have* in this book?

Draw a line through the letter "h" at the beginning of the word.

Exercise 6: I'm Worried About. . .

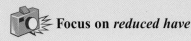 **Focus on *reduced have***

Work with a partner. Take turns playing speakers A and B.

A: Use the frame below to talk about something that worries you. Remember to link sounds, pronounce contractions, say verb and noun endings correctly, and reduce "have." Pause after each sentence for your partner's response.

B: Listen to speaker A and choose an appropriate single-word response from the following:

oh   hmm   great   yes   really

Finish the conversation by agreeing with speaker. Use rising or falling intonation to express your emotions.

> Example: my friend / He got an F on his test. / He studied before he took his test. / he
>
> **A:**   I'm worried about **my friend.**
>
> **B:**   Oh? ↗
>
> **A:**   **He got an F on his test.**
>
> **B:**   Great. ↘
>
> **A:**   **He really should** h̸ave **studied before he took his test.**
>
> **B:**   You're right, **he** should h̸ave.

1.   my car / It's making strange noises. / I… checked it out sooner. / you

2.   my job / The company's not doing too well. / I… started looking for another one. / you

3.   my garden / The flowers are wilting. / I… watered them more. / you

Exercise 7: I'm Excited About. . .

 Focus on *reduced have*

Work with a partner. Take turns playing speakers A and B.

A: Use the frame below to talk about something that excites you.

B: Use the frame below and appropriate single-word responses with rising intonation.

> Example: my grades / I got an A on my test. / I… studied like this sooner. / you
>
> **A:**   I'm excited about **my grades.**
>
> **B:**   Oh? ↗
>
> **A:**   **I got an A on my test.**
>
> **B:**   Oh! ↗
>
> **A:**   **I really should** h̸ave **studied like this sooner.**
>
> **B:**   You're right, **you** should h̸ave.

1.   my sports club / I'm having lots of fun there. / I… checked it out sooner. / you

2.   my cooking class / I'm learning lots of new recipes. / I… started cooking lessons sooner. / you

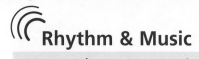

Rhythm & Music

More About Intonation

Review: Rising ↗ and Falling ↘ Intonation

What should you do if the intonation patterns in this book feel strange?

In this chapter, you will practice marked, or unusual, examples of intonation. When you practice these different intonation patterns, you may feel that you sound strange. It's normal to feel that way at first. Use the activities in this chapter to exaggerate your intonation up ↗ or down ↘ Have fun, stretch out your syllables, and make sure to open your mouth!

How should you combine intonation and stress?

When you use rising (or falling) intonation on an entire message (sentence, question, etc.), focus the intonation change on the vowel sound in the stressed syllable of a single, stressed word (the most important content word, the contrastive word, or the new information).

Practice Intonation

With a partner, practice reading these sentences aloud and changing your intonation on the stressed words.

1. Class is over. ↘   *standard sentence-level stress*

2. John drives to work, but *Mary* ↗ takes the *bus.* ↘   *contrastive stress*

3. Where's my math ↗ book?   *informational stress*

 Eye-Opener: The more you stress a word, the more your intonation changes. Use smaller intonation changes when a word receives normal, sentence-level stress. Use larger intonation changes when a word receives contrastive stress or when it is in italics.

Functions of Intonation

Using holding intonation to signal that you're not finished speaking.

Holding intonation doesn't rise and doesn't fall. It stays the same: → In the sentence below, we show that the speaker isn't finished by putting an ellipsis, or three periods (…), after the word "tonight." In speech, we show this by using holding intonation, not falling intonation: the speaker's intonation stays the same: →

1. I'm going to the movies tonight… →   (*speaker is not finished*)

2. I'm going to the movies tonight. ↘   (*speaker is finished*)

LANGUAGE STRATEGY
Using the Three Kinds of Information to Understand Intonation

1. Use sound information: Listen for rising, falling, or holding intonation.

2. Use language information: Use the chart below, and what you learn about the functions of intonation, to help narrow down the possible meanings.

3. Use background information: Use what you know about the speaker and the situation. Watch the speaker's facial expressions and body language.

USAGE NOTE: CONVERSATIONAL FUNCTIONS of INTONATION

Different intonations can accomplish the same conversational function. Look at the chart below and circle the functions, emotions, and effects that could be expressed by more than one kind of intonation. What functions or effects of intonation are you already familiar with? When do you remember hearing them or using them? Do any functions or effects of intonation surprise you? Why?

Rising Intonation ↗	Holding Intonation →	Falling Intonation ↘
Standard question intonation (rise-fall-rise): sounds uncertain **Standard "happy" intonation (rise-fall): sounds happy**	**Unfinished intonation:** more is coming	**Standard sentence intonation:** sounds certain
Possible conversational functions: •asking for information •checking understanding •asking most yes or no questions •expressing sarcasm or irony •expressing emotions (see below)	**Conversational functions:** •"holding the floor" (expressing a desire to keep talking) •expressing indecision	**Possible conversational functions:** •making statements •giving information •asking for more information •asking most "wh-" questions •asking a question you already know the answer to •expressing emotions (see below)
Can express these emotions: surprise, happiness, interest, curiosity, disbelief, shock, disapproval, etc.	**Doesn't express an emotion (default)**	**Can express any of the following or no emotion:** disappointment, disapproval, annoyance, etc.
Conversational effect: Your turn is finished. There are two possibilities: 1. Your listener responds. 2. The conversation is over.	**Conversational effect:** Your turn is not finished. There is one possibility: 1. Your listener expects you to keep talking.	**Conversational effect:** Your turn is finished. There are three possibilities: 1. Your listener responds. 2. The conversation is over. 3. You say something else (you take an extra turn).

PRONUNCIATION GOAL

When speaking, use intonation to convey a specific meaning. When listening, listen for intonation to decode the speaker's meaning.

Journal

List five questions or statements you often use at school or at work and think about their context. What conversational function are you trying to accomplish when you say these? Are you asking for new information, checking information, prompting someone else to talk, or trying to hold the floor (keep talking)? What kind of intonation should you use in each statement or question? Mark the intonation and talk about your decisions with a partner.

Exercise 8: Are You Finished Yet?

 Focus on holding intonation

1. Use the punctuation in the statement to decide if the speaker should use falling or holding intonation. Mark the intonation.

2. Work with a partner. Take turns reading statements with the appropriate intonation. Listen closely: when your partner uses falling intonation, give an appropriate response.

Statement	Response
1. a. I'm going to my grandmother's house.	Oh, that's nice.
b. I'm going to my grandmother's house…	
2. a. I'm going to the beach tomorrow.	Yeah, it's supposed to be warm then.
b. I'm going to the beach tomorrow…	
3. a. I'm going to the museum.	I was just there today!
b. I'm going to the museum…	
4. a. I'm going to the supermarket.	Can you pick me up some milk?
b. I'm going to the supermarket…	
5. a. I'm going to the mall this afternoon.	Well, have fun!
b. I'm going to the mall this afternoon…	
6. a. I'm going to the coffee shop.	Wait, I'll come with you.
b. I'm going to the coffee shop…	

3. Look at the photographs below. What details about the person's facial expressions and body language make you think he might not be finished speaking?

Exercise 9: Listening for Holding Intonation

 Focus on holding intonation

 You will hear ten complete or partial sentences. On a separate piece of paper, mark the intonation you hear for each item: ↘ (the speaker is finished) or → (more is coming).

 Eye-Opener: Some grammatical patterns carry their own intonation. Always use holding intonation in the following cases:

	Why?	Examples
1. After articles (a, an, the)	Articles always come before nouns.	He gave a → great speech. ↘
2. After adjectives in noun phrases (happy, blue, great, etc.)	These adjectives always come before nouns.	I put the blue → vase on the table. ↘
3. After directional verbs (put, give, make, etc.)	These verbs always come before objects.	I put → the blue vase on the table. ↘
4. After nonfinal items in a series	Items in a series follow each other.	I woke up, → took a shower, → and got dressed. ↘

With a partner, write additional sentences for each pattern and practice their intonation.

 Journal

English has a specific order for different kinds of adjectives. The adjectives in the sentence below have a fixed order—they can't be rearranged

Example: That's a big →, round →, red → balloon. ↘

1. Learn more about the order of English adjectives. Find a photograph of an interesting scene and write a description of it. Use many adjectives in your description, and mark your description for intonation. Read your paragraph aloud, remembering to use holding intonation after adjectives.

2. Follow the steps below to survey some English speakers on their favorite movies. Listen for holding intonation in their responses, and present your results to the class.

   • List ten movies you would like to ask people about.

   • Find some English speakers you can survey, show them the list of movies, and tell them: "I'm taking a poll for my English class. Could you tell me your three favorite movies on this list?" Keep track of how many people vote for each movie.

   • Listen for holding intonation between a person's three favorite movies (items in a series). Be careful! The responses you hear may have many pauses, fillers, or hesitations. The people you survey may not use holding intonation where you expect it.

Eye-Opener: The Effects of Incorrect Word-Level Stress

English speakers rely on syllables and stress patterns to recognize a word or message. Discuss the example below with a partner. What errors do you think the speaker made? Why didn't the listener understand?

My child's in elementary school.

AaBbC[ ]e

✓CHECKLIST

Six Things to Learn When You Learn a New Word

1. meaning (not just translation)
2. part of speech
3. etymology (derivation or related words)
4. usage (phrasal verb, count/non-count noun, transitivity, irregular forms)
5. number of syllables
6. pronunciation (including stress pattern)

Recycle Past Tense Verb Endings

Remind yourself of the three pronunciations of this ending:

Say it:	Say it:	Say it:
After:	After:	After:
Extra syllable? yes or no	Extra syllable? yes or no	Extra syllable? yes or no

Exercise 10: Context for Practice–A History of Chocolate

 Focus on word-level stress   **Recycle "-ed" endings**

1. Read the passage below to yourself. Underline all the words you recognize from earlier chapters, including words that end in "-ed" or "-ogist" and words with varying number of syllables (such as "chocolate" or "interest").

2. Choose three words from the passage to learn more about. Use the checklist above to learn the six important features of these new words. Practice saying your words aloud. Are you saying the correct number of syllables? Are you using the correct stress pattern? Teach your words to a partner or small group. Be careful with proper nouns: many proper nouns have unpredictable pronunciations and may not be in your dictionary. It's always acceptable to ask someone how to pronounce a proper noun.

3. Circle the "-ed" forms in this passage and mark their pronunciation. Practice reading the passage aloud.

Although some people say they're addicted to chocolate, others are allergic to it. However, chocolate, the popular sweet treat, has a long and interesting history. Recently, archaeologists discovered what one researcher calls "one of the most important chocolate samples in the world." At first glance, the nickel-sized piece of chocolate looks like a small chip of concrete, except the center is brown. But it's more than 1,500 years old, and it was scraped off the bottom of a pot found in an ancient Mayan tomb in Honduras. The ancient chocolate sample was displayed at well-known museums as part of an exhibition about the history and science of this highly prized, long-appreciated treat. The exhibition was called simply "Chocolate."

Even though this newly discovered chocolate sample was found in the tomb of a king, chocolate in the ancient world wasn't just consumed by royalty: Common farmers cultivated the plants and enjoyed it in drinks and stews as well.

Researchers haven't tasted the sample of ancient chocolate. After they examined it, they found the sample contained toxins from the perfumes that the Maya sprinkled around their tombs.

Adapted from "Before Kisses and Snickers, It Was the Treat of Royalty." Copyright © 2003 by *The New York Times*. Reprinted with permission.

Exercise 11: More Adjective Phrases

 Recycle "-ed" endings

With a partner, brainstorm participial adjective phrases like those in the passage above (newly discovered, nickel-sized). Here are a few to get you started:

        well educated   frequently cited   often misunderstood

Write a description of a person, place, or thing using as many of these participial adjectives and adjective phrases as you can. Have a classmate or your teacher check your description for grammar and usage. Mark your description for the sound of the "-ed" endings, for linking, and for thought groups. Then read it aloud to a classmate.

Exercise 12: Helpful Neighbors

 Recycle "-ed" endings and number of syllables   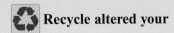 Recycle altered your

John's grandmother broke her arm last month. John is using the list below to help her write thank-you notes to the people who helped her while she was sick.

1. Write the sound of the "-ed" ending above each verb on John's list.

2. Write the total number of syllables in the "-ed" form in the box next to each item.

3. Take turns reading John's reminders aloud with a partner. Remember to link sounds, pronounce the "-ed" ending correctly, use the right number of syllables, and alter "your."

Functional Intonation and Reduced Sounds **155**

She's / He's the one who…

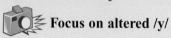

1. [2] returned your library books.
2. ☐ emptied your trash.
3. ☐ washed your car.
4. ☐ mailed your letters
5. ☐ fixed your sink.

6. ☐ cooked your meals.
7. ☐ carried your groceries.
8. ☐ watered your house plants.
9. ☐ picked your mail up at the post office.
10. ☐ emptied your trash.

Exercise 13: /y/ vs. Altered "y"

Focus on altered /y/

On your own: Read the questions in the chart aloud. Write down the sound of the letter "y" in "you": is it /y/ or is it altered "y" (/j/ or /tch/)?

With a partner: Take turns reading the questions aloud. Listen and write down the sound your partner said at the beginning of "you." Do you and your partner agree? Look back at any questions you disagree on.

	Sound of the letter "y" in "you"	Sound my partner said
1. Can't you leave early?		
2. Do you know what I mean?		
3. Shouldn't you be studying?		
4. Do you think they'll make it?		
5. Did you hear the news?		
6. Didn't you like the movie?		
7. Can you look this over?		
8. Could you lend me a dollar?		
9. Are you sure?		

Recycle linking, deletion, thought groups, "-ed" endings

1. Listen to a short talk about the Portugeuse writer José Saramago. Complete the paragraph with the words you hear. After listening, check your answers with a partner.

   The novelist José Saramago was _____ family of farmers in a small

   Portuguese village. For financial reasons he _____ high school studies and

   _____ mechanic. After trying different_____ the civil service, he

   _____ publishing company for twelve years_____ for newspapers.

   For several years he _____ translator, but _____ literary successes

   in the 1980s he _____ himself _____ own writing. In the past

   thirty years, Saramago _____ thirty _____ fiction, poetry, essays,

   and drama. He _____ numerous international prizes, including the 1998 Nobel

   Prize for Literature. Since 1992, he has _____ Canary Islands.

   http://nobelprize.org/literature/laureates/1998/biob.html

2. Read the passage above silently and decide where the thought groups are. Mark the passage for thought groups and the sound of the "-ed" past participles. Read the passage aloud to a partner.

3. Find out more about your favorite writer's life. Write a paragraph about your writer. Model your paragraph on the paragraph above, giving the following information:

   -when and where the writer was born   -early education and work experience

   -first success as a writer   -number of published works

   -international recognition   -current residence and works in progress

4. With your teacher or a partner, edit your paragraph for grammar. Mark your paragraph for linking, deletion, thought groups, and "-ed" endings. Practice reading your paragraph aloud, then read it to a small group of your classmates. Did they understand you? Invent a way to quiz their comprehension. You might write a true or false quiz, or a fill-in-the-blanks quiz. Make sure your classmates use the correct sounds of the "-ed" endings when they discuss your paragraph.

What did we do in this chapter?

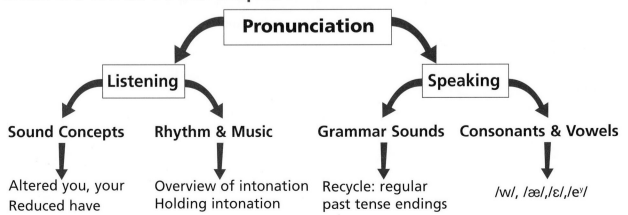

Part 1: Why Some People Understand You and Others Don't

Imagine yourself in this situation. Your ESL teacher understands you, and the people you work with every day understand you. You think your English is improving. But when you meet a new English speaker, often the new person doesn't understand you at all. You might wonder: "What's going on? *Some* people understand me perfectly and always know what I'm trying to say."

Discuss this situation with a partner. Why is it harder to explain yourself to some people?

Here are some common responses learners might have in this situation. Which of these do you think will lead to improved communication? Why?

1. "It's not my fault—I'm trying really hard to make people understand me. What's wrong with these other people?"

2. "It's just this one teacher who complains about my pronunciation. No one else has ever noticed!"

3. "Maybe I'm trying hard, but something still isn't working. I don't know why some people understand me better than others, but I know I need to work on it. What should I do differently?"

Case Study: Office Communication

An ESL learner was very pleased with his progress in English. He'd noticed that, over a period of months, his communication with his office mate seemed to have improved. His office mate now asked him to repeat himself less often. But when the learner changed offices, his new office mate asked the learner to repeat himself and clarify his meaning just as often as the old office mate had done at first.

Discuss the following questions with a partner:

1. Was the learner really improving?
2. Why did he have an easier time communicating with his first office mate than the second?

Think about it

Communication is a two-way street:

Sometimes, if listeners can't easily understand your words or meaning, they give up.

In order to communicate with them, you have to put in extra effort. Your listeners may finally understand you, but you're doing all the work.

Sometimes, even if they have trouble understanding you at first, listeners are willing to put in extra effort. Your listeners may finally understand you, but they're doing all the work.

Eye-Opener: Sometimes you may think *you* are improving, but your *listeners* may be responsible for the successful communication.

Communication should be balanced: no one should have to do all the work.

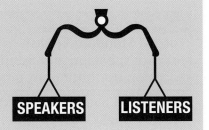
SPEAKERS   LISTENERS

LANGUAGE STRATEGY: Monitoring the Effectiveness of Your Strategies

What should you do when someone doesn't understand you? Rank the following strategies from 1 to 10 (most important to least important). Talk with a partner or a small group about your ranking. Why is one strategy more effective than another? Can you think of a time when one strategy worked or didn't work?

A. ____ Keep talking and hope your listener understands.

B. ____ Repeat what you said.

C. ____ Repeat what you said, louder.

D. ____ Rephrase your meaning in other words.

E. ____ Use intonation to express your meaning.

F. ____ Check your listener's reaction for clues.

G. ____ Use facial expressions or hand gestures to express your meaning.

H. ____ Monitor your pronunciation—check for missing grammar sounds.

I. ____ Monitor your pronunciation—check for incorrect stress or syllables.

J. ____ Monitor your pronunciation—check for incorrect consonant or vowel sounds.

Part 2: Understanding Different Styles of English

 Eye-Opener: Did you know there isn't just one English language? There are many varieties of English.

Think about it

Think about your communication in your native language. Who do you communicate with everyday? Do you speak or write the same way to everyone? What changes do you make for different people and situations?

Every language has different levels of formality and speech styles. Look at the chart on the next page. Talk with a partner about these varieties of English. How are they different? Use your own experience to discuss an example of each style.

Style of English	Uses
Formal Standard English Practice speaking and listening Focus on using thought groups and timing.	Academic writing, some business writing, job interviews, lectures, planned speeches, formal presentations
Connected Everyday English Practice speaking and listening Focus on linking and contracting sounds.	Spontaneous speech, conversations, reading aloud
Familiar Informal English Practice listening. Focus on understanding reduced and altered sounds and some dropped syllables.	E-mails or conversations with very close friends and peers

 PRONUNCIATION GOAL

Practice connected everyday English in and out of the classroom.

Exercise 1: Analyze Familiar Informal English

 Recycle Sound Concepts

Sometimes, in very informal conversations, speakers omit entire unstressed function words. You need to be able to understand the extreme reduced and altered sounds of this level of speech. Look at the different steps below, then complete the chart.

	What you hear	Number of syllables	Sound Concepts in action
Unreduced and Unaltered Original	Did you eat yet?	4	Sounds are linked
Step 1	Did you eat yet?	_____	Sounds are _____ _____
Step 2	Did you eat yet?	_____	Sounds are _____ _____
Step 3	Did you eat yet	_____	Sounds are _____ _____
Step 4	Did you eat yet? Sounds like "Jeet chet?"	2	Sounds are _____ _____

DISCUSSION OF CASE STUDY: OFFICE COMMUNICATION

The ESL learner's speech wasn't really improving, but his office mate's listening was. The office mate put in so much effort that he became better and better at understanding the learner's English.

9 Functional Intonation and Altered Sounds

Sound Concepts

Altered sounds: want to, got to, going to

Rhythm & Music

Functional intonation

Grammar Sounds

Recycle regular plural noun endings

Consonant & Vowel Sounds

/f/, /p/, /ɑ/ (odd)

 ## Sound Concepts

Altered Sounds

Diagnostic

You will hear six sentences or questions. On a separate piece of paper, write the sentences or questions you hear.

After Listening

What was difficult about this diagnostic? Did you recognize the altered verb phrase *gonna* ("going to")?

Altered Verb Phrases

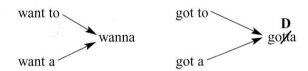

How do we mark these altered verb phrases in this book?

Circle the phrase to help you remember to link and alter the sounds.

USAGE NOTE: DID THEY SAY "WANT TO" or "WANT A" ?
When you hear the altered verb phrases "wanna/gotta", use language information to decide whether the speaker means "want/got a" or "want/got to." Listen for the part of speech of the word after "wanna/gotta":   "wanna/gotta" + noun = "want/got a"   "wanna/gotta" + verb = "want/got to"

Practice Altered Wanna, Gotta, and Gonna

Circle the altered verb phrases in the diagnostic and read them aloud to a partner.

Make sure you wrote the full, unaltered forms of these verb phrases (want a, want to, got to, got a, or going to).

Sound Concepts

Reduced Sounds

because ———————→ /bəkʌz/ (2 syllables)

because ———————→ /bəkʌz/ (2 syllables) ———————→ /kʌz/ (1 syllable)

"Because" is another unstressed function word that is sometimes reduced. You may hear either form (two syllables or one syllable). In cartoons or comics, it may be written as " 'cause," "coz," or "cuz." In writing, always use the full form: "because."

Exception: lecture notes or other personal writing

Exercise 1: Four Mini-Exercises with Gotta, Gonna, Wanna

 Focus on altered wanna, gotta, gonna

1. Invent a product. Try to sell it to someone by describing its features.

   "You're really going to like this product. It's got a lot of great features. . . ."

2. Find a photograph of a person in a magazine. Describe the person's appearance.

   "He's got a mustache and long hair. He's got a smile on his face. . ."

3. Teach someone how to do a simple task: change the oil in car, cook a meal, etc.

   "First you've got to. . . Next, you've got to. . ."

4. List things you want and what you have to do to make them happen.

   "If you want to get a good grade, you've got to study."

Exercise 2: Understanding Gotta in Context

 Focus on altered gotta   **Recycle questioning intonation and contracted sounds**

Match the comments at left to the responses at right. Mark each comment for **altered gotta**. Mark rising and falling intonation in the comments and responses. Read the dialogues aloud with a partner. Talk about the different contexts for each dialogue.

1. They've got to get a new car.   **A.** That's nice—what kind did they get?

2. They've got a new car.   **B.** Why? What's wrong with the one they have now?

3. They got a new car.   **C.** That's nice—what kind do they have?

Exercise 3: Wanna vs. Wants to

 Focus on altered wanna/gonna   **Recycle third-person singular, contrastive stress, rising intonation**

You and your friend are discussing other friends and upcoming plans. Use the frame below to discuss each the following situations.

A. **John** wants to **go to the movies** tonight.

B. Does he *really* wanna **go to the movies** tonight?

A. Well, maybe *he* wants to, but we're not gonna go.

1.	Oscar	go to the baseball game	**3.**	Peter	go dancing
2.	Carmen	go to the library	**4.**	Kim	go out to dinner

Exercise 4: What Do You Have to Do Next Week?

 Focus on altered gotta, wanna, gonna   **Recycle *altered have to***

Write a short paragraph about what you need to do next week, using the verb phrases **got to, want to, going to**, and **have to**. Write the full forms, and check your paragraph for grammar errors. Then mark each altered verb phrase, and read the paragraph to a partner.

Exercise 5: What Does She Have to Do Next Week?

 Focus on altered gotta, wanna, gonna   **Recycle *altered have to* and *reduced can, and, or***

Listen to a student talk about her plans. Every time you hear an altered or reduced form, make a mark next to it. Afterwards, add up your marks and compare your totals with a partner's. Listen again and check your totals.

Number of times you heard each form

1. altered wanna

2. altered gotta

3. reduced can

4. altered gonna

5. reduced and

6. reduced or

7. reduced because

Journal

Find a spot on a bus, train, or park bench where you can listen to English speakers for about ten minutes. Listen for the same reduced and altered forms as in exercise 5. Make a chart to keep track of how many times you hear each form. Report your results to the class. Is it easier to hear these forms now? Why do you think that is?

Consonant & Vowel Sounds

Introduction to the Sound /f/

What is the sound?

This is the consonant sound at the beginning of the word "fear," in the middle of the word "coffee," and at the end of the word "leaf."

How do you spell it?

fear coffee lau**gh** tele**ph**one

Exercise 6: Practice the Sound /f/

 Focus on the sound /f/

Read the following paragraph aloud and circle every word with the sound /f/. Be careful not to circle words with similar spellings, but without the /f/ sound.

Paralinguistic features are non-language information, conveyed primarily through physical gestures and motions, which can flesh out the meaning of a speaker's message. Though a laugh or a nervous cough is not really language, it still gives you information about a person's intent, whether in person or on the telephone. If people give you baffled expressions, they haven't understood you in some way. The clues from your listeners' facial expressions can be useful in figuring out moments of miscommunication.

How do you form the sound /f/?

The sound /f/ is a continuant, so air continues out of your mouth while you say it. To say it, touch your top teeth to your bottom lip. The sound /f/ is an unvoiced sound. Your voicebox should not vibrate when you say it.

Trouble Spots

1. Don't let spelling confuse you: whenever you see the letters "f," "ff," or "ph," always say the /f/ sound. When you see the letters "gh," you will sometimes need to say /f/ and sometimes another sound.

    Example: /g/ in ghost, /f/ in cough, silent in thought

    Go back to the paragraph above. Make sure you didn't circle words like *thought*, which has similar spelling, but a different sound.

2. Don't say /f/ as /v/. Native English speakers will usually understand this mistake, but they will notice it. Remember, /v/ is formed in the same place in your mouth as /f/, but /v/ is voiced and /f/ is unvoiced.

    Examples: leaf/leave, fine/vine, proof/prove

Introduction to the Sound /p/

What is the sound?

The sound /p/ is the consonant sound in the word "paper." The sound /p/ is formed in the same place in your mouth as the sound /b/, but /b/ is voiced, and /p/ is not. Try whispering /p/ to avoid voicing it.

How do you spell it?

drop   stopping

How do you form it?

Say the sound /p/ with both lips closed. Stop the air completely when you say it.

The sound /p/ is unvoiced.

Trouble Spots

1. Don't confuse /p/ and /f/. Let spelling help you. The letter "p" alone is never pronounced /f/. The letter "f" is never pronounced /p/.

2. Don't confuse /p/ and /b/. Let spelling help you. The letter "b" is never pronounced /p/. The letter "p" is never pronounced /b/. There are no exceptions.

3. Say the sound /p/ with a puff of air at the beginning of words and stressed syllables. You can put your hand in front of your mouth to feel the air.

Exercise 7: Practice /p/

 Focus on the sound /p/   **Recycle /b/**

Read the pairs of words aloud, remembering to practice the puff of air at the beginning of the /p/ words. Write a small "h" next to the words beginning with a /p/ sound to help you remember to say them correctly. The small "h" indicates the puff of air.

pay	bay	pill	bill
pat	bat	pace	base

Exercise 8: Word Game

 Focus on /p/ and /f/   **Recycle /b/**

Divide a piece of paper into three columns: /p/, /b/, and /f/. With a partner, copy the words below into the appropriate columns. The first pair to finish and to read their list aloud correctly wins. If a pair mispronounces /p/, /b/, or /f/, another pair has a chance to win the game.

1. copy	6. picture	11. cough	16. developing
2. bill	7. coffee	12. departure	17. stopped
3. foot	8. people	13. business	18. fill
4. better	9. laugh	14. put	19. appeal
5. pencil	10. pill	15. fine	20. telephone

Introduction to the Sound /ɑ/

What is the sound?
This is the vowel sound in the word "hot." Say the symbol: "script a."

How do you spell it?

father   stop   bureaucracy

How do you form it?
When you say this sound, your tongue is flat and your mouth is partially open and relaxed. Say this sound in the middle of your mouth.

Trouble Spots
Don't let spelling confuse you.

USAGE NOTE: CONTRASTIVE STRESS and THE WORD "THE"

What are the two pronunciations of the article "the"? When do you use each one?

1. _____   2. _____

When you use "the" to make a contrast, the stressed word "the" is louder, longer, clearer, and higher. The vowel sound in the word "the" changes:

unstressed the /ðə/ ————————→ stressed the /ði/.

Example: You hear a TV sports announcer say the following:

1. "Team X has the best record and the largest number of wins."

2. "It's not just another team; it's *the* team to watch this season."

What do you notice about this written version of the announcer's comments?

Which word receives extra stress in sentence 2? Why?

What does the announcer mean by sentence 2?

Exercise 9: Stressed "the" in Advertisements

 Focus on contrastive stress   **Recycle /ð/**

Use the frame below to write the final line of an advertisement for an imaginary new brand of a product.

(BRAND)—not just another (PRODUCT)—the (PRODUCT)

not just a
not your average
not your ordinary

Example: FreshSoap—not your ordinary soap—*the* soap!

Eye-Opener: The Sound /θ/ in Academic Contexts

Some common academic words have the difficult sound /θ/ (theta). Here are a few—can you think of any more?

theory   theme   thesis   thesaurus

 **Rhythm & Music**

Functions of Intonation

Use rising intonation to check information

LANGUAGE STRATEGY: Using Short Focused Questions to Check Information

Intonation is economical: we can use fewer words to express the same meaning.

Situation A: Someone is giving you directions. You don't understand *anything* they said. Ask a general, all-purpose question.

"What did you say?" or "What should I do?" or "Could you say that again?"

Situation B: Someone is giving you directions. You understand everything they said except for one part. Ask a short, focused question with rising intonation on the important word. Use a specific "wh-" word like "where" or "when" for best results.

You hear:	"Go to the corner and turn <mumble>."	
Ask:	"Go to the corner and turn where ↗?"	*long focused question*
	or	
	"Turn where ↗?"	*short focused question: practice in exercise 10*
	or	
	"Where ↗?"	*single-word focused question: practice in exercise 11*
Implication:	I didn't hear you—where did you say to turn?	

Exercise 10: Asking Short Focused Questions

 Focus on rising intonation

Practice asking short focused questions with rising intonation.

Example: "Open your book to page <mumble>."
             "Page what ↗?"

You hear. . . .

1. Go to the corner and turn <mumble>.

2. The party starts at <mumble>.

3. I saw a great <mumble> yesterday.

4. There's a train delay at <mumble>.

going to + verb (going to is altered: gonna)

going to + noun (going to is unaltered)

Exercise 11: Asking Focused Single-Word Questions

 Focus on rising intonation

With a partner, take turns creating sentences by combining any of the places and times below. When you are listening to your partner, imagine that you can't hear one of the pieces of information in your partner's sentence. Ask a single-word question with rising intonation to make your partner repeat the place or time.

Example

Your partner says: "I'm going to **my cousin's house next month.**" ↘

You didn't hear where. You say: "Where?" ↗

my cousin's house	tomorrow
Europe	two years from now
Vancouver	in 2007
the library	next month
L.A.	at 6:00
a party	in a couple weeks
the movies	on Thursday
a wedding	after class
the coffee shop on campus	at 6:30
the airport	on Tuesday
the mall	in May
class	in the summer

Functions of Intonation

Use falling intonation to ask for more information

Sometimes you hear and understand everything that is said to you, but you still want more information. Ask a short, focused "wh-" question with falling intonation on the important word.

You hear: "I'm going to Canada next week." ↘ *You wonder what part of Canada your friend is going to visit.*

Ask: "Where in Canada ↘ are you going?"   *long "wh-" question*
   or
   "Where ↘ in Canada?"   *shorter "wh-" question*
   or
   "Where?" ↘   *single-word focused question: practice in exercise 12*

Implication: I'm interested—tell me more details about where you're going.

Eye-Opener: In general, use falling intonation for all "wh-" questions except when checking specific pieces of information.

Exercise 12: Asking for Additional Information

 Focus on falling intonation

Work with a partner. Use a map to discuss places you would like to visit. When listening to your partner, use single-word questions with falling intonation to ask for additional information.

Example   **A:** I'd like to go to Germany. ↘

            B: Where? ↘

            A: Bavaria. ↘ Bavaria is a German state or province.

            B: Where?

            A: Munich. ↘ Munich is a city in Bavaria.

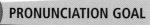 **PRONUNCIATION GOAL**

Make sure you can ask the single-word question "Where?" or "When?" with two different intonations:

     ↗ Rising: Checks understanding

         Implication: Repeat the place or time—I didn't hear or understand.

     ↘ Falling: Asks for more information

         Implication: Be more specific—I want to know more information.

Journal

Think about times when people have asked you a single-word question. What kind of intonation did they use? What was their implication? Try to think about their facial expressions when they asked the question.

Look at the pictures: which shows a person with a puzzled expression, asking for repetition? Which shows a person with an interested expression, asking for more information? Make notes about any other expressions or gestures that might accompany rising or falling intonation on single-word questions, and discuss your thoughts with the class.

Exercise 13: Asking vs. Checking

 Focus on rising and falling intonation

On your own, read the three-line dialogues below and mark the appropriate intonation.

With a partner, read the dialogues aloud. Use correct intonation: rising ↗ for checking understanding, falling ↘ for asking for more information.

Example

A: Tomorrow my friend arrives from Texas ↘ for the week.
B: When? ↘
A: In the afternoon. ↘ *"In the afternoon" is more information, so use falling intonation on "When?"*

1. **A:** Next month I'm moving to Europe.
   B: Where?
   A: Europe.

2. **A:** The test will be after spring break.
   B: When?
   A: The day we get back.

3. **A:** The U.S. Civil War took place in the mid-nineteenth century.
   B: When?
   A: In the 1860s.

4. **A:** The Olympics were in Greece last year in 2004.
   B: Where?
   A: Greece.

Write two dialogues on your own: one should ask for more information and one should check understanding. Mark the intonation and read the dialogues aloud.

 Eye-Opener: Intonation Carries Meaning

In minimal pairs, a single change in pronunciation changes the meaning of the word: light/right, berry/very, coffee/copy. The questions "Where?" ↗ and "Where?" ↘ are also minimal pairs. There is only one difference between these words: a single change in intonation changes the meaning of the word.

More Practice with Intonation and Stress

Intonation Accompanies Stress

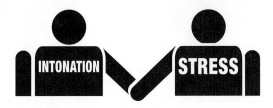

Exercise 14: Three Mini-Exercises

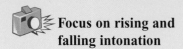 **Focus on rising and falling intonation**

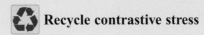 **Recycle contrastive stress**

When we stress a word to show contrast or importance, the stressed syllable of that word is longer, louder, clearer, and higher. Intonation rises and falls on a single word. Practice using rising intonation on the stressed syllables of the stressed words in these sentences. Use falling intonation at the end of the sentences.

Part 1. You have a very agreeable friend. Role-play these conversations with a partner. Use **altered you.**

   A: Where do you wanna go tonight? ↘

   B: I don't care. ↘ *Wherever* ↗ you like is fine with me. ↘

1. What do you wanna do? /Whatever…
2. Who do you wanna invite?/ Whoever…
3. When do you wanna go? /Whenever…
4. How do you wanna get there?/ However…

Part 2. You have a friend who always makes excuses for not doing what he's supposed to. You don't believe your friend's excuses. Explain your friend's excuses to someone else. Use rising intonation to show your disbelief.

   John's not gonna be able to come over today. ↘ He *said* ↗ he had to go to work. ↘

1. make it to the study group
2. come to the party
3. meet for dinner on Thursday
4. drive you to school

Part 3. You and your friend always agree on things. Use stress and rising intonation on the point of agreement. Use tag questions with falling intonation to express agreement and make conversation.

   A: That was a terrible movie. ↘

   B: Yes, it *was* ↗ a terrible movie, wasn't it? ↘

1. It's getting late.
2. This bus is always crowded.
3. That teacher always gives difficult tests.
4. She really studies hard.
5. He played a really good game.
6. That was a great speech.

 Eye-Opener: A question mark doesn't always signal rising intonation.

 **Grammar Sounds**

Recycle Regular Plural Count Noun Endings

Remember that the "-s" or "-es" plural ending has three different pronunciations. Remind yourself of these endings by completing the chart below.

Say it:	Say it:	Say it:
After:	After:	After:
Extra syllable? yes or no	Extra syllable? yes or no	Extra syllable? yes or no

Exercise 15: Context for Practice–Evolution

 Recycle plural count noun endings and intonation, thought groups

 Eye-Opener: Most of the plural nouns in the text don't have an article in front of them. Use plural nouns with no articles when speaking in general.

Below is a passage about evolution.

1. Read the passage to yourself and underline all the regular plural nouns. Decide on the correct pronunciation of the plural ending for each noun. Mark the sound of the ending above each word: [s], [z], or [Iz].

2. Mark the text for thought groups: where would you pause when reading aloud? Remember to think about holding intonation—holding the floor, not being finished, items in a series. Practice these intonation patterns with a partner.

3. Practice reading part of the text aloud to a partner.

Biologists, anthropologists, and archaeologists work together to trace humans' evolution from primates and other animals. The investigation into our origins continues, with new excavations providing more evidence about our early human ancestors and newer theories coming into favor.

Different scientists tend to focus on different areas. Some biologists are particularly interested in what early humans ate. Research questions in this area include: What did early humans' diets consist of? Did they eat leaves, meat, or berries?

Some linguists are interested in how languages evolved. Can we trace all of today's languages back to one early human language? When did tribes or groups of humans start using languages to communicate with each other? When did the first written languages emerge?

Research is also continuing to determine where early groups of humans lived. Were they concentrated into one or two main areas? When did these groups leave these so-called pockets of civilization and spread across the globe? Sometimes answers come from evidence of geological events that disrupted habitats and forced our ancestors to move.

Anthropologists are often more interested in the social aspects of how early humans lived. What kinds of family groups did they have, and what kinds of social relationships? Some researchers believe that, long before languages, our ancestors lived in highly socialized groups with complex relationships and social rules. These advanced primates may have brushed each other's fur and used other grooming techniques as the equivalent of modern conversations.

 Eye-Opener: Non-count nouns never take plural endings. Check your dictionary to see if a noun is countable or not.

Exercise 16: Plural Noun Phrases with Non-Count Nouns

 Recycle plural noun endings

Students often have problems with these common non-count nouns:

    research   evidence   vocabulary   advice

Never use plural endings with these nouns. Instead, use partitives, such as "pieces of evidence," or words like "some." The following noun phrases are common, acceptable ways to use these non-count nouns in speech and writing. These phrases are countable. Make the phrases plural and use them in sentences of your own.

1. area of research
2. vocabulary list
3. piece of evidence
4. piece of advice
5. research study
6. vocabulary word
7. word of advice
8. body of evidence
9. research topic

LANGUAGE STRATEGY: Pronouncing Irregular Plural Endings with /f/ and /v/

1. To pronounce regular plural noun endings, think back to the singular form.

   To pronounce irregular plural noun endings, work with the irregular plural form: *don't* go back to the singular form.

2. Irregular plurals with /f/ or /v/ sounds, such as "leaves" or "beliefs," are irregular in their formation *but regular in their pronunciation*.

   If you see the letter "f," say the sound /f/. The sound /f/ is unvoiced. Unvoiced sounds take unvoiced endings. Say the ending [s].

3. With a partner, list more of these irregular plurals that have /f/ or /v/ and practice saying them.

Exercise 17: Practice Pronouncing /f/ and /v/

 Focus on irregular plural endings   **Recycle /f/ and /v/**

Reread the passage in exercise 16 and circle all the /v/ and /f/ sounds. Practice pronouncing these words correctly.

Exercise 18: More Practice with /f/ and /v/

 Recycle /f/ and /v/, contracted sounds

 You will hear ten sentences. Some sentences begin with the simple pronoun subject "I." Some sentences begin with the contracted form "I've" (pronoun subject + auxiliary "have"). For each sentence, write the form you hear: "I've" or "I."

 PRONUNCIATION GOAL

Listen for holding intonation in classroom discussions to know when your classmates are pausing in the middle of a thought. Don't interrupt them—Wait until their intonation tells you they're finished.

Exercise 19: Are They Finished Yet?

 Recycle holding intonation, falling intonation, plural endings

1. Work in small groups, sitting a circle.

2. Pick a number from 1–10. Don't tell anyone your number. Write it down on a piece of paper and remember it.

3. Take turns going clockwise around the circle talking about one of the topics below. When it's your turn, list as many examples of the topic as the number you picked in step 2. Use holding intonation between examples (items in a series) and falling intonation at the end. If you are listing a series of plural count nouns (example: "dogs," "cats," "horses," etc.), be sure to say the correct plural ending.

4. Listen to your classmates' intonation to know when to take your turn. The person before you might list two examples or ten: the person's intonation will tell you when he or she is finished.

    Example: Mary is the first person in her group. Her group is listing school subjects. Mary chose the number five in step 2. When it's her turn, she says:

        "Let's see, math ➔, English ➔, chemistry ➔, biology ➔, and anthropology. ↘

1. daily chores	**5.** kinds of cars	
2. animals	**6.** U.S. states	
3. sports	**7.** South American countries	
4. school subjects	**8.** careers	

Rhythm & Music

Stress with "-ial" Suffixes

Stress Pattern: Stress the syllable before the "-ial" ending.

Here are some words that end in the suffix "-ial." What part of speech are these words? Complete the chart with words related to the example words, such as "face" for "facial" or "memory" for "memorial." Practice reading the "-ial" words and their related words aloud, with correct syllables and stress.

Spell the ending:	Say the ending:	Number of syllables in the ending	Example	Related words
-ial	/i-əl/	2	memorial trivial proverbial	
-tial	/shəl/	1	essential residential influential	
-cial or -sial	/shəl/	1	financial facial controversial	

 Eye-Opener: Different dialects of English use different stress patterns in certain words.

Example: the word "controversy," related to the "-ial" word "controversial," above.

In American English, stress "controversy" this way: **CON** –tro-ver-sy (4-I)

In British English, stress "controversy" this way: con-**TRO**-ver-sy (4-2)

If you're used to the sounds of American English, try listening to British radio or television to see if you hear any differences.

Final Chapter Activity

 Recycle intonation, thought groups

1. Choose an English speaker whose life you want to learn more about. Ask the person for an interview and permission to record his or her oral history.

2. Make a list of questions to ask during your interview. Write some questions that you definitely will ask and some questions that are possible follow-up questions, depending on the person's responses. During the interview, if the person says something interesting, prompt them to say more about that topic by using rising intonation. Your follow-up questions might include single-word questions for clarification/repetition or additional information.

3. Have a teacher or other English speaker check your questions for grammar and cultural appropriateness.

4. Practice your interview questions with a partner. Focus on these points:

   a. using holding, rising, and falling intonation

   b. using fillers, such as "uh huh," "mm," " hmm," and "oh," to show interest and comprehension

   c. letting your subject hold the floor

   d. asking for clarification if you didn't understand something

5. Interview the person and record the interview.

6. Report to the class: How do you think the interview went? Which parts went well, and which parts had miscommunication? Why?

Be prepared to play some or all of your interview recording to the class in order for your class to analyze the intonation.

What did we do in this chapter?

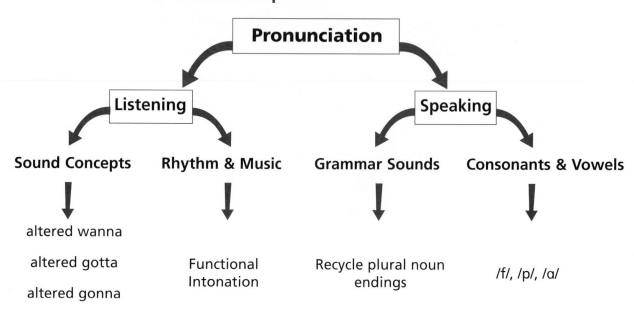

Getting Ready for Chapter 10
What You Need to Know About Intonation and Timing

 Rhythm & Music

Functions of Intonation

Use rising intonation to turn a statement into a question.

Example: George won the race. ↘   factual statement

George won the race? ↗   yes or no question

 Eye-Opener: Intonation overrides grammar.

With rising intonation, different grammatical forms can carry the same meaning:

George won the race? ↗

Did George win the race? ↗

George won the race, didn't he? ↗

Use rising intonation to get an answer, to check your understanding, or to express surprise or interest.

Examples: George won the race? ↗   Did George win the race? ↗

Use rising intonation on either grammatical form to accomplish these functions.

Exercise 1: Using Rising Intonation to Express Surprise

 Focus on rising intonation

Mark rising and falling intonation at the end of each statement or question below. Practice reading them aloud with a partner.

Example: You won the race? ↗   That's great news—congratulations. ↘

1. Your pet died? I'm sorry to hear that.
2. You're finished already? Here's another assignment.
3. You're leaving? Class isn't over yet.
4. You studied abroad? That sounds interesting.

Exercise 2: Using Rising Intonation to Express Interest

Focus on rising intonation

On a separate piece of paper, list four factual statements about your life. Exchange lists with a partner. Read your partner's statements aloud one at a time, changing them from the first person ("I") into the second person ("you"), and using rising intonation at the end. Wait for your partner to give you more information.

Example

Your partner writes: I play soccer every Saturday. ↘

You say: "You play soccer every Saturday?" ↗

If you use rising intonation, your partner responds with more information:

"Yes, I meet a few friends and we play in the park." ↘

BE CAREFUL!
If you don't use rising intonation when repeating your partner's statements, you won't sound interested. Your partner won't understand your meaning.

Exercise 3: Using Rising and Falling Intonation to Express Certainty and Uncertainty

 Focus on rising and falling intonation

On your own: Choose three vocabulary words from any of the reading passages in this text. Look them up so that you are certain of their meanings. Write each word and its part of speech on an index card. Practice reading your words aloud with correct syllables and word-level stress.

With a small group: Shuffle everyone's cards together. Take turns drawing a card at random and defining the word. When it's your turn to define the word, use rising intonation if you're unsure (uncertain) of the meaning. Use falling intonation if you're sure (certain) you know the meaning.

Keep track of each group member's scores:

If you're right and certain (falling intonation)	you get	2 points
If you're right but uncertain (rising intonation)	you get	1 point
If you're wrong and uncertain (rising intonation)	you get	0 points
If you're wrong but certain (falling intonation)	you lose	1 point

Example: The word is "primate." You think you know what it means, but you're not sure.

You say: "A kind of animal, like a gorilla or human?" ↗

You're right but uncertain. You get 1 point.

Exercise 4: Using Rising and Falling Intonation to Express Certainty and Uncertainty

 Focus on rising and falling intonation

Read the following statements. How sure are you that each statement is true? *(answers on p. 180)*

If you believe the statement is true, circle "certain." Rephrase the statement as a tag question. Use *falling* intonation.

Example: The capital of Missouri is Jefferson City, isn't it? ↘

If you're not sure or you think the statement might be false, circle "uncertain." Rephrase the statement as a tag question. Use *rising* intonation.

Example: The capital of Missouri is Jefferson City, isn't it? ↗

Work with a partner. Take turns reading the tag questions aloud and listening for final intonation.

1. West Virginia was the first state to observe Mother's Day.   certain   uncertain
2. Oregon has more ghost towns than any other state.   certain   uncertain
3. The official state beverage of Arkansas is milk.   certain   uncertain
4. The cheeseburger was invented in Colorado.   certain   uncertain
5. Suntan lotion was first developed in Florida.   certain   uncertain
6. The Genesee River in New York flows from South to North.   certain   uncertain
7. The first subway system in the U.S. was in Massachusetts.   certain   uncertain

Functions of Intonation

Use rising intonation in the middle of either/or (choice) questions

Standard yes or no questions have rising intonation at the end and no special (marked) intonation in the middle:

"Would you like cake and ice cream? ↗ " is a standard yes or no question.

"Would you like coffee or tea? ↗ " is also a standard yes or no question. This question has the word "or" in it, but it's not really a choice question. It's asking if you want something to drink, such as coffee or tea.

Remember that intonation carries meaning.

"Would you like *coffee* ↗ or *tea*? ↘ " is not a yes or no question. This question offers you a choice. It's asking you to choose either coffee or tea.

USAGE NOTE: INTONATION AND SHORTER QUESTIONS

We also use shorter forms of choice and yes or no questions: "Paper or plastic?" "Coffee or tea?" Shorter forms use the same intonation as the longer forms.

Exercise 5: Using Intonation in Choice Questions

 Focus on intonation in choice questions

Sometimes logic and background knowledge make understanding choice questions easy. Read the following choice questions and mark their intonation. With a partner, discuss where you would hear each questions. How do you know each one is a choice question? Take turns reading them aloud with correct intonation. Use contrastive stress on the two choices to help you with the intonation.

Example: Paper ↗ or plastic? ↘

1. Coffee or tea?
2. Here or to go?
3. Cash or credit?
4. Smoking or non?
5. Milk or lemon?
6. Business or pleasure?
7. Decaf or regular?
8. Aisle or window?

LANGUAGE STRATEGY
Distinguishing Between Either/Or and Yes/No Questions

Some questions look the same, but sound different, depending on whether the speaker is offering a choice or expecting a yes or no answer. Use the following strategy to distinguish between them.

1. Listen for rising intonation in the middle of the question.

2. Listen for contrastive stress on the two choices.

3. Listen for a pause before the "or."

4. Listen for falling intonation at the end of the question.

If you hear one or more of these four features, you are hearing a choice question.

If you can't hear any of these features, the question may be a yes or no question. Use your background knowledge and common sense: which meaning do you think is more logical?

Exercise 6: Distinguishing Between Choice and Yes or No Questions

 Focus on rising and falling intonation in choice and yes/no questions

 You will hear seven questions. Decide whether the question is a choice or a yes/no question. Use intonation and timing features to help you decide. Check any features you hear. Then circle the question type.

↗ Intonation in the middle	Pause before "or"	↘ Intonation at end	Question Type
1.			Choice or Yes/No?
2.			Choice or Yes/No?
3.			Choice or Yes/No?
4.			Choice or Yes/No?
5.			Choice or Yes/No?
6.			Choice or Yes/No?
7.			Choice or Yes/No?

 Journal

Spend a few minutes looking back at the exercises and readings in this book. Reflect on the following questions, write down your answers, and be ready to discuss them in exercise 2, chapter 10 (p. 186).

1. Which of the readings did you find most interesting? Why?
2. What's one new fact or piece of information you have learned from this text?
3. Which area—Sound Concepts, Rhythm & Music, Grammar Sounds, or Consonant & Vowel Sounds—did you find most interesting? Which area had the most new information for you?
4. What's one specific aspect of pronunciation (a sound, function, or concept) that you never knew before this class? What makes it important?

Answers to exercise 4: all items are true

10 Timing and Linked Sounds

Sound Concepts	Rhythm & Music	Grammar Sounds	Consonant & Vowel Sounds
Vowel-to-vowel linking	*Timing and pauses: spoken punctuation*	*Recycle regular past tense verb endings*	/k/, /g/, /r/

 ## Sound Concepts

Linked Sounds

Diagnostic

You will hear eight phrases. Listen and write the phrases you hear.

After Listening

What was difficult about listening to these phrases? What patterns do you see in your list of phrases?

Introduction to Vowel-to-Vowel Linking

How do we mark vowel-to-vowel linking in this book?

Link the vowel sound at the end of one word to the vowel sound at the beginning of another word. Use a small /w/ or /y/ sound to help you link the vowels smoothly. Mark the linking and write a small "y" or "w" over the linked sounds.

Examples: do͜ over, see͜ it.

When do we not use vowel-to-vowel linking?

When the first vowel sound is /ə/, /ʌ/, or /ɑ/, don't link it to the next vowel sound. Combining these vowel sounds with other vowels is difficult even for native speakers of English.

Examples: I went to the **law office** today.

There's a **sofa in** the living room.

Practice Vowel-to-Vowel Linking

Mark the phrases in the diagnostic above for vowel-to-vowel linking and read them aloud to a partner.

 Eye-Opener: Vowel-to-Vowel Linking Within Words

Sometimes two vowel letters in a row make one vowel sound (one syllable): "real." Sometimes they make two different vowel sounds (two syllables): "re-AL-i-ty."
You can't predict these pronunciations. Use your dictionary to help you when you learn a new word.

In words of two or more syllables, if one syllable ends with a vowel sound, and the next syllable begins with a vowel sound, say a slight /w/ or /y/ sound in between the two vowels (like vowel-to-vowel linking).

Word	Syllable Breaks	Say it
reality	re-AL-i-ty	re-ᵞAL-i-ty
cooperation	co-op-er-A-tion	co-ʷop-er-A-tion
ambiguous	am-BIG-u-ous	am-BIG-u-ʷous
period	PER-i-od	PER-i-ᵞod
diagram	DI-a-gram	DI-ᵞa-gram

Exercise 1: Vowel-to-Vowel Linking

 Focus on linked sounds

Use the word bank at right to complete the sentences grammatically.

Mark the vowel-to-vowel linking in each item.

1. She told it <u>to him</u> over dinner.

2. He got around _____ at last.

3. They _____ their notes every night.

4. John _____ great place for dinner.

5. Don't _____ if you don't mean it.

6. I didn't _____ at the store.

7. _____ go there.

8. _____ you here?

9. _____ going there.

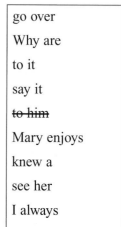

go over

Why are

to it

say it

~~to him~~

Mary enjoys

knew a

see her

I always

Consonant & Vowel Sounds

Introduction to the Sound /k/

What is the sound?

This is the consonant sound at the beginning of the word "can." It can appear in the beginning ("can"), middle ("because"), or end ("sick") of a word.

How do you spell it?

king   can   rock   accept   stoma**ch**   quarter   box

How do you form it?

Form the sound /k/ in the back of your throat. It's an unvoiced sound.

Trouble Spots

1. Sometimes the letter "k" is silent, as in "knee," "know," and "knife." It doesn't make any sound. You need to memorize these exceptions.

2. Don't let spelling confuse you! Words like "accept," "box," "text" and "stomach" all have the /k/ sound, but not the letter.

3. Don't drop the /k/ sound at the end of words like "think" and "sink."

   "think" without the /k/ sounds like "thing"

   "sink" without the /k/ sounds like "sing"

Introduction to the Sound /g/

What is the sound?

This is the consonant sound at the beginning of the word "go." It can occur at the beginning ("go"), middle ("beginning"), and end ("big") of words.

How do you spell it?

    go   **gh**ost   **gu**ess   exi**s**t

How do you form it?

Form /g/ exactly like /k/, but let your vocal cords vibrate for /g/: /g/ is voiced.

Trouble Spots

1. Don't say /k/ (unvoiced) instead of /g/ (voiced) at the ends of words. Without the voiced /g/, "bag" sounds like "back."

2. Sometimes the letter "g" does not make the sound /g/. There is no /g/ sound in the following words: following, sing, singer, king, ring, bring, thing, running, walking.

Journal

Voicing carries meaning. In English, using a voiced or an unvoiced sound can be the difference between two words: cold/gold, fine/vine, etc. Other languages use pitch (or tone), length, aspiration (the puff of air at the beginning of a word), or other features to distinguish between different sounds. Think about your language. What features distinguish between different sounds and words? Are there some words in your language with more than one acceptable pronunciation? Does your language have a lot of minimal pairs? Write about your reflections and share them with a partner or a small group in class.

Introduction to the Sound /ʔ/

What is the sound?

This is the sound in the middle of the expression, "Uh-oh!, " which English speakers say when something bad or unexpected happens. Say this symbol: "glottal stop."

How do you spell it?

Spell this sound with a space or a hyphen (no letter), as in "Uh-oh!"

Spell this sound with the letters "t" or "tt," as in mountain, button, kitten, and cotton.

How do you form it?

The glottal stop is the sound of saying nothing, for a very brief moment, with your glottis (the space between your vocal cords) closed. The glottal stop is the opposite of the sound /h/. The sound /h/ is the smooth, connected sound of breath escaping. The glottal stop is not smooth: when you say a glottal stop, you can't link sounds.

Trouble Spots

1. Don't use glottal stops before or after a complete word. Some languages allow glottal stops at the beginning or end of words. In English, we only use a glottal stop in the middle of a word.

   Examples: mountain, uh-oh

2. Some English learners have trouble with syllables that end in a consonant sound, so they say a glottal stop instead of the final consonant. The result is English that sounds choppy and unfinished.

3. Don't be afraid to use glottal stops in words with the letter "t" before the sound /n/: kitten, button, mountain. The glottal stop is a standard consonant sound — saying /t/ instead of a glottal stop makes you sound very formal.

Journal

Watch a television comedy or drama and listen for the expressions in the chart below. Take notes and report your findings to the class.

Expression	Sound	Meaning (can vary with intonation)
uh-uh (strong-weak)	/ʔ/	generally negative
uh-oh (strong-weak)	/ʔ/	generally negative
uh-huh (weak-strong)	/h/	generally positive

Rhythm & Music

Introduction to Timing

Diagnostic 2: Part 1

You will hear one side of a short conversation. After each sentence, decide which of the two statements below is true.

1. **a.** There are two people eating breakfast.   TRUE   FALSE

   b. There are three people eating breakfast.   TRUE   FALSE

2. **a.** Mary wants someone to drive Bill to work.   TRUE   FALSE

   b. Mary wants to know if Bill is driving to work.   TRUE   FALSE

3. **a.** Mary is talking to Bill.   TRUE   FALSE

   b. Mary is talking to George.   TRUE   FALSE

4. **a.** Mary wants Bill to answer the phone.   TRUE   FALSE

   b. Mary wants someone to bring her the phone bill.   TRUE   FALSE

After Listening

What was difficult about listening to the sentences and deciding which statements were true? What clues did you use when listening?

Diagnostic 2: Part 2

Read along as you listen to the entire story again, with more details and the other half of Mary's conversation. Listen to the complete conversation as you read the text below. The speaker will pause at the same places.

Mary, who works as an accountant, and her husband Bill, who's a lawyer, were eating breakfast before going to work. *(check your answer to 1)*

"Are you driving, Bill?" Mary asked.

"Yes, I took the train yesterday, but I'm taking the car today," Bill answered. *(check your answer to 2)*

"Are you driving George?"

"No, he's not coming in today, but I'm driving Pete, because his car's in the shop." *(check your answer to 3)*

"Okay, well, have a nice day," Mary said as she walked toward the door.

The phone rang just as Mary was going out the door.

"Can you get the phone, Bill?" Mary asked. *(check your answer to 4)*

Compare answers with a partner. Do you agree? What clues helped you figure out what was going on?

 Eye-Opener: The message is in the music: Timing and pauses carry meaning.

The first time you heard the conversation, you had to rely completely on *sound information* in order to understand what was happening. There was no context, or background information. The second time you listened, you heard more details with more background information.

For instance, the first time you heard the conversation you knew that Mary's husband's name was Bill, and you knew that the phone rang. The second time you listened, you could also use language information to understand what was happening. The sentences and punctuation on the page helped you know to whom Mary was speaking.

Practice Pauses

Listen to the conversation again for pauses while following along with the text. While you listen, put a slash (/) wherever you hear a pause. Remember that pauses are the spoken version of punctuation marks.

Timing and Pauses

How do we know where to pause?

Pause slightly at the end of every thought group.

Pause at most punctuation marks. This chapter explains some of them in more detail.

Pause before and after contrastively stressed words.

Are all pauses the same length?

No. Some pauses are large and some are small. Mark small pauses with one slash: / and large pauses with two slashes: //. The "Sounds of Silence" boxes in this chapter tell you when to use small and large pauses.

THE SOUNDS of SILENCE

Use a large pause when addressing a person directly.

"Are you driving today or getting a ride, // Bill?"
"Bill, // are you driving today or getting a ride?"
"Are you driving today, // Bill, // or getting a ride?"

Don't link sounds across these large pauses.

Exercise 2: Direct Address in Small Groups

 Focus on pauses   **Recycle intonation**

You will need your journal entry from Getting Ready for Chapter 10 (page 180). Sit in a circle with a small group and use the activity below to discuss your responses to the journal entry. In this activity, practice addressing your group members by name.

1. Write your name on an index card, and then shuffle all the cards together. Put the cards face down and take turns drawing a card.

2. One person starts the discussion by explaining his or her response to question 1 in the journal. The person who started the discussion then turns the floor over to the person whose name is on his or her card. Remember to use pauses around the person's name and contrastive stress on the *you.*

3. When everyone in your group has shared their responses to question 1, repeat your discussion for the remaining questions.

> Bob: "Well, I really liked the reading about the origin of chocolate, because I love
>
> chocolate. **How about *you*, Ana? Which one did *you* like most?"**
>
> Ana: "I agree, Bob, I liked that text, but my favorite reading was the borrowed words.
>
> I thought that was neat. **How about *you*, Theresa? Which one did *you* like most?"**

Journal

Other journal activities in this book referred you to radio or TV talk shows, which are a good place to listen for specific language features. Listen to a talk show and note how the host and guests use pauses before and after each other's names when they address each other. Share your findings with the class.

THE SOUNDS of SILENCE

Use a small pause between people, items, or units in a group.
Use a large pause between groups.
  "I'm going to Chicago to visit my friends Maria, / Carla, / and Steve // and
  my grandparents."
Items within a series or group: Maria, Carla, and Steve
Two separate groups: 1. my friends Maria, Carla, and Steve
                           2. my grandparents

Exercise 3: Grouping Your Classmates

 Focus on large and small pauses

Practice using large and small pauses as you group your classmates into pairs. List your classmates' names in alphabetical order. If you don't know what letter someone's name begins with, ask: "Is that with an A?" or "Does that start with an E?" Decide which students should work together. If your class has an odd number of students, there will be one group of three. Make a list of the pairs (and group of three). Your list may look something like this:

Ben, Arnold   Annie, Paul   Debbie, James, Carl

Take turns reading your list of groups aloud. When it's your turn to read, use a small pause between the two names in a pair. Use a large pause between pairs or groups. Don't gesture or use any function words (and, then, so, next) to help: timing alone carries your meaning.

Example: Ben / Arnold // Annie / Paul // Debbie / James / Carl //

When your classmates read their lists, find your partner and stand next to him or her. The student reading the list checks that everyone is with the correct partner. Be careful! If you don't notice the difference between a large and small pause, you'll end up with the wrong partner.

Exercise 4: How Many Items Are There?

 Focus on small pauses

Listening to pauses tells you how many items are in a list. Work with a partner. Close your book as your partner reads the phrases below. Listen for your partner's pauses: how many items is your partner saying?

1. fish, tank, and fish food
2. baseball cap and gloves
3. picture, frame, and nails
4. dress, shoes, and purse
5. computer monitor and keyboard
6. can opener and blender

THE SOUNDS OF SILENCE

Use large pauses to separate additional information in a sentence (apposition).

Mary, / an accountant, / and Bill   three people: small pauses, items in a series

Mary, // an accountant, // and Bill   two people: large pauses, apposition

When you see a phrase like "Mary, an accountant, and Bill," you don't know if there are two or three people unless you have background information. Listen for the length of the pause in order to understand the meaning.

When you see a phrase like "Boston, Massachusetts, and San Francisco," you *do* know how many places there are because you have background information. You know that Boston is part of Massachusetts; it doesn't make sense to list a city, its state, and another city this way.

Boston, // Massachusetts, // and San Francisco

     Two cities (one with its state): large pauses, additional information (apposition)

Exercise 5: Two or Three?

 Focus on large and small pauses

Each group below could consist of either two or three people, depending on the length of the pauses. Mark the timing: // for large pauses and / for small pauses.

Work with a partner. Close your book and listen as your partner reads the phrases below. Listen to the length of your partner's pauses: how many people is your partner speaking about?

Three People	Two People
Heather, a teacher, and Miriam	Heather, a teacher, and Miriam
Miriam, a mathematician, and Heather	Miriam, a mathematician, and Heather
Ivan, a student from Russia, and Seth	Ivan, a student from Russia, and Seth

Exercise 6: One or Two?

 Focus on pauses   **Recycle rising intonation**

 You will hear six phrases. Do you hear one unit or group, with no pauses or marked intonation? Or do you hear two separate choices, with a pause and marked (rising) intonation? Check the column you hear. The first one is done for you.

One Unit (Yes/No Question)	Two Choices (Either/Or Question)
1.	✓
2.	
3.	
4.	
5.	
6.	

THE SOUNDS OF SILENCE

Use large pauses at parentheses or dashes (additional information).

"Many American writers // (including Hemingway and Fitzgerald) // were concerned with the problem of individual identity and purpose."

"It's not a big deal — // no problem."

Don't link sounds across these large pauses.

Exercise 7: Parentheses

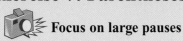 **Focus on large pauses**   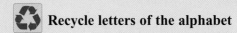 **Recycle letters of the alphabet**

Read the sentences below aloud, using large pauses at parentheses. Write additional sentences that explain other acronyms from chapter 1 (p. 4).

1. The UN (United Nations) is meeting today at its headquarters.

2. The UAE (United Arab Emirates) delegation will be presenting to the committee.

3. H_2O (hydrogen dioxide) is commonly known as water.

4. The CEO (chief executive officer) will be meeting with the chairman of the board.

5. Please enter your PIN (personal identification number) after the beep.

6. CDs (compact discs) have replaced tapes in many cities in the world.

THE SOUNDS OF SILENCE

Use large pauses at quotation marks.

"Everyone take out your books," // said the teacher, // "and look at the following exercise."

Don't link sounds across these large pauses.

Exercise 8: Who's Talking?

 Focus on large pauses

 You will hear four sentences. Listen and circle the sentence you hear.

1. a. "The anthropologist," said the student, "made an interesting discovery."

   b. The anthropologist said the student made an interesting discovery.

   c. The anthropologist said, "The student made an interesting discovery."

2. a. "The newspaper," said the reporter, "was biased."

   b. The newspaper said the reporter was biased.

   c. The newspaper said, "The reporter was biased."

3. a. "Stephanie," said Brady, "is running for Congress."

   b. Stephanie said Brady is running for Congress.

   c. Stephanie said, "Brady is running for Congress."

4. a. "The book," said the writer, "was ambitious."

   b. The book said the writer was ambitious.

   c. The book said, "The writer was ambitious."

Eye-Opener: Intonation Accompanies Stress

Sometimes we use quotation marks around a sarcastic, insincere, or untrue word or phrase.
Use rising intonation and extra stress on the word or phrase in quotation marks.
Don't forget the large pauses at the quotation marks.

Examples: The "poor" CEO only made half a million dollars last year.

Some of the "healthy" meals at fast food restaurants are still very bad for you.

When you hear sentences like these, you might also hear the phrases "quote-unquote" or "so-called"
or see speakers drawing quotation marks in the air with their fingers.

 Journal

Watch a TV talk show and listen for the timing features you have learned.
Take notes on the speaker's pauses, stress, intonation, and hand
gestures/facial expressions. Report your findings to the class and
discuss them.

Exercise 9: Putting It All Together

 Focus on timing and pauses   **Recycle Sound Concepts, syllables, stress,
intonation; all noun and verb endings**

Choose a newspaper article to read aloud. Use the checklist on the next page to prepare for your reading.

Practice at home and then record yourself, or be ready to read aloud in class.

✓ CHECKLIST

How to Prepare to Read a Text Aloud

Read a text silently first in order to become familiar with it. You need to understand a text completely in order to use correct sentence-level stress, intonation, and timing. Then use the list below to practice reading the text aloud. The list reminds you of all the things you need to pay attention to, from individual words to phrases to sentences. Read your text aloud six times, stopping after every number on the checklist to monitor your progress.

If something is difficult for you to say or to remember to say, mark it on the text. Use any system that's helpful to you. When you're ready, try to put it all together.

1. Word-Level Pronunciation/New Vocabulary Words

   a. Number of syllables
   b. Syllable structure
   c. Consonant and vowel sounds
   d. Word-level stress

2. Word-Level Noun and Verb Endings/Grammar Sounds

   a. -ed endings (past tense, passive voice, past participles)
   b. -s/ -es endings (plurals and third-person singular present tense)
   c. -'s and -s' endings (possessives)

3. Word-Level and Phrase-Level Sound Concepts

   a. Linking
   b. Deletion
   c. Reduction
   d. Alteration
   e. Contractions

4. Sentence-Level Stress

   a. Normal sentence-level stress
   b. Contrastive stress

5. Sentence-Level Intonation

   a. Normal sentence-level intonation
   b. Questions and questioning statements
   c. Intonation for special purposes (emotion)

6. Phrase-Level and Sentence-Level Pauses and Timing

   a. Thought groups
   b. Pauses at punctuation

      i. Small pauses
      ii. Large pauses
      iii. Difficult punctuation marks: quotation marks, parentheses

 **Grammar Sounds**

Exercise 10: Peer Dictation

 Recycle "-ed" endings

Write a paragraph about what you did on a trip, vacation, or family visit. Include all appropriate "-ed" (regular past tense) endings, and be sure you know how to pronounce them. Mark your paragraph for thought groups and pauses.

Work with a partner. Take turns reading your paragraphs aloud. Pause at the end of each thought group to give your partner time to write what you said. When it's your turn to listen, write exactly what your partner said, as in any dictation exercise. Did your partner say any "-ed" endings? Make sure you wrote them down whenever you heard them. Compare your paragraph with the original. If there are any differences, try to decide why.

 **Sound Concepts**

Linked Sounds

Remember that linking helps us to connect words smoothly. What are the three kinds of linking you have learned so far? _____ _____ _____

Consonant Sounds Linked to Consonant Sounds

We also link consonant sounds to consonant sounds when they are formed in different places in your mouth. Practice holding the first consonant and linking it smoothly to the second, even though your mouth will change position.

> Example: I waited for you.

Trouble Spots

1. If you don't say final consonant sounds, consonant-to-consonant linking won't work.

2. If you add extra sounds to the ends of words, consonant-to-consonant linking won't work, and your sentence rhythm will be wrong.

Exercise 11: Consonant-to-Consonant Linking

 Focus on consonant-to-consonant linking

Read the following sentences to yourself and mark the sentences for consonant-to-consonant linking. Then take turns reading the sentences aloud to a partner.

1. I bought some apples.
2. I wanted the job.
3. It took ten minutes to do it.
4. The prize was presented by the mayor.
5. The speech was at nine.
6. I revised my thesis statement.

 Eye-Opener: Even native English speakers find many of these groups of consonants difficult.

Exercise 12: The Mysterious Castle

 Focus on consonant-to-consonant linking

 Recycle past tense endings, individual consonant sounds, syllable structure, standard sentence-level stress

1. Look at the words in column A. Be sure you can pronounce these words with the correct syllable structure and number of syllables.

2. Write the final sound of each word (the sound of its past tense ending) in column B.

3. Write the number of syllables in each word in column C.

4. Combine the verb from column A and the object from column D into a verb phrase in column E. Mark this phrase for linking.

5. Look at the linking in column E. List the linked consonant sounds (not letters) in column F and write the total number of linked consonant sounds in column G.

A	B	C	D	E	F	G
Verb	Past Tense Sound	Syllables	Object	Verb Phrase	Linked Consonant Sounds	Number of Linked Consonant Sounds
used	[d]	1	the map	used the map	z + d + ð	3
missed			the turn			
circled			the block			
entered			the castle			
dropped	[t]		the flashlight			
turned			the key			3
opened			the door			
climbed		1	the stairs			
flipped			the switch			
crossed			the room			
unlocked			the cabinet	unlocked the cabinet		
discovered			three jewels		r + d + θ + r	

6. Look over your completed chart, and circle any linked verb phrases in column E that you think will be difficult to say. Practice reading the linked phrases in column E aloud with a partner. Don't add extra syllables or delete necessary consonant sounds. Practice until you're ready to go to step 7.

7. Work in a small group to make up a story with the verb phrases in column E. Take turns using one of the verb phrases in a sentence with the subject "I." Add any adverbs or connecting words (first, then, after that, next, finally) you wish. Keep the rhythm of the story going. Stress the content words, not the function words. Remember to say the past tense endings correctly, to pronounce the consonant sounds, and to link consonant-to-consonant sounds. When your group is finished, try telling the story faster or with even more expression (intonation).

 **Sound Concepts**

Review, Reflect, and Recycle

Discuss these questions with a partner:

Why is the consonant-to-consonant linking in exercise 12 (above) so difficult to say?

Why do you think English speakers link, reduce, delete, alter, and contract sounds?

 Eye-Opener: Every language has its own version of these Sound Concepts. Linked, reduced, deleted, altered, and contracted sounds help us speak more easily and quickly.

LANGUAGE STRATEGY: Using Sounds and Sound Concepts for Easier Pronunciation of Consonant Groups

There are two kinds of consonant groups:

1. within a word (consonant clusters)

2. across words (consonant-to-consonant linking)

Focus on the following sounds and Sound Concepts for easier pronunciation of these consonant groups.

Linked Sounds

Use all kinds of linking as much as you can. Linking helps your speech sound smoother. Look at the exercises and examples above to practice consonant-to-consonant linking.

Individual Consonant Sounds

When you need to say the sounds /t/, /p/, or /k/ in a group of consonants, don't make a puff of air for these sounds (don't aspirate them). These sounds are easier to say in groups when your mouth, teeth, and tongue form, but don't complete the sound. Native English speakers do this without thinking. Practice with the sentences below:

| Stop smoking! | I dropped the flashlight. | Thanks for the help. |

Reduced Sounds

Native English speakers often reduce, and sometimes omit, consonant sounds in the middle of large consonant groups. In the following examples, the sound (not letter) in bold is usually very hard to hear when native speakers say the word. English speakers don't consciously avoid saying these sounds, but the combination of consonants is so difficult—such a tongue-twister—that the consonants disappear.

months	3 consonant sounds: n + θ + s
sixths	4 consonant sounds: k + s + θ + s
discovered three	4 consonant sounds: r + **d** + θ + r
fixed the	4 consonant sounds: k + s+ **t** + ð
let's stay	4 consonant sounds: t + s + **s** + t

Exercise 13: Listening for Syllables and Consonant Groups

 Focus on consonant-to-consonant linking

 Recycle unstressed function words, past tense endings

 You will hear sixteen phrases. On a separate piece of paper, write the phrase you hear.

Rhythm & Music

Using Stress and Syllables with Negative Prefixes

English has six negative prefixes. These prefixes don't change a word's part of speech or stress pattern, but they *do* add an unstressed syllable. Make sure you say this unstressed syllable at the beginning of the word.

1.	im	possible	impossible
2.	in	appropriate	inappropriate
3.	il	logical	illogical
4.	ir	regular	irregular
5.	un	reasonable	unreasonable
6.	non	returnable	nonreturnable (sometimes "non" is hyphenated)

These prefixes are usually unstressed. But when you're making a contrast, stress the negative prefix.

A: That's possible.

B: No, that's *im*possible.

Exercise 14: Positive or Negative?

 Focus on unstressed syllables in negative prefixes

 Listen to the following sentences and decide whether or not you hear a negative prefix. Use the three kinds of information to help you make sense of what you hear.

1.	reasonable	unreasonable		**6.**	logical	illogical
2.	reasonable	unreasonable		**7.**	logical	illogical
3.	reasonable	unreasonable		**8.**	logical	illogical
4.	possible	impossible		**9.**	regular	irregular
5.	possible	impossible		**10.**	regular	irregular

Final Chapter Activity

 Recycle Sound Concepts, stress in words, thought groups and timing, noun and verb endings

Context for Practice: Compound Nouns and Noun Phrases

 1. You will hear a paragraph about the way stress works in English compounds and phrases. Before listening, look back at page 62 (Chapter 4) to remind yourself of stress in compound nouns and noun phrases. Then listen and complete the paragraph with the words you hear.

In English, a compound is often _____ hyphen or by running its two _____ ,

but _____ also _____ with a space between the two components _____

they were still separate words…. _____ simple _____ tell whether

something _____ compound _____ phrase: compounds generally have stress on

the _____ (phrase) phrases on the second. A "dark róom" _____ room

_____ dark, _____ dárkroom (compound word) is where photographers work,

_____ darkroom _____ lit when the photographer is done. A "black bóard"

(phrase) _____ necessarily a board _____ black, but some bláckboards

(compound word) _____ even white. Without _____ punctuation _____

guide, some word strings can be read either as a _____ as a compound, _____

following headlines:

Squad Helps Dog Bite Victim

Man Eating Piranha Mistakenly Sold as Pet Fish

Juvenile Court to Try Shoot Defendent

Stephen Pinker, *The Language Instinct*, Harper-Perennial 1994

2. After listening, talk with a partner about the ideas in this passage. What are the two possible meanings and stress patterns in the author's three example headlines? Look back at chapter 3 and ask other English speakers if you're not sure.

3. Use the oral reading checklist (page 191) to mark the passage and practice reading it aloud. Make sure you can read it aloud in natural connected speech.

4. Work with a partner. Where did you mark thought group boundaries, large pauses, and small pauses? Discuss any disagreements, and read the paragraph aloud together (in unison) until you and your partner are both pausing at the same places, producing the same number of syllables, and placing stress on the same words.

5. With your partner, get together with another 1–2 pairs. Combine pairs to form a group of 4–6 students. Together, continue reading the text aloud and working on your phrasing and stress.

What did we do in this chapter?

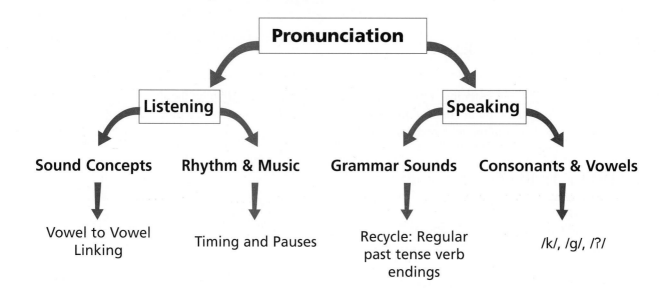

Assessment Section 3: Unit 3 (Chapters 8–10)

Part 1: Listening and Thinking About Listening and Speaking

Listen to the student presentation on silence for overall comprehension. The student's classmates may interrupt to ask questions during the presentation.

When you are finished listening, work with a partner or in a small group on the following activities. Your teacher may ask you to concentrate on one or more of the activities at a time. Your teacher may also ask you to listen to the lecture again.

ACTIVITY 1: Rhythm & Music

Was it easy to tell who was speaking, even though you weren't looking at the group of people? Why? Did you notice the interruptions? How can you describe them in terms of intonation, stress, and timing?

ACTIVITY 2: Sound Concepts

Find examples of the following Sound Concepts from the discussion and write them in the chart. What was their context? Were they easy to notice at first?

Sounds are reduced	Sounds are altered	Sounds are contracted

Part 2: Speaking

ACTIVITY 1: Read Aloud

Turn to the audio script (p. 216) at the back of this book. Working in a small group, read the students' discussion aloud, taking turns playing the different roles. Your teacher may ask you to record your group. Your group should focus on three things:

1. Timing (small and large pauses, and pauses between turns)

2. Intonation (rising, falling, and holding)

3. Stress (contrastive and informational)

ACTIVITY 2: Focus Sounds

List the individual consonant and vowel sounds from this unit in the box.

Unit 3 Focus Sounds

Go back to the speaking diagnostic you took in chapter 2 (p. 21). With a partner, circle every word with one of the focus sounds listed in the box. Practice reading the diagnostic aloud. Are you saying the focus sounds correctly?

Part 3: Thinking About Listening and Speaking

ACTIVITY 1: Write and Reflect

What did you think about the style of class discussion on the CD? Was this discussion like any other student presentations you've ever given or listened to? Why or why not? Would you have felt comfortable asking questions during the presentation? Which questions or contributions would you have felt most comfortable volunteering?

What did you think about the content of the student's presentation? Have you ever noticed fast talkers or slow talkers, or thought about the problems when people with different conversational styles interact? What about the idea of "good" and "bad" silences? What have you noticed about other people's body language when they're silent?

ACTIVITY 2: Quiz Yourself

1.   When do you need to use small pauses?

2.   When do you need to use large pauses?

3.   What's the difference between rising, falling, and holding intonation? What are some situations in which you might hear each kind of intonation?

4.   When do we use a glottal stop in English? Why do some students overuse it?

5.   What are your continuing pronunciation problems? Where do you need to focus your efforts in the future?

6.   Which log entries are you able to say correctly at this point in the semester? What helped you?

Appendix 1: International Phonetic Alphabet (IPA) Chart and Mouth Diagrams

Use this chart as a reference tool only. Go back to the listed pages for more information.

Sound	Name of the Symbol	Key Word for This Sound	Other Symbols for This Sound	Pages for Reference
This is the symbol used in this text for this sound.	*This is how to refer to this sound.*	*The bold letters in this word make this sound.*	*Other textbooks or dictionaries may use these symbols for this sound. Add your dictionary's symbols here.*	*Look at these pages for an introduction to this sound.*
Unvoiced Consonant Sounds				
/θ/	theta	**th**ink		Chapter 1, p. 10
/t/	t	**t**ime		Chapter 3, p. 38
/s/ *	s	**s**it		Chapter 4, p. 65
/h/	h	**h**ave		Chapter 6, p. 102
/sh/ *	sh	**sh**e	ʃ	Chapter 6, p. 101
/tch/ *	tch	**ch**air	tʃ	Chapter 6, p. 101
/f/	f	**f**our		Chapter 9, p. 164
/p/	p	**p**ull		Chapter 9, p. 165
/k/	k	**c**ome		Chapter 10, p. 182
Voiced Consonant Sounds				
/ð/	eth	**th**en		Chapter 1, p. 10
/d/	d	**d**ime		Chapter 3, p. 38
/z/ *	z	**z**ip		Chapter 4, p. 66
/b/	b	**b**e		Chapter 5, p. 86
/v/	v	**v**ery		Chapter 5, p. 86
/y/	y	**y**es		Chapter 5, p. 87
/j/ *	j	**j**u**dg**e	dʒ	Chapter 5, p. 87
/zh/ *	zh	mea**s**ure	ʒ	Chapter 6, p. 101
/D/	altered /t/	be**tt**er	ɾ	Chapter 7, p. 119
/r/	r	**r**ight		Chapter 7, p. 121
/l/	l	**l**ight		Chapter 7, p. 122

* These sounds are sibilants (hissing sounds).

Sound	Name of the Symbol	Key Word for This Sound	Other Symbols for This Sound	Pages for Reference
Voiced Consonant Sounds (cont'd)				
/w/	w	**w**ay		Chapter 8, p. 145
/g/	g	**g**o		Chapter 10, p. 183
/ʔ/	glottal stop	uh-oh		Chapter 10, p. 183
/ŋ/	engma	thi**ng**		Not in this book
/m/	m	**m**ake		Not in this book
/n/	n	**n**o		Not in this book
Vowel Sounds (all vowels are voiced sounds)				
/ə/	schwa	**a**bove		Chapter 4, p. 59
/iʸ/	E	b**e**	/i/, /iy/	Chapter 5, p. 86
/I/	capital I	need**e**d		Chapter 5, p. 85
/aI/	I	**eye**	/ay/	Chapter 5, p. 84
/uʷ/	oo (or script u)	t**o**	/uw/	Chapter 6, p. 111
/ʌ/	inverted V	ab**o**ve		Chapter 6, p. 111
/ʊ/	upsilon	p**u**t		Chapter 7, p. 122
/eʸ/	A	m**a**ke	/e/, /ey/, /eI/	Chapter 8, p. 146
/ɛ/	epsilon	g**e**t		Chapter 8, p. 147
/æ/	ash	**a**t		Chapter 8, p. 146
/ɑ/	script A	st**o**p		Chapter 9, p. 166
/ɔ/	open O	b**o**ss		Not in this book
/aw/	ow	n**ow**	/əʊ/	Not in this book
/o/	O	n**o**	/ow/	Not in this book
/ɔy/	oy	b**oy**	/ɔI/	Not in this book

Mouth Diagrams:
How to Form Vowel Sounds

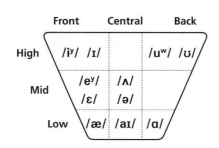

Key Features of English Vowels

Rounded Vowels

Tense Vowels

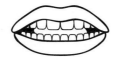

Lax Vowels

Mouth Diagrams: How to Form Consonant Sounds

1. Unvoiced: /θ/
   Voiced: /ð/

2. Unvoiced: /t/
   Voiced: /d/

3. Unvoiced: /s/
   Voiced: /z/

4. Unvoiced: /p/
   Voiced: /b/

5. Voiced: /y/

6. Unvoiced: /tch/
   Voiced: /ʝ/

7. Unvoiced: /f/
   Voiced: /v/

8. Unvoiced: /h/
   Voiced: /ʔ/ (glottal stop)

9. Unvoiced: /sh/
   Voiced: /zh/

10. Voiced: /r/

11. Voiced: /l/

12. Voiced: /w/

13. Unvoiced: /k/
    Voiced: /g/

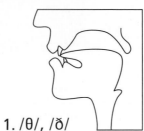

1. /θ/, /ð/

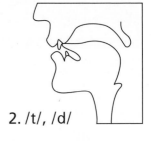

2. /t/, /d/

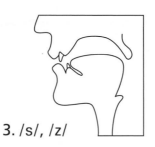

3. /s/, /z/

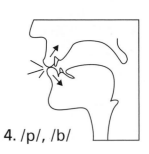

4. /p/, /b/

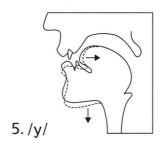

5. /y/

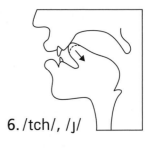

6. /tch/, /ʝ/

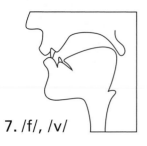

7. /f/, /v/

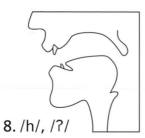

8. /h/, /ʔ/

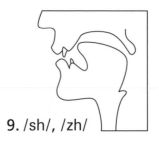

9. /sh/, /zh/

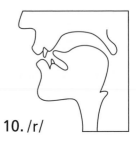

10. /r/

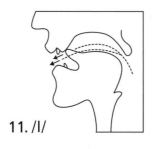

11. /l/

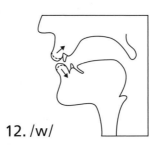

12. /w/

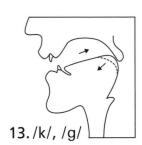

13. /k/, /g/

Language Strategy: Pronouncing Commonly Confused Consonant Sounds

If you know you commonly confuse two different consonant sounds, use the following strategy. Some commonly confused pairs: /b/ and /v/, /r/ and /l/, /sh/ and /tch/, /p/ and /f/, /v/ and /w/.

Step 1: Define the problem

Which two English consonant sounds do *you* confuse? **sound 1:_____ sound 2:_____**

Write your sounds next to the words "sound 1" and "sound 2" in the folllowing steps. Answer the following questions about *your* sounds to try to pinpoint your confusion.

Step 2: Think about your language

1. Does your language have sound 1 (_____)? Write a word with this sound:_____

   If you use an alphabet, what letter(s) do you use to write this sound?

   Does this letter (or letters) *always* make this sound?

2. Does your language have sound 2 (_____)? Write a word with this sound:_____

   If you use an alphabet, what letters do you use to write this sound?

   Does this letter (or letters) *always* make this sound?

3. Does your language have a sound very similar to sound 1 (_____) or sound 2 (_____)?

   Write a word with this sound:_____

   If you use an alphabet, what letters do you use to write this sound? _____

   Does this letter (or letters) *always* make this sound?

Step 3: Think about English

1. What letter or letters make sound 1 (_____)?

   Does this letter (or letters) *always* make this sound?

2. What letter or letters make sound 2 (_____)?

   Does this letter (or letters) *always* make this sound?

Step 4: Think about your strategies for saying these sounds and your success

1. How competent are you at pronouncing sound 1 (_____) and sound 2 (_____) correctly? How often do you get them right?

   > nearly all the time   sometimes   almost never

2. How conscious are you of pronouncing sound 1 (_____) and sound 2 (_____) correctly? How much do you have to think about them?

   > a lot   a little   not at all

Step 5: Find yourself on the Four Levels of Competence (p. 25)

1. You get sound 1 (_____) and sound 2 (_____) correct "nearly all the time," and you think about the problem "a little" or "not at all."

   > ⟶ *Level 4:* Unconscious Competence. Don't worry about these sounds any more.

2. You get sound 1 (_____) and sound 2 (_____) correct "nearly all the time" or "sometimes," and you think about the problem "a lot."

    ———▶   *Level 3:* Conscious Competence. Your strategy is working. Eventually, you'll be able to say these sounds correctly without even thinking about them.

3. You get sound 1 (_____) and sound 2 (_____) correct "sometimes" or "almost never," and you think about the problem "a lot."

    ———▶   *Level 2:* Conscious Incompetence. Your strategy isn't working: you need to change strategies. Look below for suggestions.

4. You get sound 1 (_____) and sound 2 (_____) correct "almost never," and you think about the problem "a little" or "not at all."

    ———▶   *Level 1:* Unconscious Incompetence. You need to think more about how to say these sounds. Look at the list of strategies below, and start using one or more of them.

| Level 4: Unconscious competence |
| Level 3: Conscious competence |
| Level 2: Conscious incompetence |
| Level 1: Unconscious incompetence |

 Eye-Opener: There's a big difference between level 2 and level 3. If you're at level 2, enter these sounds into your logbook. If you're at level 3, you're on the right track.

Strategies for Matching a Consonant Sound to the Correct Letter(s)

How to Remember Which Commonly Confused Sound to Say in a Word

Before using the following strategies, make sure you can pronounce your pair of sounds correctly.

1. Let spelling help.

Sometimes sounds are confusing only when you imagine them in a non-English alphabet or writing system. Visualize your sounds in English words and English letters.

    Example: In English, the letter "b" never makes the sound /v/; the letter "v" never makes the sound /b/.

Many pairs of English consonants follow this pattern. What about your pair of sounds?

2. Use model words.

Find a model word for each of your sounds that is easy for you to remember.

    Example: Use the words "left" and "right" as models for the sounds /l/ and /r/. If you know a word has an /l/ or an /r/ sound, but you can't remember which, use your model words to help. If you get the sound wrong, switch to your other model word.

What are your model words? Fill out the chart below.

	Example sound 1: /l/	Example sound 2: /r/	Your sound 1: _____	Your sound 2: _____
Model Word:	left	right		
Focus Letter:	l	r		

3. Use clues from your listeners.

If you know that a pair of sounds is difficult for you, pay attention to your listeners' reactions when you say words with these sounds. Look back at "Clues for Communication Breakdowns" (page 79). These clues tell you that you may have chosen the wrong sound: you may have said sound 1 (_____) when you needed sound 2 (_____). Pay attention to your listeners' reactions to know when you need to switch sounds.

To help you locate pronunciation errors, read aloud the paragraph below (and on p. 21). Your teacher may photocopy this page for each student, and use it to circle words you mispronounce when reading aloud. Your teacher may return the marked-up copy to you, but will not address a particular pronunciation problem until after it is introduced in class. At that point, return to this page and enter the relevant problem in your logbook.

Name: _____ **Date:** _____

Last June, Veronica and Greg moved to Ithaca (a city in upstate New York). She was interested in studying Spanish at a four-year college, and he wanted to get a job. Veronica had already applied to some colleges and universities, so she started school right away and really liked her classes. But Greg had trouble with his job search.

"I've looked at job listings in newspapers and even used Internet job lists for months," he complained. "None of it's done any good."

Some people at Veronica's school said that local libraries could be good sources of information, but nothing helped Greg. They started to think he would never find something. Finally, after a year, he found a job in one of the offices at Veronica's college.

"It's really great—now, he works right on campus," Veronica said, "and in between my classes, I can even meet him for lunch."

Notes to teachers:

1. If a student has problems with individual consonant sounds or noun and verb endings, circle the sound or ending. For example, if a student mispronunces the /y/ sound in "York," or the "-ed" in "liked," circle the "Y" or the "ed."

2. If a student adds or omits a sound (by adding an extra syllable at the beginning of "Spanish" or at the end of "college," by omitting the final /t/ in "right" or the contracted "s" in "it's," etc.), mark the error with a small minus sign.

3. If a student's stress, intonation, or timing is nonstandard, mark the appropriate place. For example, if a student pauses strangely mid-phrase, mark a large slash. On the other hand, if a student reads straight through parentheses or quotation marks without pausing, circle the ignored punctuation to mark the error. If one or more words or syllables are stressed inappropriately, mark a stress mark over the incorrectly placed stress, such as "complained" or "job listings."

4. Unless your students are not making any of the above errors, you may want to ignore errors with vowel sounds.

Appendix 3: Grammar Cross-Reference

Use the following list of grammar topics to cross-reference the exercises and activities in this book with your grammar book or course syllabus.

Use the script below to practice without the audio or to check your listening comprehension.

Chapter 1

p. 2–Language Strategy

a b c d e f g h i j k l m n o p q r s t u v w x y z

p. 6–Mini-Lesson 1

Example: Tell her I'll meet her.

1. Is everybody here? Where's Albert?
2. Susan and Catherine are here, but Albert's missing.
3. Where is he? Is he in his office?
4. No, he's not.
5. Is he on his way? Try him on his cell phone.
6. Meanwhile, can we meet without him?

p. 11–Exercise 8

Example: Oh no! (upset)

1. What do you know about that? (curious)
2. What do you know about that? (sarcastic)
3. What do you know about that? (surprised)

Chapter 2

p. 19–Section A

1. Please tell her I'm coming.
2. This is it!
3. Is it black or white?
4. Please take off your jacket.
5. Are you in a hurry?
6. Take care of yourself!
7. What's up?
8. Do it right away.
9. Will you help him?
10. Won't you help me?
11. Give him his book.
12. How much is room and board?
13. Let's call her up.

p. 20–Section B

Part 1

1. sports
2. right of way
3. change of plans
4. one in a million
5. half a dozen
6. team

Part 2

Example: Wow! That's some hot dog!

1. The patient, said the doctor, is late.
2. Do you have the phone bill?

Part 3

1. She gave me *three* CDs.
2. Bring me *those* four tools.

Part 4

1. Great!
2. Great.

Part 5

1. This train's usually on time, isn't it? (uncertain)
2. He's a great cook, isn't he. (certain)
3. It isn't time to go, is it? (uncertain)
4. You'd like to go to Europe, wouldn't you. (certain)

Part 6

1. I like to cook.
   What? (What do you like to cook?)
2. I used to live in Los Angeles.
   Where? (Where did you say you lived?)
3. I'm going on vacation next month.
   When? (When are you going, specifically?)

p. 27–How a Pronunciation Log Works

Student 1 (Japanese speaker): su-peech. The President gave a su-peech. su-peech.

Student 2 (Spanish speaker): es-peech. The President gave an es-peech. es-peech.

Student 3 (Korean speaker): speech-ee. The President gave a speech-ee. speech-ee.

p. 28–Practice Using a Logbook

Student 4 (Spanish speaker): ice. He has beautiful blue ice. ice.

Student 5 (Chinese speaker): look. Yesterday we look at the blackboard a lot. look.

Student 6 (Spanish speaker): use-ed. Last week I bought a use-ed car. use-ed.

Chapter 3

p. 35–Diagnostic

1. What's up?
2. What's a vowel?
3. What time is it?
4. Take care of yourself!
5. Please take off your shoes.
6. Time's up!

p. 42–Log Reminder: Problems with syllables

Listen to one student say the word *five*.
Student 1 (Chinese speaker): fi. fi. I can say consonant-vowel syllables, but I have problems with consonant-vowel-consonant syllables.
Listen to another student say the word *brand*.
Student 2 (Japanese speaker): boo-ran-do. Boo-ran-do. I can say consonant-vowel but not consonant-consonant. I can say consonant-vowel-consonant syllables but only if the final consonant sound is /n/.

p. 46–Exercise 8

1.	pronounced	6.	researched
2.	looked	7.	used
3.	waited	8.	listened
4.	realized	9.	returned
5.	married	10.	asked

p. 51–Final chapter activity

In college I was a language major, so I studied a lot of languages—I learned Russian, and a little French and German, and in high school I'd studied Spanish. After college I decided to go to Europe for the summer. I was really excited about my trip and about getting to use my languages. First I visited my friend in Spain, but right away I realized I didn't know enough Spanish. Everyone talked so fast! I had a hard time understanding anything, but at least my friend helped out. After a week in Spain I took a train to France. On the train I looked up phrases in my French book. But when I asked a woman for directions to my hostel, she laughed at my French and I couldn't understand her—everyone sounded like they were swallowing the ends of their words. I was awfully embarrassed about my accent. By the time I got to Russia, I was getting really worried about everything I said. I practiced all night on the train, and I was shocked when someone actually understood me when I spoke!

Chapter 4

p. 55–Diagnostic

1. He's late.
2. Where is he?
3. Is he on his way?
4. Is he in his office?
5. Should I call him up?
6. Try him on his cell phone.

p. 59–Diagnostic 2

1. They have to change plans.
2. He has the right of way.

p. 64–Diagnostic 3

1. You can always take the train to the airport.
2. You can never be too careful.
3. He can drive us to the airport, can't he?
4. Yes, he can.

p. 70–Exercise 14

Zach works downtown, but he lives in the suburbs and commutes. He can get to the city in lots of ways. Sometimes he drives, but it's not worth the trouble. There's too much traffic in rush hour, and it's too expensive to park his car. So he catches the bus at the corner and takes it downtown. When he travels for business on a Monday, he flies out on Sunday because he can get to the airport in forty minutes. The same trip takes him an hour on Monday.

p. 72–Final chapter activity

Charles Lindbergh was the first person to fly across the Atlantic Ocean, in a plane called the *Spirit of St. Louis*. In 1932, his baby son was kidnapped: he was snatched from his crib. They had checked on him at 8:00, and he was fine, but by 10:00 he was gone. The kidnapper used a homemade ladder to get to his room. The Lindberghs received a ransom note, and delivered the money, but three months later, the baby's body was discovered in the woods. The police investigated, and the crime was solved when the ransom money was used in New York by a man named Bruno Hauptmann. When they discovered more ransom money in his wallet, they searched his house and found another $10,000. His trial lasted several months, and throughout his trial he maintained his innocence. He was convicted by a jury and sentenced by a judge. Hauptmann's trial was called "the trial of the century" because so many people sympathized with the Lindberghs and were interested in the case.

p. 74–Assessment Section 1: Listening

You may have thought that language is just speech, but it isn't: not all languages use sounds. Around the world, and throughout history, many different varieties of natural sign languages have always existed, none of which uses speech.

The linguist Steven Pinker writes a succinct summary of what sign language actually is: "Contrary to popular misconceptions, sign languages are not pantomimes and gestures, inventions of educators, or ciphers of the spoken language of the surrounding community. They are found wherever there is a community of deaf people, and each one is a distinct, full language, using the same kinds of grammatical machinery found worldwide in spoken languages. For example, American Sign Language, used by the deaf community in the United States, does not resemble English, or British Sign Language, but relies on agreement and gender systems in a way that is reminiscent of Navajo and Bantu."*

Just as we can describe the individual sounds of a spoken language like English by talking about voicing and the place and manner of articulation, sign languages also have three important components for describing individual signs: hand shape, location, and direction of motion. As Pinker states, a sign language has a grammar of its own, and uses its own rules for combining signs to make phrases and sentences.

Roughly 10% of deaf babies are born to deaf parents; the rest are born to hearing parents, which makes the decision about whether or not to teach the children sign language, and if so, when, a much-debated issue. All babies, including the deaf, begin to babble orally soon after birth. They babble in random consonant and vowel sounds at first, and then in consonant-vowel (CV) syllables. At around 6–8 months, a hearing baby begins to produce groups of repeated CV syllables, which can be called reduplicated babbling. A hearing baby whose native language allows CVC syllables soon produces those, as well. This kind of babbling isn't just for play, or amusement; it's also a step toward speech, and listening to themselves helps hearing babies become accustomed to the structure of their own language.

Deaf babies, on the other hand, stop babbling orally at about the same time. However, if deaf babies have been exposed to sign language, they begin to babble with their hands, learning the structure of their parents' or caretakers' sign language.

Earlier in this textbook, you learned that speaking helps listening, and that when a person is learning a language, he relies on his own output—his production—in order to help his listening (his perception). This theory accounts for why deaf babies suddenly stop babbling: they aren't getting any feedback, and they can't hear themselves, so there's no reason for them to continue.

In one famous case, a deaf family with a hearing child decided not to use sign language with their child. They argued that their child would acquire speech faster if he never learned signs. The child was exposed to educational programs on TV, which were his only source for spoken language. But when he was around the age of three, it was discovered that he couldn't speak at all: he hadn't acquired either speech or sign language, because he lacked interactions with speakers of either language. This example is often used to show that mere exposure to a language is not enough: in order to learn it, you need to use the language, in interaction with other speakers.

*Steven Pinker, *The Language Instinct*. Harper-Perennial 1994

Chapter 5

p. 81–Diagnostic

1. He washed his hands with soap and water.
2. Did he eat his ham and eggs this morning?
3. She offered him a cup of coffee.
4. He drinks his coffee with cream and sugar.
5. He leaves the house at a quarter of nine.

p. 86–Exercise 4

1.	live/leave	6.	it/it
2.	feel/fill	7.	eat/it
3.	leave/live	8.	feel/feel
4.	live/live	9.	it/eat
5.	fill/fill	10.	leave/leave

p. 88–Exercise 6

1.	yellow/yellow	6.	juice/juice
2.	use/use	7.	vote/vote
3.	yellow/Jello	8.	mayor/mayor
4.	major/mayor	9.	juice/use
5.	boat/vote	10.	major/major

p. 95–Final chapter activity

1. [If you ever go to the state of Vermont,] [you should visit Ben & Jerry's ice cream factory.]
2. [You can take a tour] [and sample a few of their many flavors.]
3. [At the end of the tour,] [you can vote for your favorite flavor.]
4. [There are lots of other things to see and do in Vermont.]
5. [The state of Vermont] [is a major tourist destination,] [with many small towns and villages.]

Chapter 6

p. 99–Diagnostic

1. Do you want to see a movie with me?
2. I'll help you in a minute.
3. Will you be here tonight?
4. Do you know what I mean?
5. Can you give me a hand?
6. See you later!

p. 103–Diagnostic

1. Should I get the shirt *with* buttons or *without* buttons?
2. How about *with* the buttons?
3. Well, should I get the *short*-sleeved one or the *long*-sleeved?
4. Well, I like short-sleeved shirts.
5. Ok, do you like the *blue* or the *white?*
6. *I* like the *yellow.* Can we go now?

p. 107–Exercise 8, part A

1. Do you know today's *date?*
2. Do I need extra postage for this?
3. Is there *any* research on this topic?
4. Do you know today's date?
5. Can I have that pizza with pepperoni?
6. Do I need *extra* postage for this?
7. Is there any research on this topic?
8. Can I have that pizza *with* pepperoni?

p. 107–Exercise 8, part B

The speaker has contrastive stress on the word "date," so we know that there's a contrast between the date and something else—maybe the day of the week? Maybe the speaker already asked someone the day of the week, and is now trying to get additional information, or maybe the speaker asked the same question once before, and got an inappropriate answer. Now he's being more specific: I know it's Tuesday (for example), but I don't know if it's the 15th or the 16th or…

p. 108–Diagnostic 2

1. I have an appointment tomorrow.
2. I have to see the doctor tomorrow.
3. Do you have a meeting with your advisor?
4. Do you have to meet with your advisor?

p. 109–Exercise 11

1. I have to meet him at 10:00.
2. I have a meeting at 10:00.
3. I have a problem to solve.
4. I have to problem solve.
5. They have to turn in their homework tomorrow.
6. They have homework due tomorrow.

p. 109–Exercise 12

Parents around the world have a similar hope for their children. Usually they want their children to have a connection to their culture. Some parents feel that their children have to be musical or have to succeed academically. Some sociologists and psychologists have a theory about how children develop in relation to these goals. According to the theory, children have to feel accepted by their friends. As a result, children may have a different perspective on life than their parents.

p. 112–Diagnostic 3

1. What do you do on the weekends?
2. Where do you go to do your laundry?
3. When do you get to the airport?

p. 114–Exercise 15

1. Do you have to go home so early? (F)
2. He wasn't sure what to do next. (C)
3. I have to do my homework after this. (C)
4. Why do you like living in Boston? (F)

p. 115–Exercise 16

1. I'm going to return to my country next year.
2. Two of my friends are related to each other.
3. I applied to two schools last month.
4. She decided to find a better job.

CD 2: Getting Ready for Chapter 7

p. 118–Diagnostic

A: Hey, did you see that article in the paper about teaching sign language to a baby?

B: No, I missed it—what was it about?

A: It said that you can communicate with babies by sign language when they're very young.

B: But how are they going to learn sign language?

A: You teach it them before they can talk.

B: So they can tell their parents when they're hungry?

A: Yeah, that's the idea.

Chapter 7

p. 119–Preview

1. letter **2.** meter **3.** better

For number 1, you may have written: mail, stamps, envelope, or related words.

For number 2, you may have written: parking meter, taxi meter, or related words.

For number 3, you may have written: good, best, worse, bad, feel.

p. 119–Diagnostic

1. You'd better tell her right away.
2. The soda machine's out of order.
3. Tell her I'm better.
4. I'll meet her in an hour.
5. Let her know I'm here.
6. My pen ran out of ink.
7. I bet her I'd do better.

p. 123–Diagnostic 2

1. I'd like to travel.
2. I like to travel.
3. I like to dance.
4. I'd like to dance.
5. I need your help.
6. I'd need your help.

p. 126–Exercise 9

Hi, Mr. Smith. Fred said you wanted me to fill you in on what I've done. Well, I've filed the reports like you asked, and I've updated the database. I'm contacting the customers now, and then I'll talk to the salespeople. I'm still planning the next conference, and after that I'll set up a new meeting. I'd reprogrammed the database last month, remember. Later on, I'd like to talk to you more about the new changes.

p. 126, 127–Exercise 10

1. Where's the book?
2. The book's on the counter.
3. Next to the paper?
4. No, *under* the paper.
5. I've already looked under the paper.
6. Well, look *again*.

(See answers on p. 127)

p. 129–Exercise 14

1. John said he'd take his car and meet us at dinner.
2. Paul's having a party at his apartment later.
3. Steve'll meet her at his office after work.
4. Bill offered to loan us his lecture notes.

p. 133–Exercise 18

1. That's some medicine.
2. That's *some* music.
3. That's *some* medicine.
4. That's some paper.
5. That's *some* paper.
6. That's some music.

p. 135–Final Chapter Activity

Okay, today we're gonna talk about the universality of human emotions. First of all, let me say that this theory is attributed to Paul Ekman, a professor of psychology who's known as "the world's most famous face reader."
Dr. Ekman's based at the University of California Medical School at San Francisco, but he's done research all over the world. Dr. Ekman says he's always been interested in emotions, ever since he was a teenager. And, being a photographer since he was twelve, he just naturally decided to look at facial expressions. In Ekman's view, it turns out there're seven basic human emotions: anger, sadness, fear, surprise, disgust, contempt, and happiness. All of these emotions have clear facial signals. There're actually 43 facial muscles that combine to reveal these emotions.

Ekman's theory helped resolve a debate between evolutionary science and anthropology—on the one hand, scientists who follow the ideas of Charles Darwin have always believed that human facial expressions were universal. On the other hand, anthropologists like Margaret Mead thought the opposite. So, back in 1965, Ekman decided to investigate this. The first thing he did was to show pictures of facial expressions to people in a number of different countries, including the U.S., Japan, Argentina, Chile, and Brazil. It turned out that everyone judged the expressions in the same way—everyone thought the happy face was happy, etcetera. It seems like he proved his point—human emotions are universal. However, it could be argued that all of the people he studied had been influenced by Western movies and television. So, Ekman needed what he called a group of "visually isolated people." In other words, what he needed was people who'd never seen TV or modern media.

Ekman found his second group of subjects in Papua New Guinea—a remote island in the South Pacific. It just so happened that Papua New Guinea was the ideal place to do this kind of investigation: it's very isolated, and had people who, at the time Ekman visited, hadn't been exposed to the modern world. Ekman did two things in New Guinea: first, he showed his subjects the same photos of facial expressions he'd shown the earlier groups, and found that they were judged exactly the same way. Next, he asked the people in New Guinea to pose with expressions of the seven different emotions on their faces, and he recorded them, and later showed them to people in the West. Americans and other Westerners perfectly understood the facial expressions and emotions of the people from Papua New Guinea. Therefore, not only did they identify correctly the Western expressions and emotions, but Westerners correctly interpreted their expressions. Ekman had the proof he needed.

Ekman's theories have implications for different aspects of our lives. First of all, he argues that, in his words, "emotions work from the outside in, as well as the inside out." What he's saying is that if you really manage to arrange all of your facial muscles into the expression of, say, happiness or anger, then you will actually feel that emotion to a certain degree. This isn't as easy as it sounds, though, because for instance, with smiling, in order to show happiness, there's a certain muscle around your eyes that must be moved in order to truly feel happy—and, if you're just trying to smile, you're probably not moving that muscle. So, Ekman believes you can learn to tell the difference between a real smile, and a fake smile. On the other hand, anger or disgust are easier emotions to experience merely by arranging your face into the right expressions.

Another thing Ekman's trying to do with his theories is to help improve the emotional balance of schoolteachers and other people in high-pressure jobs. In fact, he received a $50,000 grant from the Dalai Lama to investigate this. Dr. Ekman says that meeting the Dalai Lama and working with him has led him to study the emotions of Buddhist monks. In addition, he's sharpened his own ideas by contrasting them with Buddhist beliefs.

One final application of Ekman's theories is to the world of computer-generated graphics. Dr. Ekman's been asked to be a consultant with animators in the technology departments of several movie studios that use high-tech computer graphics to create realistic emotions on their characters' faces.

Overall, Ekman's theory of the universality of these seven human emotions, and the facial expressions that reveal them, is an important one for modern psychology and sociology, with many useful applications for education and science.

p. 139–Assessment Section 2

Everyone knows that communication breakdowns can be frustrating, and that they can sometimes have negative consequences in academic or business contexts. However, in some particular high-stakes cases, communication breakdowns can have life-or-death consequences. Take, for example, the case of air traffic controllers communicating with airplane pilots via radio: without visual contact, the controllers and pilots have no way of relying on paralinguistics (gestures, facial expressions, or other body language). So as a result, clear spoken communication becomes vitally important.

In author Steven Cushing's recent book called *Fatal Words*, the problem is described this way: "because of the confusions and misunderstandings that can readily arise as a result of such specifically linguistic phenomena as ambiguity, unclear reference, differences in intonation. . ., [l]anguage-related misunderstandings of various kinds have been a crucial contributing factor in aviation accidents and potential accidents."

Because of the way sounds are linked, reduced, deleted, altered, and contracted in connected speech, an air traffic controller's instructions to a pilot can sometimes be difficult to interpret. Think of the very small difference in sound, but the huge difference in meaning, between the phrases "right way" (meaning the correct direction) and "right of way" (meaning that you don't have to worry about someone else entering your lane). "Right way" has two syllables, and "right of way" has three, but the unstressed, reduced function word "of" in the middle of the second phrase can be very difficult to hear.

Here are some real-world examples of miscommunications taken from Cushing's book: In one case, a pilot's instructions were to remain "on the deck," which means in line for take-off. The pilot thought he'd heard "*off* the deck," meaning he should take off immediately. Unstressed function words like the prepositions "on" or "off" can be very hard to hear, as you know, so that pilot's error was understandable.

In another case, a pilot currently at 10,000 feet, who was supposed to be landing soon, heard the copilot say what he thought was, "Cleared to seven," so he descended to 7,000 feet. Upon reflection, [he] realized that the copilot's "Cleared to seven," had really meant "that our assigned runway was TWO seven—Not that we were cleared TO seven [thousand feet]." So, the co-pilot had said "two," the number and the stressed content word, but the pilot had heard "to," the preposition and the usually unstressed, reduced function word. He'd almost caused an accident before he realized the error.

Steven Cushing, *Fatal Words.* University of Chicago Press, 1997

Getting Ready for Chapter 8

p. 141–Diagnostic Parts 1 and 2

1. Coffee or tea?
2. Paper or plastic?
3. For here or to go?
4. Soup or salad?
5. How are you doing?
6. Where are you living?
7. When are you leaving?
8. What are your plans?

Chapter 8

p. 143–Diagnostic

1. Did your friend arrive?
2. Could you meet me later?
3. Put your coat on.
4. I don't know what you mean.
5. I asked your friend to dinner.
6. Would you mind giving me a hand?
7. Send your application in right away.
8. I fixed your car already.
9. I'll let you know soon.

p. 148–Diagnostic 2

He should have listened to the weather forecast last night. If he'd listened, he would have taken his umbrella, and he wouldn't have walked to work today. He would have taken his car, and his shoes wouldn't have gotten wet. He might not have caught a cold, and he could have saved himself a lot of trouble.

p. 153–Exercise 9

1. I'm going to catch a plane to Chicago.
2. I'd love to, but first I have to finish my report.
3. I lost my shopping list. . .
4. I'm meeting Fred tonight.
5. I'm going to catch a plane to Chicago. . .
6. Would you like some coffee or tea. . .
7. I'm meeting Fred tonight. . .
8. Would you like some coffee or tea?
9. I lost my shopping list.
10. I'd love to, but first I have to finish my report. . .

p. 157–Final Chapter Activity

The novelist José Saramago was born in 1922 to a family of farmers in a small Portuguese village. For financial reasons he abandoned his high school studies and trained as a mechanic. After trying different jobs in the civil service, he worked for a publishing company for twelve years and then for newspapers. For several years he supported himself as a translator, but since his literary successes in the 1980s, he has devoted himself to his own writing. In the past thirty years, Saramago has published thirty works of fiction, poetry, essays, and drama. He has been awarded numerous international prizes, including the 1998 Nobel Prize for Literature. Since 1992, he has lived and worked in the Canary Islands.

http://nobelprize.org/literature/laureates/1998/biob.html

Reflecting on Chapters 1–8

p. 160–Exercise 1

Step 1. 4 syllables; Sounds are altered (altered /y/)

Step 2. 4 syllables; Sounds are altered (altered vowel in *you*)

Step 3. 3 syllables; Sounds are deleted ("Di" in *Did*)

Step 4. 2 syllables; Sounds are deleted (/ə/ in altered *you*); Sounds are linked (/ʤ/ and /ə/)

Chapter 9

p. 161–Diagnostic

1. Do you want to meet in an hour with the customer?
2. Do you want to meet in an hour with the customer?
3. He wants to, but he's not going to be here today.
4. I got a package in the mail today.
5. I've got to thank my friend when I see him.
6. I've got a busy day ahead of me.

p. 163–Exercise 5

I took a look at my schedule for this week, and I want to get everything done tomorrow if I'm going to be ready for school. I've got to get a good night's sleep tonight, 'cause tomorrow's going to be a busy day. I've got to register for classes, but first I've got to meet with my advisor and we're going to choose my classes. I don't know if I want to take three or four classes, cause I have to work too. Then I want to go to the financial aid office, 'cause I've got to make sure my paperwork goes through. If it doesn't, I'll have to check up on it later. After that I'm going to meet my friend and his wife for lunch, 'cause I haven't seen him in awhile. I don't know where we want to go—the deli or the pizza place, but I'm going to be hungry. After lunch I've got to go to work. I've got to hurry, or else I'll be late. Then I have to go to the bookstore and buy my books, so I don't have to buy them next week. Yeah, it's going be a busy day. Well, got to go—see you!

p. 174–Exercise 18

1. I forgive them.
2. I followed her.
3. I've often heard that.
4. I've given them.
5. I failed the test.
6. I've always said it.
7. I always said it.
8. I forgot it.
9. I often heard that.
10. I've got it.

Getting Ready for Chapter 10

p. 180–Exercise 6

1. Do you want to get together on Monday or Tuesday? (y/n)
2. Did you go to high school here or abroad? (choice)
3. Do you want an appointment on Monday or Tuesday? (choice)
4. Is that property residential or commercial? (choice)
5. Do you live near an elementary school or a middle school? (y/n)
6. Would you like to meet to study or go over our notes? (y/n)
7. Is your son in elementary school or middle school? (choice)

Chapter 10

p. 181–Diagnostic

1. lay over
2. buy it
3. see her
4. I am
5. do it
6. to it
7. knew a
8. go out

p. 184–Diagnostic 2

Part 1

1. Mary, an accountant, and her husband were eating breakfast before going to work.
2. "Are you driving, Bill?" Mary asked.
3. "Are you driving George?"
4. "Can you get the phone, Bill?"

Part 2–p. 185

Mary, who works as an accountant, and her husband Bill, who's a lawyer, were eating breakfast before going to work. (check your answer to 1)

"Are you driving, Bill?" Mary asked.

"Yes, I took the train yesterday, but I'm taking the car today," Bill answered. (check your answer to 2)

"Are you driving George?"

"No, he's not coming in today, but I'm driving Pete, because his car's in the shop." (check your answer to 3)

"Okay, well, have a nice day," Mary said as she walked toward the door.

The phone rang just as Mary was going out the door. "Can you get the phone, Bill?" Mary asked. (check your answer to 4)

p. 188–Exercise 6

1. coffee or tea (choice)
2. Monday or Tuesday (y/n)
3. doctor or dentist (y/n)
4. magazines or newspapers (y/n)
5. paper or plastic (choice)
6. baseball or football (y/n)

p. 189–Exercise 8

1. The anthropologist said, "The student made an interesting discovery."
2. The newspaper said the reporter was biased.
3. "Mary," said John, "is running for Congress."
4. "The book," said the writer, "was ambitious."

p. 195–Exercise 13

1. caused the concern
2. cause of concern
3. change direction
4. changed direction
5. change of direction
6. fixed a pipe
7. fix a pipe

8. fixed the pipe

9. asks many questions

10. asks as many questions

11. ask many questions

12. stop it

13. stopped it

14. stops it

15. look at it

16. looked at it

p. 195–Exercise 14

1. That's an unreasonable idea.

2. That's a reasonable idea.

3. That's unreasonable.

4. That's an impossible goal.

5. That's a possible goal.

6. That's an illogical conclusion.

7. That's a logical conclusion.

8. That's illogical.

9. That's a regular occurrence.

10. That's irregular.

p. 196–Final Chapter Activity

In English, a compound is often spelled with a hyphen or by running its two words together, but it can also be spelled with a space between the two components as if they were still separate words…There is a simple way to tell whether something is a compound word or a phrase: compounds generally have stress on the first word, phrases on the second. A "dark róom" (phrase) is any room that is dark, but a "dárk room" (compound word) is where photographers work, and a darkroom can be lit when the photographer is done. A "black bóard" (phrase) is necessarily a board that is black, but some "bláckboards" (compound word) are green or even white. Without pronunciation or punctuation as a guide, some word strings can be read either as a phrase or as a compound, like the following headlines:

Squad Helps Dog Bite Victim

Man Eating Piranha Mistakenly Sold as Pet Fish

Juvenile Court to Try Shooting a Defendant.

p. 198–Assessment Section 3

Student presenter: Okay, so today I'm going to talk to you about some interpretations of silence in certain U.S. classrooms. My research comes mainly from a book called *Perspectives on Silence*, edited by Deborah Tannen and Muriel Saville-Troike, sociologists and linguists. You can follow along with the outline I gave you on your handout. In general, Tannen classifies voices as either "fast-talkers" or "slow-talkers," although she points out that "fast" and "slow" are relative terms. So, one group of "slow-talkers" might be considered "fast-talkers" by an even slower group of "slow-talkers." These conversational styles vary according to culture, age, ethnicity, and location. In conversation, fast-talkers generally interrupt each other more, allow for more overlapping speech, and don't like long pauses in between turns. Slower talkers tend to allow for longer pauses in between turns, and it means they don't interrupt each other as much. Think about the English voices you know: you can probably think of some fast-talkers and some slow-talkers, or some who are in the middle. Fast-talkers usually don't interrupt people and overlap in order to offend them, but rather to connect with them—to show that they have a similar story or experience, and that they're interested in the other person. Yes, did you have a question?

Second student: Yeah—so, what you're saying is… that… a slow-talker and a fast-talker—well, wouldn't they have problems talking to each other?

Presenter: Yes, exactly—slow-talkers might misinterpret fast-talkers, and think that they're being rude, when that isn't the intention, but it's still really hard for them to know that. And sometimes a fast-talker might think a slow-talker is being rude, if they're silent too long or if they don't really show enough of what the fast-talker thinks is interest. This whole situation gets really complicated when you have elementary school classrooms, where there's a teacher and about thirty kids who could have all been raised with different conversational styles and cultural backgrounds.

If you look at the handout I gave you guys, there are two examples of student-teacher dialogues.

In the first one, the teacher says, "What were you doing?" when a student has misbehaved. The student is silent, but look at the description of her body language: she looks up at the teacher, raises her eyebrows, bows her head a little, holds up her hands, and sort of shrugs. This is "good" silence to the teacher, who just says, "Okay. But don't do it again," and that's the end of it.

Look at the next example, on page 2, and—

Third student: Page what?

Presenter: Sorry, I'm on the top of the second page here, in Example B. Okay, so here the teacher's talking to another student, who also misbehaved, and asks the student again, "What were you doing?" This time, the student is silent but has completely different body language: the student's head is up, with their chin and lower lip out, eyebrows close together sort of frowning. The student looks down and to the side, not really at the teacher, and has one hand on her hip. To the teacher, this is a "bad" silence, and the teacher doesn't accept it; she says, "Answer me," and then waits, but the student remains silent, and doesn't change her body language. You can tell the teacher's getting angrier, because she's saying, "I asked you a question… Answer me… I said answer me!" Uh-oh—this kid's in trouble! So, what do you think the difference is between these two cases? How can you tell the difference between good or bad silence?

Fourth student: Uh, maybe it's the body language, like you said, that's the difference—if the second student had looked up, then it would have been okay for the teacher.

Fifth student: I think the teacher probably thought the second student was challenging her, you know, sticking out her chin and looking away, refusing to meet the teacher's eyes. I know that's not the same in all cultures, but maybe that's what was going on here.

Presenter: Interesting—so, the first student, who was looking up at the teacher, that wasn't challenging her?

Fifth student: No, maybe the teacher thought that was acceptance. It's kind of like, "I know I did something wrong, and I'm sorry," but the second kid didn't do that, for whatever reason, and that was the problem.

Presenter: Uh-huh, I think something like that probably was going on here. Let's look at the next example on your handout…

Tannen and Saville-Troike, *Perspectives on Silence*. Ablex Publishing 1985

Some parts of pronunciation are difficult for most students, no matter what their native language is. Many students have trouble with:

- linked, reduced, deleted, altered, or contracted sounds (the Sound Concepts)

- verb and noun endings (Grammar Sounds)

Sometimes pronunciation mistakes are related to a student's native language. English language learners with the same native language often share some of the same mistakes.

Think about it—which mistakes do speakers of *your* native language tend to make? Look at the list of trouble spots below. Read the examples next to each mistake and check the box next to the mistakes *you* make.

Rhythm & Music Trouble Spots

1. Syllable Counting (see p. 31)

❑ Is it hard for you to think of your native language in terms of syllables? If so, you might have trouble counting syllables. Some Chinese or Japanese students find it hard to think of English one-syllable words like *one* and *words* as a single syllable.

2. Syllable Structure (see p. 39)

❑ Does your language allow fewer possible syllables than English? If so, you may have problems pronouncing consonants at the beginnings or ends of English syllables.

❑ Do you add sounds to the beginning of syllables? Sometimes Arabic, Indian, or Spanish students add a vowel sound (and an extra syllable) to the beginning of words like *stop* and *spring*.

❑ Do you add sounds in the middle of syllables (between consonant sounds)? Some Arabic, Farsi, or Turkish speakers add a vowel sound (and an extra syllable) between the final consonants in *next*.

❑ Do you add sounds at the end of syllables? Sometimes Japanese or Korean students add a vowel sound (and an extra syllable) at the end of words like *hot* or *lunch*.

❑ Do you delete sounds in the middle of a syllable (in a consonant cluster)? Some Korean students don't say the /w/ sound in words like *quote*, *question*, and *language*.

❑ Do you delete sounds at the end of a syllable? Some Chinese, Vietnamese, or Thai speakers delete the final sounds in words like *wife*, *page*, or *lunch*.

3. Word-Level Stress (see p. 60)

❑ Do you consistently use the wrong stress in words? Sometimes French or Farsi students consistently stress the final syllable of English words like *academic* and *category*. Other students tend to stress the *first* syllable of English words.

❑ Do you have trouble with secondary stress in words? Some Greek or Russian students don't use any secondary stress in English words.

4. Standard Sentence-Level Stress and Timing (see p. 63)

❑ Do you stress every syllable in a sentence equally? Some Spanish or Brazilian Portuguese students make all the syllables in an English sentence equal.

❑ Do you tend to stress the last word in every sentence, instead of the most important content word or the new information? Some Hungarian speakers do this.

❑ Do you have trouble making content words stressed (strong) and function words unstressed (weak)? Some German speakers put too much stress on English function words like *and*, *or*, and *but*.

Consonant & Vowel Trouble Spots

1. Individual Consonant Sounds

❑ /θ/ and /ð/: Some Chinese, French, and Italian students change /θ/ to /s/ or /t/ and /ð/ to /z/ or /d/ (see p. 200)

❑ /h/ at the beginning of words: Sometimes French, Portuguese, or Creole speakers don't pronounce the /h/ sound at the beginning of words like *have* and *here*. (see p. 200)

❑ /w/ at the beginning of words: Some Japanese, Korean, or Spanish speakers have problems with the sound /w/ at the beginning of words like *work*, *would*, and *woman*. (see p. 201)

❑ /l/ after another consonant sound: Sometimes Chinese speakers have trouble distinguishing between words like *cue* and *clue*. (see p. 200)

❑ voiced sounds (instead of unvoiced) at the end of words: Some German or Catalan speakers say unvoiced sounds instead of the voiced sounds at the end of words, so that /v/ or /z/ in *leave* or *phase* sounds like /f/ or /s/ *(leaf or face)* instead. (see p. 200)

2. Commonly Confused Consonant Sounds

Which pairs of consonant sounds are difficult for you? Learn how to solve these problems by using the Language Strategy: Pronouncing Commonly Confused Consonant Sounds (Appendix 1).

❑ /p/ and /f/: Some Korean students confuse the words *copy* and *coffee*.

❑ /p/ and /b/: Sometimes Arabic speakers pronounce the word *people* with the sound /b/.

❑ /v/ and /b/: Some Spanish speakers confuse the words *berry* and *very*.

❑ /v/ and /w/: Some German, Russian, or Indian students confuse the words *vine* and *wine*.

❑ /l/ and /r/: Some Japanese speakers mix up these sounds in words like *light* and *right*.

❑ /tch/ and /sh/: Some Spanish students confuse the words *chip* and *ship*.

❑ /y/ and /j/: Sometimes Scandinavian or Spanish students pronounce the sound /y/ as /j/ in words like *year*.

❑ /v/ and /f/: Some Arabic or Chinese speakers use the sound /f/ instead of /v/ in words like *leave*.

❑ /s/ and /z/: Sometimes Chinese or Portuguese speakers pronounce the word *rise* with the sound /s/ instead of /z/.

3. Individual Vowel Sounds

❑ Does your language have fewer vowel sounds than English? If so, you may have problems with specific vowel sounds. (see Appendix 1 and individual sections)

Name: _____

Everyone has different pronunciation problems. Use this page to record yours.

Word/phrase	How to say it	How did I say it?	What was my mistake?	Other examples	Pages to look back at
speech	speech (1 syllable)	su-peech (2 syllables)	separating the consonant cluster	su-trong/ strong	pp.13-14, p. 54

Review your log entries above. Where are your errors?

Sound Concepts   Rhythm & Music   Grammar Sounds   Consonant & Vowel Sounds

Use the index to find pages in the textbook that deal with each topic. Cross-references to other entries in the glossary are indicated by the use of italics.

background information: (see the *Three Kinds of Information*)

competence: (see the *Four Levels of Competence*)

connected speech: Connected speech is linked speech. It's everyday speech, without space between separate words. It's not fast speech.

consciousness: (see the *Four Levels of Competence*)

consonant: English has twenty-one consonant letters and about thirty consonant sounds. Use the mouth diagrams and consonant confusion strategy (Appendix 1, p. 201–203) for more help.

consonant cluster: A group of two or more consonant sounds in the same syllable, written CC, CCC, etc. English uses more consonant clusters than many other languages.

content word: The word that gives you the information (content) of the phrase (nouns, verbs, etc.) Content words are usually *stressed.*

continuant: A consonant sound that lets air continue, with friction; sometimes called a fricative.

contrastive stress: Extra *stress,* or emphasis, on any word in a sentence in order to make a contrast with something said or implied.

diphthong: A vowel sound with two parts.

distortion: The natural changes that make it hard to understand spoken English: as a result of linked, reduced, deleted, altered, and contracted sounds, English doesn't sound the way it looks.

Four Levels of Competence: A way of understanding your progress, moving through four levels or stages: 1) unconscious incompetence (making mistakes and not knowing what they are); 2) conscious incompetence (still making mistakes but being aware of them); 3) conscious competence (no longer making mistakes, but still needing to pay attention to them); 4) unconscious competence (the goal: no longer making mistakes and not needing to think about them).

freeze-frame: When you correctly pronounce something difficult, stop and "freeze-frame" in order to remember how you said it.

function word: Grammatical words like prepositions (such as *in, on, at,* etc.) and articles (such as *the, a, an*) that connect content words to make sense. Function words are usually un*stressed* and may have deleted, reduced, altered, or contracted sounds.

Grammar Sounds: One of the main sections of this book, with a focus on verb and noun endings (regular past tense, third-person singular present, plural count nouns, and possessives). Use the checklists (inside front cover) for more help.

informational stress: Extra *stress* or emphasis on any word in a sentence in order to highlight the new and important information.

intonation: The melody of a language. Words, sentences, and questions can rise or fall in *pitch.* This means your voice gets higher or lower, just like notes in music.

language information: (see the *Three Kinds of Information*)

minimal pair: Two words (or sometimes sentences) with different meanings, but with only one pronunciation difference between them

motor memory: Your body "remembers" how to say a consonant or vowel sound. Learning a new way to say these sounds may feel strange until you make a new motor memory.

paralinguistics: The non-language information you observe in conversations, including facial expressions and body language

pitch: The musical note or tone of a syllable, word, phrase, or sentence. Changes in pitch lead to rising or falling *intonation.*

Rhythm & Music: One of the main sections of this book, with a focus on *syllables, stress, intonation,* and *timing*

schwa: The sound of the vowel in most unstressed syllables; a relaxed vowel sound made in the middle of your mouth, like the sound of the first syllable in the word *about.* Written with this symbol: ə

segment or segmental: One aspect of pronunciation, focusing on individual consonant and vowel sounds

sibilant: The hissing consonant sounds in English. Some sibilants are voiced sounds: /z/, /zh/, /j/. Some sibilants are unvoiced sounds: /s/, /sh/, /tch/.

Sound Concepts: One of the main sections of this book, with a focus on the linked, reduced, deleted, altered, and contracted sounds you will hear in connected speech. Use the list of Sound Concepts (inside back cover) for more help.

sound information: (see the *Three Kinds of Information*)

standard sentence-level stress: In normal English sentences, stress the *content words* and not the *function words.*

stop: A consonant sound that completely stops (or blocks) airflow

strategy: A plan or system to attack a problem. You need to be aware of your pronunciation problems, and you need to have a plan for how to solve them. If your strategy isn't working, you may need to use another one. Use the Fast Track list of strategies (inside front cover) for more help.

stress: When you make a syllable louder, longer, clearer, and higher, you stress, or emphasize it. English has standard word-level, phrase-level, and *sentence-level stress*. Stress carries meaning: *contrastive stress* and *informational stress* add extra meaning to words, phrases, and sentences.

suprasegmental: One aspect of pronunciation, focusing on the *Rhythm & Music* of a language

syllable: A syllable is a rhythmic beat. An English syllable almost always has a vowel sound. Syllables can be strong (stressed) or weak (unstressed).

syllable structure: A way of thinking about the consonants and vowels that make up *syllables* in English and other languages. We sometimes talk about syllables in terms of their *consonant* sounds (C) and vowel sounds (V), not letters: CV, CVC, CCVC, etc.

thought groups: A meaningful phrase or group of words in a single sentence. Usually, you pause after each thought group.

Three Kinds of Information: Use the Three Kinds of Information to increase listening comprehension: 1) Background Information, what you know about a topic; 2) Language Information, what you know about the language and how it works; 3) Sound Information, what you actually hear.

timing: The use of *thought groups* and pauses to control the pace of a language

unvoiced sound: (see *voiced sound*)

voiced sound: These sounds are produced by vibrating your vocal cords. Voicing can be the only difference between two different sounds or words. Turn your voicebox on for voiced sounds and off for unvoiced sounds.

vowel: English has five vowel letters, but fourteen different vowel sounds. Spelling doesn't help you think about most English vowel sounds. Use the mouth diagram of vowel sounds (Appendix 1, p. 201) for more help.

Index